MAKING ORGANIZATIONAL CULTURE GREAT

JENNIFER A. CHATMAN
AND GLENN R. CARROLL

MAKING
ORGANIZATIONAL
CULTURE
GREAT

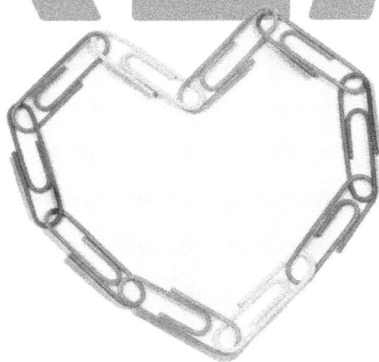

MOVING BEYOND
POPULAR BELIEFS

Columbia Business School
Publishing

Columbia University Press
Publishers Since 1893
New York   Chichester, West Sussex
cup.columbia.edu

Library of Congress Cataloging-in-Publication Data

Names: Chatman, Jennifer author | Carroll, Glenn author
Title: Making organizational culture great : moving beyond popular
beliefs / Jennifer A. Chatman, Glenn R. Carroll.
Description: New York : Columbia University Press, [2026] |
Includes bibliographical references and index.
Identifiers: LCCN 2025035597 | ISBN 9780231221375 hardback |
ISBN 9780231221368 trade paperback | ISBN 9780231563697 epub |
ISBN 978023156527I PDF
Subjects: LCSH: Corporate culture
Classification: LCC HD58.9 .C4857 2026 |
DDC 658.4—dc23/eng/20250902
LC record available at https://lccn.loc.gov/2025035597

Cover design: Noah Arlow
Cover image: Shutterstock

GPSR Authorized Representative: Easy Access System Europe,
Mustamäe tee 50, 10621 Tallinn, Estonia, gpsr.requests@easproject.com

To Russell, Ava, and Sonya — *JAC*

To Lihua and Lishan — *GRC*

CONTENTS

PREFACE

As career-long cultural analysts and educators, we have been fortunate to teach, and to facilitate discussions among, literally thousands of students, executives, and entrepreneurs in hundreds of class sessions over the years. We have also visited scores of firms and other business organizations, talked with many executives, managers, and employees, advised many leaders, and trained hundreds of groups of assembled staff. As scholars, we have read and published hundreds of articles, scoured many books, and obsessively followed the business press and other media.

Across our careers, we have witnessed profound changes in the way that the Western business world regards organizational culture. Before about 1980, many leaders denied its existence, or at least its importance—organizational culture was not something that many of them deemed worthy of deep thought or as meaningful enough to implement or shape. (Of course, there were exceptions like Goldman Sachs, Nordstrom, and Disney, where culture played a dominant role in managing the enterprise.)

The emergence and fast dominance on the world stage in the 1980s of the powerful multinational Japanese corporations changed perceptions of culture. Think Toyota, Sony, Honda, Mitsubishi, and the like. Not only were these companies fierce and successful competitors in many Western markets, including the United States, they apparently were managed in a fundamentally different way from the average American company. For the most part, they were managed culturally, relying heavily on internal cultural systems to control and coordinate much behavior. At the time, the cultural mode of management seemed to many observers far superior to the conventional Western management models used at firms like Ford, General Electric (GE), and International Harvester.

After intense self-reflection and scrutiny, American managers began to realize that the old way had to change, and new ways must be embraced. Foremost among these changes was the intentional designed use of cultural systems to shape and guide behavior within firms. The transformation has been so complete that we venture now that no well-respected executive would dare to publicly voice the view that culture is irrelevant, that it does not matter (even if they hold this belief deep in their heart). Today, organizational culture is widely regarded as important and powerful in managing an organization. And, for some leaders, including many atop leading high-tech companies, culture eclipses all the other aspects of management in determining outcomes.

While denial about culture's impact on organizations has waned dramatically, leaders are still uncomfortable and uncertain about how to develop and manage it. We see this in our classes, consulting engagements, and discussions with executives, managers, and entrepreneurs. The typical discomfort comes from a lack of basic understanding about culture, as well as concerns that taking proactive steps to define and manage culture will backfire and make things worse. For whatever reason, culture has too often been sanctified, and as a result, many managers do not feel knowledgeable or powerful enough to change the rites or the script.

The situation that we have described is both commonplace and troublesome. Organizational leaders, the very people entrusted with developing and managing the culture, often feel uneasy about embracing the task, leaving it to others or letting it languish on its own.

Our primary aim in writing this book is to offer guidance on how to manage organizational culture to those individuals charged with leading and directing organizations, and teams of people within them, including divisions, departments, and other units. Throughout the book, we will refer to these individuals in charge of others at various times in almost interchangeable ways, as "executives," "leaders," "managers," "bosses," and "entrepreneurs."

Our guidance covers a range of critical topics, from crafting a culture that helps an organization execute on its strategy to ensuring that the culture is responsive and adapts over time. We offer guidance in a particular way—by sorting out among popular beliefs what is true about culture, what's not true, and what appears ambiguous or unresolved. We do so by highlighting and translating relevant social science theory and research. We also discuss many real-world examples and incidents, drawn from a variety of companies and industries. Some of these cases and stories may be familiar and frequently discussed in the context of culture, but a fair number are new, providing less familiar material and insights. We believe that this approach will enable managers to prioritize what really matters, to understand what is consequential, and to know what to ignore and leave behind.

As a manager, you need to behave *consistently, comprehensively, and coherently* in scientifically known ways to get the results that you want by managing organizational culture. Our goal in writing this book is to make culture comprehensible and actionable and to review and explain the known ways of leading and managing an effective culture in an organization.

ACKNOWLEDGMENTS

To write this book, we incurred many debts of gratitude to family, colleagues, students, friends, and others. The list is long, and we apologize for its incompleteness, for surely, we have forgotten some key contributions from others over the years.

First, we appreciate the educational institutions that employ us and pay us to live as scholars and educators. We regularly feel lucky to be on the faculties of the business schools at the University of California (UC), Berkeley, and Stanford University. Moreover, we derive individual support from the Paul J. Cortese Distinguished Chair of Management and the Bank of America Dean's Chair (Chatman) and the Adams Distinguished Chair of Management (Carroll). Chatman also benefits from the support of the UC Berkeley Center for Workplace Culture and Innovation.

At both institutions, we are fortunate to benefit from the top-notch colleagues of our respective organizational behavior groups. When it comes to organizational culture, we both learned an enormous amount over decades from our longtime colleague and mentor, Charles O'Reilly. Charles studied culture long before culture was a cool topic, and we are grateful to have benefited from his insight and wisdom for so long. We also continuously learn from our colleagues at Berkeley and Stanford, including especially Cameron Anderson, Erica Bailey, Frank Flynn, Michele Gelfand, Amir Goldberg, Mike Hannan, Laura Kray, Helena Miton, Don Moore, Aruna Ranganathan,

Juliana Schroeder, Jesper Sørensen, and Sameer Srivastava, among others. We benefited greatly from close critical readings of the manuscript by John DeFigueiredo, Charles O'Reilly, and Sameer Srivastava.

We would also to thank our many illustrious coauthors and colleagues whose culture-related work enables and inspires us: Sigal Barsade, Dave Caldwell, Elizabeth Canning, Michele Duguid, Carol Dweck, Lindy Greer, Mike Hannan, J. Richard Harrison, Laura Kray, Arianna Marchetti, Mary Murphy, Maggie Neale, Jeffrey Pfeffer, Jeff Polzer, Ed Schein, Ben Schneider, Barry Staw, Bob Sutton, and Mike Tushman.

Doctoral students support faculty in more ways than those outside academia could imagine. We have been lucky to work with a host of talented students in producing research underlying this book, many of whom have moved on to become successful professors at other institutions. At Berkeley, these students have included Alice Boisnier, Derek Brown, Yixi Chen, Andrew Choi, Bernadette Doerr, Frank Flynn, Jack Goncalo, Hope Harrington, Jessica Kennedy, Richard Lu, Eliot Sherman, Sandy Spataro, Dan Stein, Salem Sulaiman, and Anna Yan. At Stanford, they have included Sobhana Alturi, Anjali Bhatt, Kara Luo, Abraham Oshtose, Paul Vicinanza, and Lara Yang. At Northwestern, they have included Etty Jehn, Elizabeth Morrison, and Jeff Polzer.

Audrey Jones, Angela Shu, and Harshita Somani provided excellent editorial services. And Emily Tinnei Chen did a truly remarkable job of organizing the figures and getting copyright permissions from all over the world.

We dedicate the book to those closest to us and who manage our cultures. From Jenny, this is Russell, Ava, Sonya, Otis, and Raven, who inspire her and keep her laughing every day. From Glenn, this is Lihua and Lishan, but Lola and Iko get honorable mention.

MAKING ORGANIZATIONAL CULTURE GREAT

1

POPULAR BELIEFS ABOUT CULTURE

Culture baffles even the most experienced managers. Even those who take on the challenge of leveraging their organization's culture for strategic success often feel mystified, uneasy, or skeptical.

There are plenty of good reasons for this discomfort. First, culture is not a tangible phenomenon that you can readily see. Second, managers typically receive little or no training in creating or managing culture, unlike their training on tasks like manipulating a spreadsheet or reporting financial outcomes. And few managers are social scientists.

Yet the stakes—using culture to accelerate your organization's success or, conversely, letting cultural inertia doom your organization—are high. Most people—especially executives and other top leaders—believe that culture matters enormously for how an organization operates and performs, both in the short and long term.

Consider the findings of prominent management consulting firms. For example, a 2021 survey of 3,243 executives in forty-two countries by consulting firm PwC found that "81 percent of respondents who strongly believe their organization was able to adapt during the 12 months before our survey was conducted also say their culture has been a source of competitive advantage."[1] Similarly, Deloitte's survey of 1,308 adults and executives in 2012 found that "94 percent of executives and 88 percent of employees believe a distinct workplace culture is important to business success."[2] A study by Korn Ferry found that "91 percent of executives agree that improving corporate culture would increase their organization's value" and "80 percent of executives ranked culture among the five most important factors driving valuation."[3] Likewise, Heidrick & Struggles' 2021 survey of 500 CEOs at companies with a minimum of $2.5 billion in annual revenue found that "82 percent of CEOs . . . surveyed said they had focused on culture as a key priority over the past three years."[4]

Academic researchers report similar findings. John Graham and colleagues surveyed 1,348 CFOs and other finance executives around 2020. They found that "91 percent of executives consider corporate culture to be 'important' or 'very important' at their firm."[5] Similarly, Glenn Carroll and Lara Yang surveyed 1,926 managers and nonmanagers in the United States about cultural beliefs, perceptions, and experiences. They found that about half the respondents reacted positively to the statement, "In general, culture is more important to organizational performance than strategy or operating model."[6]

Despite the professed importance of culture, a Gallup poll found that only 21 percent of employees report feeling connected to their company's culture.[7]

OUR APPROACH

We wrote this book to help managers develop and manage culture so they can improve their organization's performance.

We do so by helping to sort out what's what with respect to culture, to consider several of the most salient popular beliefs about culture, and to offer our evaluations as professional social scientists, one of us (Chatman) a psychologist and the other (Carroll) a sociologist. We have been researching organizational culture for decades.

Our main goal in writing this book is to offer guidance on how to manage organizational culture effectively to those who are responsible for leading and directing organizations and the teams of people within them, including divisions, departments, and other units. We recognize at the outset the difficulty of trying to define culture. Academic definitions often extend broadly to include symbols, behaviors, norms, values, and language. For example, pioneering culture researcher Ed Schein defined organizational culture as "the pattern of basic assumptions which a given group has invented, discovered or developed in learning to cope with its problems of external adaptation and internal integration, which have worked well enough to be considered valid, and therefore to be taught to new members as the correct way to perceive, think and feel in relation to those problems. . . . It is the assumptions which lie behind values and which determine the behavior patterns and the visible artifacts such as architecture, office layout, dress codes, and so on."[8] Yet we view it as counterproductive for managers to worry about definitional debates. We suggest using a simpler, more straightforward definition of culture as "a system of shared values that define what is important, and norms that define appropriate attitudes and behaviors for organizational members."

Culture can also be hard to identify "in the wild." To see culture in action can be like trying to spot camouflaged animals in the jungle. Adding to the challenge, culturally relevant behaviors can be ambiguous, frequently spawning multiple interpretations.

And members of an organization's culture can claim to have a certain culture, but the reality of that culture can be quite different from what people say it is.

Mainly, we aim to offer guidance on how to manage organizational culture—ranging from crafting a culture that helps an organization execute on its strategy to ensuring that the culture adapts over time. We do so in a particular way—by sorting out what is true about culture, what's not true, and what appears ambiguous or unresolved.[9] We believe that this approach will enable managers to prioritize what really matters, to understand what is consequential, and to know what to ignore and leave behind.

To illustrate our approach, consider the issue of measuring culture quantitatively. Many managers wonder whether measuring culture is a good idea, and if so, how and when they would do so. Others wonder whether their hiring processes should evaluate a person's fit to the culture, and if so, how they can avoid bias and discrimination in the process. And, of course, managers wonder about culture's impact on organizational performance and how they can ensure that culture helps rather than hinders people trying to accomplish organizational goals. These questions often challenge managers as well as social scientists. But they become even harder to answer, if not impossible, without a solid understanding of the behavioral realities of culture, which requires looking beyond the popular beliefs to find what's true about culture.

STRONG CULTURE ORGANIZATIONS

We pay particular attention to a culture's strength, a widely used social science term that is sometimes misunderstood.

Specifically, social scientists define a *strong culture organization* by two pronounced features. First, its members hold a high consensus around the appropriate norms, values, and beliefs of the organization. In other words, people agree about "the right thing to do at this organization." Second, members display a high intensity of commitment to those norms, values, and beliefs, such that people will act on their own to ensure that others comply. Imagine being taught on the assembly line the "right" way to do things by your fellow worker or being scolded by your peer when violating a normative expectation of timely attendance at meetings. In both cases, the targeted employee is being instructed and sanctioned by a peer rather than a boss. This self-managed aspect of strong culture organizations is part of their appeal, and systematic research (reviewed in chapter 7) shows that strong culture organizations indeed require fewer managers to operate effectively—operationally, they are simply more efficient.

Note that by this definition, a strong culture organization does not depend on any specific norms or practices (often called "cultural content") to make it strong—all that's required is high agreement and high intensity. Another way of saying this is that cultural strength is independent of cultural content. Accordingly, you can find examples of strong culture organizations with virtually any cultural content. Indeed, in this book we will review examples of strong culture organizations engaged in manufacturing, service delivery, research, terrorism, religion (including cults), policing, military activities, and more. We will see strong culture organizations that are large and small, old and newly founded, across a variety of industries and operating in many different countries.

For example, among commonly recognized strong culture organizations are the following well-known organizations:

- Southwest Airlines, with its breezy culture of fun and teamwork
- The Unification Church, aka the "Moonies," a religious cult that draws people in and won't let them go easily
- Nordstrom, the Seattle-based department store known for exceptional customer service
- Goldman Sachs, the long-successful investment banking firm that drives performance through information sharing
- Navy SEALs, Green Berets, Special Weapons and Tactics (SWAT) teams, military-like special forces, who perform highly specialized and immensely difficult tasks for national defense
- Amazon, the internet-based retailer and cloud service company who seeks to provide consumers with anything they might want to buy online
- Netflix, the video-streaming service whose culture has enabled it to transform its business model from sending DVDs in the mail to now producing its own entertainment content
- Google, the information technology company built on internet search who selects people based on sheer curiosity
- Uber, the ride-hailing platform that dominates most US urban markets

FIVE POPULAR BELIEFS

We organized this book around five common popular beliefs about culture. We focus on these specific beliefs because they come up most frequently in our consulting activities and classroom teaching. The beliefs capture many of the key challenges that managers face in using culture to improve organizational performance and to sustain performance at high levels.

The discomfort that many managers feel about culture often leads to misdirected efforts to learn more about culture or to engage consultants and other experts. While we applaud any attempt to gain more knowledge, we think that the biggest challenge that leaders face in managing culture is not intellectual but behavioral. Once you learn to ignore the munificent and often imprecise babble about culture—the underlying forces involved in building and maintaining a strong culture hold little mystery, at least to social scientists.

Cultures get built and sustained through a variety of well-studied and well-known social and psychological processes. For the most part, social scientists do not question or debate the ways that these processes operate; they reside in the scientific canon as accepted facts. Most important, these processes are not mysterious or technical: You can readily learn and remember them. For example, the relevant managerial levers include culturally selective hiring, intense early socialization, aligning compensation and other incentives, and communicating expectations throughout the organization. The payoff can be substantial because understanding and implementing these processes will enable you to enhance your organization's well-being and performance.

By contrast, what is difficult—exceptionally so in our estimation—is the ability to act and behave *consistently* in ways that advance your goals as a manager in using these processes. Acting consistently day in and day out, meeting after meeting, activity after activity, in the presence of many different people holding many different positions and playing many different roles, requires self-discipline, deliberateness, and personal presence. Jack Welch, the highly successful long-term CEO at GE, famously said that good leaders had to be "relentlessly boring." Welch was not advocating that a leader be boring when speaking or acting (he passionately believed the opposite) but he appreciated that if an intelligent and engaged leader repeats the same message consistently hundreds, perhaps thousands, of times, then it will likely get boring to the leader himself. Welch was warning against being harmfully inventive by modifying the message to make it interesting to the leader.

A second difficulty lies in ensuring a *comprehensive* approach to managing culture. That is, leading through culture involves using a variety of managerial levers that affect a variety of processes. While there may be some absolute no-no's, there is no magic bullet, no single way to build and sustain an organization's culture. You must attend to several or many levers and processes at once if you want to manage the culture effectively. It's not just about incentives, training, or culturally selective hiring—it's about orchestrating a wide range of the levers at your command. The challenge rests with juggling many balls to the same end, some of which may be easy for you and some which you will find hard.

Finally, offering a *coherent* narrative about these consistent and comprehensive practices ensures that members of your organization understand without ambiguity why you wish to cultivate a particular culture, with specific behavioral norms. What do various groups in the organization—the executive team, managers, individual contributors, and others—think you and they will gain by following this particular culture with these values and norms? The narrative contains both formal scripted chapters as well as informal spontaneous ones. Cultural coherence provides the logic for coordination across organizations, something essential for getting big things done.

So, in our view, success in managing culture does not require you to become a rocket scientist—defining and figuring out difficult unsolved problems. Instead, the challenge involves performing on point. Perhaps an orthopedic surgeon represents a better metaphor—a knowledgeable professional who executes time and time again in a consistent, comprehensive, and coherent way. Managers need to behave consistently, comprehensively, and coherently in scientifically known ways to get the results that they hope for in managing organizational culture. Our goal in writing this book is to demystify culture, to offer clarity about the known and proven ways of leading and managing an effective culture.

The book will demonstrate that managing through culture typically differs from conventional management in numerous ways. For example, leading through culture involves culturally selective hiring for fit rather than just focusing on skills. New hires are socialized to the culture, and motivational messages aim to inspire instead of offering higher pay. Leaders are often treated like peers, information is shared widely, and peers are involved in supervision as much as bosses. Rules in strong culture organizations also tend to general and generative rather than specific and detailed. Strong culture organizations typically manage through social control—peer pressure or normative sanctioning—rather than heavy doses of formal control, consisting of rules, policies, and defined procedures.

PLAN OF THE BOOK

We aim in this book to better inform you about culture to make you an even more effective leader. We use as our point of departure five common popular beliefs about culture. The popular beliefs that we hear regularly from managers and others are the following:

- Culture shows great inertia, it doesn't change much, and you as a manager can't really change it. We examine cases including Apple, Ford, and Roche.

- Culture can be managed only from the top down, using authority. It's all about managers imposing their will on employees and forming the culture themselves. We examine cases including Southwest Airlines, Salesforce, AMD, Boeing, Lululemon, WeWork, and Lyft.

- Culture consists of soft, fuzzy, and ambiguous phenomena; thinking about culture remains elusive and cannot be measured objectively. We examine cases including the Navy SEALS, Netflix, NXVIM, and Synanon.

- Culture benefits only those who fit in, so-called aligned employees benefit from culture while some valuable others are neglected. We examine cases including Disney, Google, Cisco, Axon, and Maersk.

- Culture can make people happy, but it does not matter for business performance. Culture does not affect the bottom line. We examine cases including Dreyer's Grand Ice Cream, Uber, and the Ryder Cup.

While some of these popular beliefs may be true, we show that others carry only an element of veracity. For example, with respect the belief that culture is inert, we provide cases demonstrating that culture can change, but leaders need to be deliberate and have a plan. As for the top-down belief, we show that culture can be created and strengthened by people and forces other than the CEO or senior leaders, but CEOs and senior leaders typically play leading roles. With respect to the belief that culture is soft, we describe cases where culture would be described as tough rather than soft; we also show that culture can have an enormous impact both on financial performance and people's behavior. Concerning the fit popular belief, we show that lower levels of cultural fit, at least among a subset of members, can instigate innovation and culture change, even though high person-culture fit offers distinct advantages to organizations and employees. Regarding the popular belief about culture mattering on the bottom line, we review examples and studies making clear that culture matters to the bottom line, but its impact can be nuanced and indirect. The ultimate verdict on the popular beliefs shows that even though they have some veracity at times, following them blindly surely leads to many missed opportunities, as well as to mistakes—sometimes terrible ones.

We chose these specific beliefs because, in our experiences in consulting with and teaching executives and business students, we have seen many people get hung up on and confused by these beliefs. We suspect that the discomfort that many managers feel about managing culture arises from their doubts about these popular beliefs. Once managers better understand the reality behind these beliefs, we think that being deliberate in developing and managing culture becomes less daunting.

Accordingly, after starting in chapter 2 with an extended case example of effective cultural management, we organize the next part of the book and its chapters around these popular beliefs. So, in the next five chapters, 3 through 7, each tackles one of the popular beliefs and addresses it head on, using specific examples as well as social science theory and research. After running through those ideas, we then take a full march in chapter 8 through the various ways that leaders of strong culture organizations manage their cultures. This includes looking at an extensive set of specific managerial levers used to set up, design, develop, and maintain a strong culture organization. Finally, in chapter 9, we offer some concluding remarks.

If you read the chapters in order, we think that the experience provides a coherent narrative. But many readers will already know a fair amount about culture, especially some specific issues. In that case, it may make sense to skip some chapters and go straight to the topic of primary interest, leaving the skipped chapters for later. That is, we do not think that this book needs to be read in the assigned chapter order. We hope that you find our assessment of the five popular beliefs helpful as you develop and manage your organization's culture!

2

COOKING UP CULTURE

"**J**ennifer's culture." That's what they called it.

The term referred to Senior Vice President Jennifer Cook's proposal to bring together the four units in a new division that CEO Ian Clark had asked her to run at Genentech following its merger with Roche (figure 2.1). The new division was named Genentech Immunology and Ophthalmology, "GIO" for short.

GIO included four product franchises: Actemra (rheumatoid arthritis), Rituxan (rheumatoid arthritis), Lucentis (wet age-related macular degeneration, an eye disease), and Xolair (allergic asthma). To say that it was not obvious that these four franchises should be grouped together in a single division would be an understatement. They had different histories, the products were at different stages in their life cycles, and the teams had different cultures. Xolair and Rituxan were mature Genentech brands with modest growth prospects and a strong sense of history and identity; Lucentis was a Genentech brand with a robust life cycle, significant growth potential, and an already-strong culture; and Actemra was a Roche brand in launch mode with an extensive life cycle and significant growth potential, but its culture was less cohesive, and it had a variety of product launch challenges.

FIGURE 2.1 Jennifer Cook

To complicate matters even more, GIO was established amid the Roche-Genentech merger, which had led to layoffs, disruptions, and uncertainty, as well as multiple leadership changes. The new GIO division was a collection of stray cats and dogs, each fending for itself. Each of the four franchises reported acceptable sales numbers, "but as a group, they didn't have a strong sense of shared identity," said Cook.

Because of GIO's disparate franchises, Cook felt that it was especially critical to evaluate and develop the division's culture to succeed over the long run. She believed that cultivating a shared culture that would connect the franchises and foster cross-franchise learning was the key to GIO's ability to deliver better business results. With the ambitious five-year goals that Ian Clark had set for GIO—essentially to triple the business—Cook felt significant pressure to unlock GIO's potential and rev up its performance quickly. And she knew that GIO wouldn't get there just by increasing the performance of each unit.

DISPARATE IDENTITIES

Cook was not making her assessment in isolation. When she asked senior leaders what they needed, their responses revealed a surprisingly clear yearning for a shared sense of identity and purpose. She said: "The big challenge was how we think about coming together . . . [because the] group . . . sees each other so rarely."

Khurem Farooq, head of rheumatology, added: "We talked about the fact that the franchises essentially existed on their own, that there was no real common goal or common value set that brought them together. We were all a part of the GIO business unit, but what are the commonalities that bring us together because the products don't as much when compared to oncology."

Given these assessments, Cook asked, "Why not find out what unites us, what we have in common, and what could be helpful to us?" She didn't want to fabricate something artificial, but she did want to find opportunities to see how the franchises might share knowledge and help each other out. This, she thought, could be a path to tripling the business in five years.

After getting her senior leaders on board, Cook began to discuss culture with a broader group in GIO. She knew that she needed to engage the entire GIO organization to help define and create the culture.

In the fall of 2010, she introduced the culture idea to the entire organization through multiple live onstage communications and workshops. "This was daunting," she said. "I had to explain what culture is, why are we doing this, and how are we going to approach it. There were a number of skeptical people who had heard about culture too many times before, and understandably they had a 'flavor of the day' cynicism. I had to directly acknowledge those doubts and try to convince them the change could be real this time. I also knew the only way to really convince people was to demonstrate the change, not just talk about it."

GIO's operations lead, Ashwin Datt, also heard from the skeptics: "There were a lot of people in the organization who felt that they had heard this culture business before, and it was loud enough that we acknowledged that. People also said that they had real problems and wanted real solutions to fix those problems."

In her communications to GIO employees, Cook focused on what brought the franchises together. According to Datt: "People could have come away with a feeling that we were just put together because Genentech has bio-oncology and everything else [is] not in bio-oncology. I'm not saying that was how the decision was made, but to be fair, it was close. But it does make sense to put the new emerging areas together, and what Jennifer did was to take the time to really understand and look for commonalities. We are all in a chronic disease environment, we have a lot of opportunities to impact patients, we all have competition in our brands, and we all have challenges to explain to our health-care practitioners and payers on our value propositions. Early on, the focus was to sort out the vision of GIO."

PRESSURE TO GROW GIO

Ian Clark held high ambitions for the newly formed GIO division, even though the restructuring was not based on any identified strategic links or deep analyses suggesting that the franchises should be grouped together. He asked Cook to triple the collective businesses, from $1 billion to $3 billion in revenue, and he also wanted GIO to triple the number of patients served—those with chronic diseases like rheumatoid arthritis, asthma, and glaucoma—all within a five-year window. And Clark wanted Cook to fully integrate the four franchises, particularly given that two of them had been competitors and at least one was underperforming. These became known as the "3, 3, and 3 goals" (300,000 patients, 3 franchises, and $3 billion annual revenue by 2015). Cook believed that these goals could be achieved only by bringing the franchises together.

These challenging goals put a significant amount of pressure on Cook, and when she approached Clark with her idea of achieving them by focusing on culture, Clark was, by any measure, underwhelmed. He was not a big believer in using culture to achieve strategic success. To his credit, he refrained from discouraging Cook as she pursued the culture change path, but he didn't actively support her either.

Cook understood that GIO's cultural transformation would need to simultaneously provide purpose and cohesion to GIO members, but, critically, it would also need to push strategically relevant performance—growing revenue, consolidating and integrating the franchises, and serving considerably more patients.

"YOU CHOOSE IT"

In a bold stroke, Cook chose to combat the cynicism from those who called it "her culture" with an ownership challenge. "I tried to shift that sense of ownership and accountability to them. After all, the culture was chosen by them, defined by them, based on their vision of what it would take for us to be successful," she said. "I kept repeating, 'You choose it,' which became a theme because our culture is made up of all the choices individuals within it make every day," she added.

"It's not about what I say that shows up on a piece of paper or that we stick on a website. It's about what our people literally choose to do every day, and if we're not making the choices that are aligned to what we say matters, then we're not living this culture."

Cook added: "Employees already know what they want. They know what they wish for and what they think would be a good culture, but they don't really have a way to communicate it, and they may not even be conscious of it—it could be subliminal, but it is there. I like the idea of harnessing what is in their minds, because we hire extraordinary people, true knowledge workers. Why not ask them what they think?"

SURVEYING GIO

As part of this process, Cook conducted a GIO-wide organizational culture profile (OCP) assessment with 550 employees to "get data and try to understand it." The OCP (described further in chapter 5) is a quantitative culture assessment tool (developed by Jennifer Chatman and Charles O'Reilly) that asks respondents to rank fifty-four validated, standard attributes of culture from most to least characteristic. The OCP can identify gaps between the current and the strategically needed culture.

Everyone at GIO was asked to rank the fifty-four cultural attributes for both the current GIO culture, to understand what the current culture was emphasizing, and GIO's future, strategically desired culture, to describe the culture that would ideally be in place if GIO were fully executing on its five-year strategy. The fifty-four attributes roll up into eight higher dimensions. For example, the dimension "intensity" aggregates the following attributes: being aggressive, hard-driving, fast-moving, urgent, and competitive. And under the focus on people dimension are these attributes: being people-oriented, being supportive, having respect for individuals, and sharing information freely.

The OCP survey at GIO showed gaps in four dimensions between the current and desired cultures that were particularly relevant to Cook's strategy for GIO: **innovativeness** (which Cook labeled "courageous" to fit with Roche's language around innovation), **focus on people, integrity**, and **patient orientation**. These four dimensions showed the greatest gaps between GIO's current and future desired cultures and the greatest alignment with GIO's five-year goals (see figure 2.2). Two other dimensions that had gaps as well—but in the opposite direction, meaning that they were being emphasized more in the current

culture than GIO members thought strategically necessary—
were **intensity** and **drive for results**.

Cook's OCP survey was quantitative, data driven, and analytical. According to Datt: "Jennifer wanted to use data to help
us think about what matters. From my experience, even within
Genentech where other organizations have tried to do culture
change, what is unique about the GIO process is that she took
what is at the very heart of who we are as a company—being
science driven, being data driven, having a hypothesis, as well as
running an experiment—and said that if we do that with culture
to support our business objectives, what would we do?"

Cook labeled the four identified gaps as GIO's "Cultural Pillars," and they became the focus of subsequent culture change
efforts at GIO. Based on the OCP results, it was clear that people needed to make behaviors in these areas more prominent in
their work lives. They also wanted these principles to motivate
and guide employees' everyday actions. And Cook viewed these

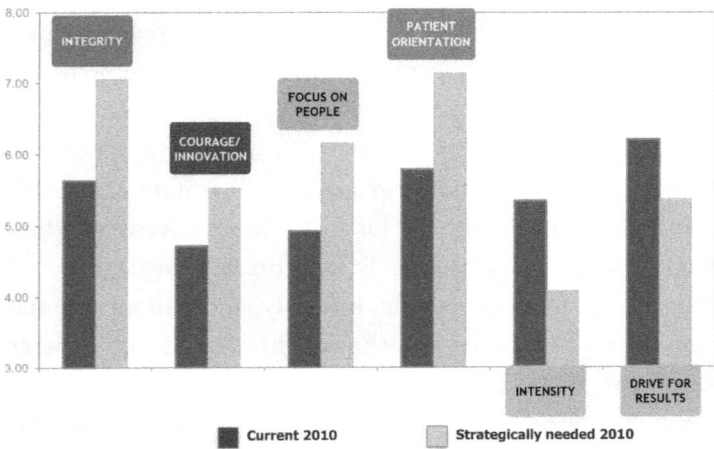

FIGURE 2.2 Key gaps between current and strategically needed culture

priorities as the pathway to achieving GIOs ambitious five-year business goals.

The two cultural dimensions that GIO staff wanted to see less emphasized—intensity and drive for results—helped Cook and her senior leadership team (SLT) round out their understanding of the current culture at GIO. Cook explained: "The way I read the survey results was that people already understood that they're on the hook to drive results. We're a sales and marketing team, and we know we're accountable for a revenue number. But our people want to be more inspired; the four things we wanted more of are all inspirational, and the two we wanted less of are more basic business terms. Interestingly, if people are given an opportunity to work on something they care about and that could make a difference, they don't see that as demanding intensity and drive; they see it as opportunity. This isn't about how hard people are willing to work. They're willing to work ridiculously hard. It's the difference between what you tell them to do versus what you let them do."

GIO'S VISION

Cook met with her extended leadership team (ELT) to share the OCP results at an offsite meeting. The ELT considered the six culture gaps and the ways that they showed up in people's behaviors. For example, GIO's staff were almost singularly focused on bottom-line quarterly results. They talked about it, they planned for it, and they felt immense pressure to hit their numbers, and thus they prioritized driving for results over just about everything else. This orientation explained the intensity and drive for results findings from the OCP. This focus was, of course, incompatible with the courage and innovation—the ability to swing for the fences or growing by working smarter rather than just harder—that would be required to grow the business threefold within five years. From these discussions, the group formulated a new GIO vision statement, shown in figure 2.3. The ELT created this vision statement, which, as Cook noted, came directly from "our people's words."

As Cook recalled, "[The ELT] took reams of survey and focus group information and assembled a vision statement out of our employees' words. We didn't want to collect our senior leaders in a room and just state our vision. . . . We wanted to take the prior statement and make it more inspirational and connect more to what we identified that we care about in order to make it more meaningful."

Combined with the five-year strategic goals, Cook and her leaders were able to develop a comprehensive rationale for why instilling the strategically needed culture—those four Cultural Pillars—was so important. Figure 2.4 shows a visual depiction of the rationale. Connecting vision culture and strategy (the five-year goals) represents remarkable coherence, and it also helps employees connect the dots to their own performance.

> GIO is a **HIGHLY SKILLED TEAM** of sales and marketing professionals who have the **PASSION & ADAPTABILITY** to succeed in our complex health care environment. We bring breakthrough medicines that provide **MAXIMUM LIFETIME IMPACT** to patients suffering from chronic immunologic and ophthalmologic diseases.

FIGURE 2.3 Genentech's GIO vision

GIO Vision

GIO is a
HIGHLY SKILLED TEAM
of sales and marketing professionals
who have the
PASSION & ADAPTABILITY
to succeed in our complex health
care environment. We bring
breakthrough medicines that provide
MAXIMUM LIFETIME IMPACT
to patients suffering from chronic
immunologic and ophthalmologic
diseases.

GIO Strategic Goals

3 FRANCHISES

$3 BILLION

300,000 PATIENTS

GIO Culture

FOCUS ON PEOPLE

COURAGE/ INNOVATION

PATIENT ORIENTATION

INTEGRITY

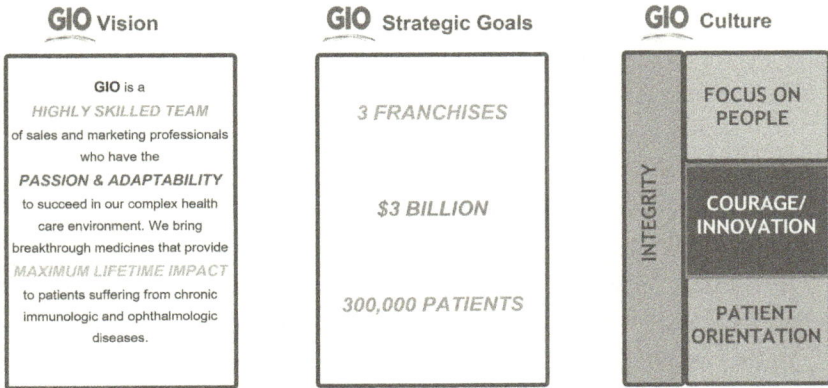

FIGURE 2.4 Genentech's GIO *Vision* drives *Strategy*, which *Culture* enables.

Copyright © 2013 by Regents University of California. Used by permission.

BUILDING ON THE VISION

In December 2010, Cook met again with the ELT to drill down into the survey results to build out the Cultural Pillars. The Trium Group, a management consulting group, was brought in to help move things forward.

At this meeting, the team developed a "Culture Placemat" (a term that they coined because the document was laminated and was the size of a placemat that one could eat lunch on) for each pillar. Each placemat explicitly defined its pillar, as well as its associated behaviors and outcomes, mindset shifts, and evidence. The goal of the placemats was to make the culture changes behaviorally specific so people had a vivid understanding of these new expectations.

For example, the Culture Placemat defined the Courage/ Innovation Pillar as follows: "We challenge the way things are done with new ideas, fostering an environment where creativity and persistence are rewarded." The placemat also listed a specific example of a relevant behavior: "Engage in rigorous debate about what will serve the patient." And it included an example of a mindset shift from the current culture: "I believe my reputation and self-worth are on the line when I suggest a new approach. Being wrong leaves me diminished," to move toward a more intentional culture, focused on courage and innovation: "I believe rejection is about the idea, not about me." See figure 2.5 for more details about the placemat for the Courage/Innovation Pillar.

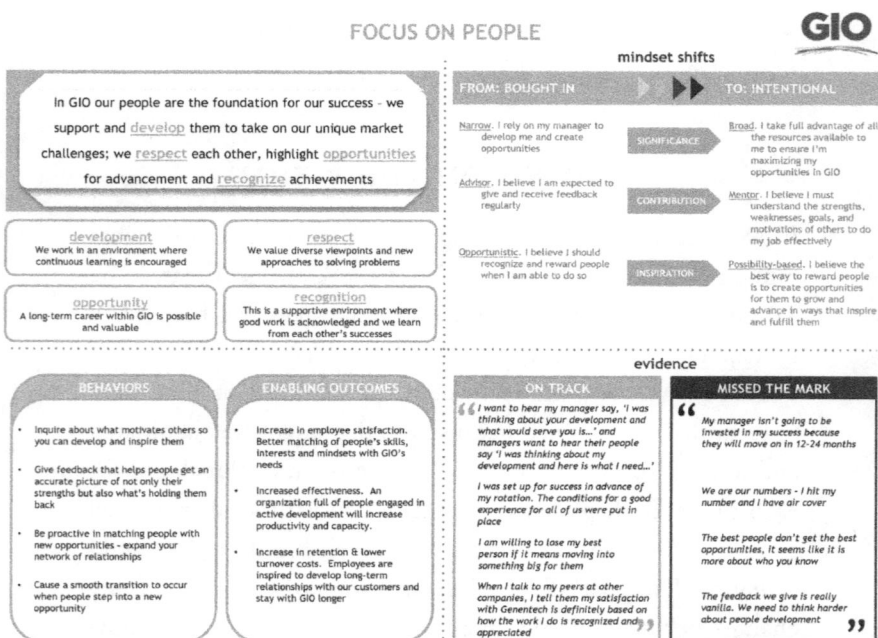

FIGURE 2.5 Culture Placemat for the Courage/Innovation Pillar

Copyright © 2013 by Regents University of California. Used by permission.

Cook wanted the placemats to be very specific to GIO's needs because words like "courage" or "innovation" can seem generic and vague, and not very tailored to the setting. She said, "I love the placemat for Courage/Innovation in that the words on the placemat include 'persistence' and 'creativity', not what you would think of necessarily. Creativity for innovation, yes, but 'persistence' is a different word than 'courage.' Yet, those are the specific words that we need because of the business we're in— with our products for chronic diseases, you have to overcome many biases and a multitude of choices physicians have at their disposal, as well as what can sometimes be a lack of urgency; this contrasts with an area like oncology where patients may have only months to live and fewer therapeutic choices."

In January 2011, Cook went further into the organization. She called a meeting with the eighty-eight GIO line managers during the Sales and Marketing Managers' Meeting (SAMM) to present the results from the survey and to get their buy-in. She also rolled out the new vision statement as a test drive before the larger annual National Sales Meeting (NSM) a few weeks later, which would include all GIO employees. The goal was to generate personal insights and garner commitment before going to the rest of the organization. Tara Jewett, who was the associate director of GIOs business unit operations, said, "The prior meeting with senior leaders was critical for alignment before going into this January manager meeting because the senior leaders were going to facilitate the SAMM meeting."

DEVELOPING MANAGERIAL LEVERS

Two weeks later, Cook and Chatman presented the results of the GIO-wide survey to all the GIO employees at the Las

Vegas NSM. Right after the presentation, the meeting shifted into a highly organized workshop with the goal of surfacing the specific actions that would shift the culture. To come up with new practices and behaviors to shift the culture, the 500 GIO employees were organized around five specific culture levers drawn from management research: Performance Management, Communication, Reward & Recognition, Training, and Recruiting.[1] "We adopted these levers knowing that they would work to change behavior," said Cook. Jewett added: "These change levers are a framework on how to operationalize change in each one of the pillars."

At the meeting, Cook gave the organization small, simple cards that listed the five levers and asked everyone to pick a lever that they were interested in and propose a tactic to address it. As a result, the groups were naturally mixed with people from different franchises across GIO.

Next, four ballrooms were organized into cross-franchise teams, with three senior leaders and an outside consultant in each room. The facilitators' goal was to "inspire possibility about what we can create together in GIO in terms of our business and culture." Their objectives were to "clarify how culture shows up in our daily work" and to help "brainstorm ideas about how we can reinforce GIO's desired culture."[2]

People brainstormed ideas such as putting patients versus sales numbers first in e-mail communications, restating how sales were quantified from "vials sold" to "patients helped," and starting meetings with an inspirational story of a real patient who benefited from the medicines provided by GIO. "We wanted to get people using this concept and to realize it's not ambiguous or fuzzy, but actually quite tangible and day-to-day," said Cook. At the end of the workshop, everyone received a bracelet on which the four pillars were printed—one of many efforts to make the four pillars omnipresent.

"We were nervous about doing a workshop for over 500 people, but we did it anyway," said Cook. "Logistics alone were complicated, and we worried that people would be frustrated if their ideas weren't put to use." Jewett said: "The message to us was that people wanted to be more inspired, to feel valued, and to see the right behaviors role-modeled consistently."

The workshop was a huge success, generating over 500 ideas for closing the gaps between the current and the strategically needed culture. Jewett and her team organized and synthesized the ideas into fifty concepts called "The Nifty 50." On the process, Jewett said: "We took the 500 ideas and grouped them not only by the pillars, but also by the change levers within those pillars. From there, themes rose to the top in terms of the volume or intensity of demand." A few ideas were: "Open meetings with a quick patient story," "Create a GIO 'culture corner' on the GIO Portal," and "Introduce culture awards related to our four Cultural Pillars."

On the levers, Cook said: "I like to say that the [culture assessment] tool [and the levers] are catalysts, but not the answer. The value was in the discussions we had because words are just words. What does 'needing more integrity' actually mean? We were already really patient-focused, but people said we needed to be more patient-focused, so what did that mean? We had to take apart the meaning and dive into it as the first step. The culture assessment tool gives you a quantitative, tangible, and trackable set of things to talk about, but it doesn't give you the answer. That's still up to the group to figure out."

Datt was amazed by how successful the workshop was. He believed that its success arose from the very structured approach to engaging people so that ideas came out, communicating and filtering the ideas quickly within the organization, and encouraging people to sign up to volunteer to work on various initiatives identified at the NSM, as described next. "This is something I hadn't experienced before," he said.

Also at the workshop meeting, Cook and her team rolled out the vision, goals, and culture or "all the rest of it" (shown in figure 2.4). It was part of the plan to have the vision, goals, and culture all described at one time. "They have to relate," she said.

The vision connected to the culture and to GIO's five-year goals. "From the outset, Jennifer framed culture in the context of the business objectives," said Datt. "From the get-go, it was about articulating what makes GIO and how we are different from the other business units. She was very mindful and structured in her approach to discussing the benefits of the different franchises being together as a business unit, and from there taking the staff forward to focus on the goals and objectives that we have to deliver over the next three to five years that are going to be critical for success for Genentech and Roche."

Cook's leadership staff then organized cross-franchise initiative teams around each of the change levers and key initiatives culled from the GIO-wide workshop. They sought volunteers in the ELT to serve as leadership "sponsors." Initially, there were nine teams, each with about fifteen people.

Within the Communication lever, for example, a Culture Advisory Board was formed; within Reward & Recognition were the Culture Awards team and the Noncompensation Rewards & Recognition team; within Training were New Hires, Development Center Program, and Rotations teams; within Performance Management was a Development Planning Skills team; and within Recruiting was a Recruiting team. Figure 2.6 gives an example of some of the detailed work conducted on the levers. Note that each initiative team had a mission statement; it recorded its current year accomplishments; if the initiative lasted for multiple years, the team stated its next-year goals; and each had a sponsor. Table 2.1 underscores the comprehensiveness of the culture change process at GIO.

TABLE 2.1 CULTURE CHANGE INITIATIVES AT GENENTECH (GIO)

Initiative Team	Mission	Prior-Year Key Accomplishments	Next-Year Objectives
Culture Advisory Board	• Create culture awareness and provide a sounding board for cultural progress and issues.	• Develop a Genentech Culture Logo (Q3 2011), vote (Genentech 2011), and reveal (NSM 2012).	• Design and deliver a culture awareness campaign. • Provide insight into our culture evolution. • Serve as an advisory group on key questions. • Create and manage a "Culture Corner" on the Genentech Portal.
Recruiting and New Hire	• Integrate Genentech culture awareness and expectations with new hires.	• Create the New Hire Welcome Letter and Video from leaders.	• Merge Recruiting and New Hire initiative teams, given synergies.
	• Ensure consistent focus on Genentech's desired culture with interview candidates through our screening and hiring process.	• Add a Culture component to New Hire Road Map and CORE Training.	• Enhance internal recruiting training and communication and pull-through.

(continued)

TABLE 2.1 (*continued*)

Initiative Team	Mission	Prior-Year Key Accomplishments	Next-Year Objectives
	• Develop tools to enable culture-related assessments.	• Incorporate Genentech culture into training. • Create Genentech "Discovery Guide" for internal use. • Create recruiting interview questions.	• Examine the feasibility of the external "Genentech Discovery Guide." If viable, develop "Discovery Guide 2.0" for use with external candidates. • Explore the feasibility of assigning each new hire a "buddy." • Involve Genentech in selecting new hires. • Pull through a recommended Genentech/ NSM New Hire reception with a Genentech leader.
Noncompensation Rewards & Recognition	• Recognize people for excellent work and behavior outside the formal awards process.	• Launch Genentech Noncompensation Rewards & Recognition tool and program on Genentech Portal	• Create Communication and pull-through campaign re: the "Culture in Action" Tool on Genentech Portal. • Explore other recognition types and make recommendations.

People created relationships across franchises in the initiative teams. Cook said: "The cocktail hours don't do it. Mixers don't do it. People tend to connect with the people they already know, and it doesn't create a new network. But if you give people something specific to do that they care about, they form relationships."

It was also important to Cook to allow people to choose what to work on so that they cared about it. She also offered them visibility by encouraging them to make presentations to senior leadership—opportunities that they would not have had otherwise. And, of course, the culture change work was done in the context of the work that the GIO division already needed to do—it was not an add-on.

The initiative teams pushed GIO's cultural transformation in a variety of ways. For example, the Recruiting team focused on defining what "recruiting" meant, which led to the question of how to hire people to "fit the culture." This included developing questions that emphasized the four Cultural Pillars that hiring managers could use to assess an applicant's fit with the needed culture at GIO. Derrick Webster, a human resources (HR) consultant at GIO, said: "We created a list of behavioral questions that we thought would screen for our cultural attributes. We came up with a long list and distilled it down to nine questions. [We use] . . . these questions [as] we prepare . . . our interview strategy."

The other initiative teams developed similar specific culturally based templates, routines, and measures for their managerial levers, including On-Boarding, Training, Development, Job Swap, Development, Branding, Recognition and Rewards, Culture, and Performance Management, among others.

COOK'S EVOLVING ROLE

As the culture changed, Cook's role expanded. Not only did she oversee the effort and advise those deeply engaged in it, she also became a visible symbol of the new GIO culture. GIO's successful culture efforts depended on Cook demonstrating and exemplifying the culture. In other words, Cook needed to "walk the talk." According to Farooq, "One of the big reasons for the success of this culture effort was because Jennifer demonstrated and lived it in her day-to-day practice. It wasn't something that you saw on the odd occasion, but it was something you saw daily in terms of how she did things."

Cook ensured that the culture initiative teams' work was embedded in everything that GIO did. She gave the initiatives attention when everyone was together on stage. Every initiative team displayed a poster during the cocktail hour at business unit meetings to show colleagues what they were doing. "Many of these people also presented on stage at meetings and were highly visible," said Farooq.

Cook consciously tried to live the Focus on People Pillar by being accessible. "I act on that all the time and always say 'yes' if people just want advice or time from me," said Cook. She held culture team office hours, when any of the teams could just show up and get advice and support or get a milestone approved. Cook's SLT were also available for its own office hours.

Every month or so, the initiative teams could dial into a call and speak directly with Cook and the SLT to give updates on what they had been working on. "This showed everyone that what they were working on was a priority for the organization," said Farooq.

Cook's "you choose" mandate resonated. "Jennifer never told people what they should do, but rather she allowed us to go to her," said Datt. "She would ask questions and provided insight and support through open office hours. She didn't tell us what to do or what not to do, but she asked us what we were trying to achieve, how we thought we could make it happen, and provided other alternatives. The ideas came from the organization, and Jennifer and the SLT viewed themselves as removing roadblocks."

Cook also changed how she ran her leadership meetings. She listened more, and she consistently incorporated the pillars into each agenda item. Farooq said: "I saw how Jennifer's leading by example on culture changed the environment that I was working in. She would always turn around in meetings and say, 'Well, hold on for a second, what's the right thing to do here, how do we make things easier for people, how do we change things, and so on.' She very much lived what she practiced and demonstrated elements of the culture that she had talked about in her day-to-day situation."

Moreover, Cook tied her own personal performance goals to her culture efforts. "I have a lot of product and business goals each year, but I chose to include these culture efforts as a specific business unit strategy goal in my first year," she said. "I told my team that I was being assessed on how this goes so that they knew it was real."

Note that GIO, under Cook's leadership, developed an approach that was immensely consistent. Starting with measuring the culture, connecting it to GIO's vision and strategic goals, surfacing levers to emphasize the Cultural Pillars across the organization, and Cook's behavior as a leader, the culture that GIO was developing was clear and easy for members to see. Her deliberateness, not only in the practices that she supported for others but in holding herself accountable, is a positive example of influencing the culture from the top down while relying on massive amounts of input and advice from people in all parts of the organization, as discussed further in chapter 4.

CULTURAL CHANGE AND IMPACT

The culture change efforts had a rapid and positive impact on GIO. Leaders and staff reported a noticeable change in morale and engagement within just a month. This alignment among team members is a topic discussed fully in chapter 6. And, miraculously, GIO met its ambitious five-year goals—tripling revenue, serving three times more patients, and consolidating the four drug franchises into three—within, not five years, but eleven months! These bottom-line results—real business results—suggest that culture is not "soft." Rather, it is a "hard" business practice that can have a significant impact on the bottom line, a topic we consider in chapter 5.

Cook and many others in GIO attributed this astonishing growth to the culture change efforts, noting that culture change was not an add-on, but rather was part of the work that they needed to do—a way of focusing on the exact behaviors that would enable the organization to hit its strategic goals. Note that this case flies in the face of most people's views about culture—that it can't possibly change quickly. We discuss the issue of cultural inertia and how to break it in chapter 3.

When Cook delivered the news to the GIO team that it had hit its five-year goals—four years early—and to ask what it wanted to do next, team members enthusiastically replied that they wanted to "go to 4!" That is, service 400,000 patients and generate $4 billion in annual revenue.

Cook assessed the GIO culture using the OCP again the next year and found that people, patients, and integrity had moved upward in the current culture, closing those gaps that had previously existed. The Courage and Innovation Pillar had not moved as much as she hoped. But Cook also saw tangible evidence that the culture norms were helping GIO people in their day-to-day decision making. In fact, her most prized outcome was that GIO's external reputation was elevated within Genentech. Previously, the two oncology divisions had been viewed as the best places to work within the company, but now people from oncology were clamoring to move over to GIO because it had become such an exciting place to work. Notably, GIO's engagement score went from a low of 67 to 84, one of the highest scores within Genentech.

In 2013, Cook got a huge promotion and left GIO to become the head of clinical trials worldwide for Roche. People in the unit such as Khurem Farooq, Cook's successor, kept moving GIO in the desired direction. The impact was clear and positive. When GIO readministered the OCP survey in 2015, the findings showed significant progress in closing the gaps for Integrity, Focus on People, and Patient Orientation. Similarly, GIO culture showed a marked decrease in emphasizing intensity and the drive for results. Of the cultural pillars, only Courage/Innovation had failed

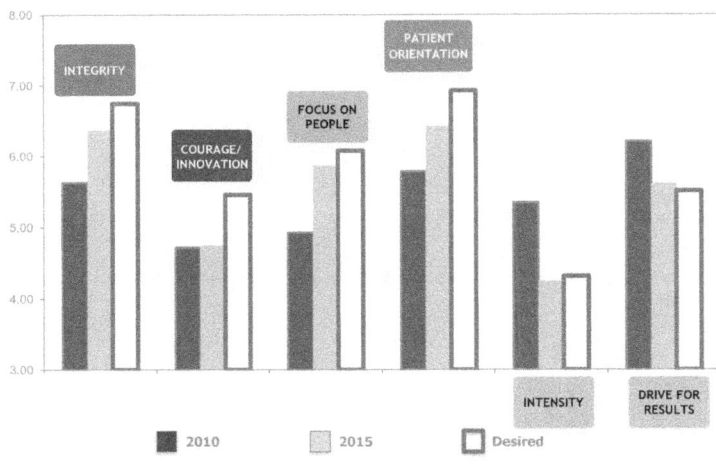

FIGURE 2.6 GIO makes significant progress toward strategically needed culture.

to move in the desired direction. See figure 2.6 for a comparison of GIO culture in 2010 and 2015. Employee engagement also soared, as annual surveys showed (see figure 2.7).

Moreover, GIO saw a noticeable steady upward tick in sales over the entire period of the culture shift. As figure 2.8 shows, the compound annual growth rate (CAGR) rose an annual average of 12 percent from 2010 to 2017. All-important outcome measures showed that not only had Cook's effort succeeded in changing the culture at GIO, it also made a positive difference in the bottom line for the company.

USING CULTURE TO MANAGE

Business leaders have long been at least somewhat aware of the importance of organizational culture, with early pioneers

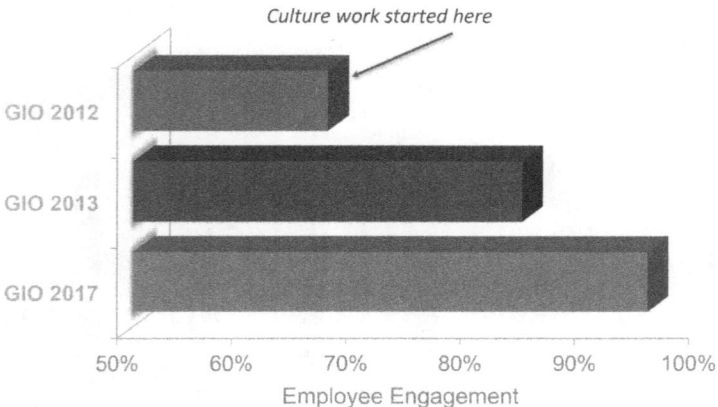

FIGURE 2.7 Measurable impact on GIO engagement, which increased to >90 percent. Note: Two brands were added to the business unit over the interval, but the original brands still exceeded their goal.

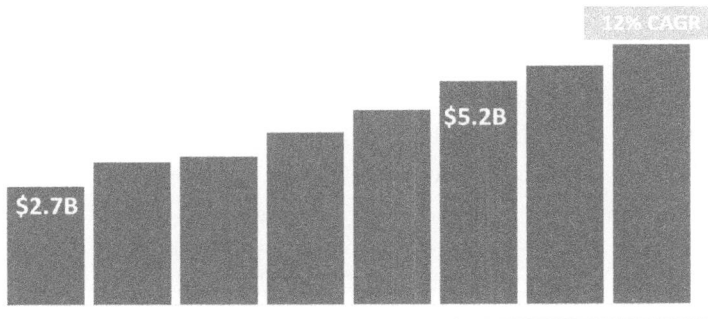

FIGURE 2.8 Clear Business Impact at GIO with All Brands
Delivering Robust Growth

of strong-culture companies dating back at least to when the tightly knit Goldman Sachs was founded in 1869. But Western interest in culture as a management issue massively increased in the 1980s with the immense success of culturally driven global Japanese businesses such as Honda, Sony, and Toyota.

Today, leaders of high-tech successes like Google, Apple, and Salesforce credit their unique cultures as important elements of their companies' strong performance. Spectacularly successful start-ups like Airbnb also serve as cultural models for new entrepreneurs hoping to become the next unicorn. Recent research reports that thousands of senior executives believe that organizational culture is one of the top three factors that affect a firm's value.[4]

Looking at other companies as models can be helpful, of course. But a common problem is that people often focus on what social scientists call "cultural content." Cultural content is the actual behaviors that people exhibit inside an organization. In Silicon Valley, the many perks—the free food, the beer blasts, the personal services—often become the center of attention in culture content.

Cultural content represents only one aspect of managing culture, however. Culture is really about a much broader set of behaviors—the ways that people develop, sanction, and enact norms, how information is transmitted and interpreted, the everyday habits of how work gets done, and how much people agree and care about upholding the culture.

Managing organizational culture involves much more than setting content around values and norms—it's also about setting up and monitoring systems, training and socializing people, and evaluating people as you hire, reward, and fire them. These elements reflect the strength and intensity of the culture, which can be completely distinct from its content. For example, you could imagine two organizations whose cultures both emphasize collaboration, but in one, the collaborative norms are only weakly adhered to, while in the other, collaboration is deeply embedded in everything that people do. The content is the same, but the strength of the culture varies. People will undoubtably experience these cultures differently, and the organizations will experience different benefits from their cultures.

When contemplating building or changing an organization's culture, many managers find it tempting to try to copy the culture of a successful firm. Learning from others, and even borrowing ideas, are often great ways to accelerate growth. But for at least two reasons, it is misguided to think that you can avoid the hard work of designing your own culture by simply using what another organization does.

First, culture proves very difficult to copy. Consider Southwest Airlines, the poster child for efficient airline passenger service. Numerous other airline companies have tried to copy Southwest without success—and Southwest has even invited them to come and study their approach directly. But none of the other airlines have been able to get close to reproducing the Southwest culture in their own organizations.

Second, developing a successful organizational culture depends on aligning it with other key organizational factors—your strategy, your vision, and your institutional context. What works well in one time and place may not in another. In short, developing a strategically effective, strong, and adaptive culture means that you have to do the hard work yourself, figuring out what your organization needs and how to create practices and behaviors that get you there. To work well, the culture needs to be comprehensive, consistent, and coherent.

Jennifer Cook did not copy or even borrow much from another culture, including the one at Genentech. Instead, she and her team built their culture based on collectively perceived strategic needs to help GIO achieve a sense of identity, gain more unity, and integrate across seemingly disparate teams and markets.

POPULAR BELIEFS ABOUT CULTURE

Of course, culture can be a huge challenge for many managers for a host of reasons. We think that one of the biggest is how difficult it is to navigate through the many popular beliefs—some true, some false—about culture that abound today.

In chapter 1, we identified five popular beliefs that we hear about frequently: (1) culture shows great inertia; (2) culture can only be managed from the top down, using authority; (3) culture consists of soft, fuzzy, and ambiguous phenomena; (4) culture benefits only those who fit in; and (5) culture can make people happy, but it does not matter for business performance.

If she had embraced these five beliefs, consider what Jennifer Cook likely would have done (or not done) at GIO. She would *not* have viewed culture change as a legitimate pathway to achieving the growth goals that Ian Clark had set for GIO. She would have viewed unifying the disjointed units at GIO as important. And she would have presumed that the culture change process would take a long time—much longer than eleven months. She might have autocratically imposed some new norms, believing that culture comes autocratically from the top. She may not have bothered to try to measure what was going on culturally. She certainly would have minimized the time and effort that she and her staff devoted to culture change.

Instead, in her successful efforts to transform GIO and improve its performance in record time, Cook ignored many of these popular beliefs and managed around others. Obviously, she possessed good knowledge and intuition about behavioral matters, especially culture. But she was surely not born with this intuition. Much of it came from her education and her prior work experience. In business school, she took relevant classes and studied hard and she practiced culture change in the smaller organizations she led prior to GIO.

Cook also managed admirably through the behavioral difficulties that we pointed to in chapter 1. Specifically, she was consistent in her approach to people and to culture change. For example, she served as a beacon of the culture change personally. She also launched and oversaw a comprehensive effort to change and manage the culture, addressing almost every aspect of the business in doing so. Finally, Cook used a coherent narrative about what the issues with culture were, why and how they needed to change, and how the change related to GIO's strategy and vision.

Prior to leading GIO, Cook had gained valuable experience initiating culture-related efforts in other parts of Genentech.

In 2001, in a small department of fifteen people called Market Planning, she measured its culture using the OCP as part of a process to assess the organizational culture. Her goal was to bring that team together and give them a sense of shared purpose. This process helped to determine what the group stood for and how its members could better deliver on their business goals by working toward the culture that they desired.

"We did the audit and got clear and actionable results," said Cook. "New leaders have since guided that group, staying true to the organizational culture work we began. Today the group has grown to 75 people, yet the foundations of their culture persist and support them in delivering strong performance."

In 2006, Cook launched another culture effort in a portfolio management group that started with 85 people and grew to 200 people a few years into the process. She once again used the OCP to assess the current and desired future cultures aligned with the group's business purpose. The group had four departments that were highly interdependent, and yet it began with the impression that they did not have much in common. The effort lasted three years and was organized and driven through volunteer workgroups created with specific initiatives around driving culture change.

"This was the first time I had created workgroups because we wanted people to get involved and work on what they cared about," said Cook. Two years into the effort, she resurveyed the group and found that the specific culture attributes that they were working on had improved significantly.

In this effort and her other initiatives, Cook engaged with expert consultants and academics. Obviously, she learned a lot through her education and experiences. She is an enlightened manager of organizational culture.

SUMMARY

In this chapter, we wanted to vividly show how you can manage organizational culture. We wanted to show that managing culture is both possible, compelling, and profitable for both leaders and employees.

In leading GIO, Jennifer Cook brought together a disparate set of people working in different markets, with different client bases, to form a common identity and unified culture. She did so deliberately through both systematic and informal methods, using data as well as influence techniques to convince people that this approach could be beneficial. The results that she achieved were nothing short of profound. In chapter 8, after considering each of the popular beliefs that she navigated through, we will return to Cook's efforts and discuss them in terms of how she used specific managerial levers so that you, too, have the tools to improve your culture.

Our goal in this book is to try to bring you, as a leader and manager, up to Jennifer Cook's level of knowledge and expertise so you can effectively manage and even improve your culture. We do so by taking on the five common popular beliefs about culture. You don't have to be the leader of your organization. Instead, you only need to have a clear-eyed view about what's true and not true about organizational culture. Our choice of these specific beliefs draws on our culture research, experiences in teaching executives and business students, and advising organizations and managers over many years.

If you are like most students of culture whom we have met, your discomfort about managing culture arises from legitimate concerns about how to think about the five popular beliefs. So we take them on directly and organize the book around them. Once it is clear what's true and what's not among the popular beliefs, we hope that managing your culture will become much easier.

MANAGERIAL TAKEAWAYS
FROM THIS CHAPTER

- You can successfully manage organizational culture.
- Cultural initiatives can address general managerial problems like weak identity and a lack of connection among employees who need to work together.
- Managing organizational culture requires diligence and behavioral consistency from the leader and leadership team.
- Managing organizational culture requires including employees in identifying and even designing relevant culture change initiatives.
- Using culture assessment tools, focus groups and consultants can be helpful in figuring out where your culture is today and where it needs to go.
- Managing culture successfully requires attending to many details of beliefs, norms, and practices.
- Successfully managing culture can dramatically improve morale and motivation—and organizational performance.

3

IS CULTURE INERT?

I would meet with one of the vice presidents and we would discuss a particular problem and what needed to be done. We'd agree on a course of action.

And nothing would happen. Nothing. It was as if the conversation had never taken place. No follow-through . . . no explanations . . . no reports. And these were the top executives of the company.

That's a quote from Gil Amelio (figure 3.1), recounting his experiences as the newly installed CEO of Apple in early 1996. Previously CEO of National Semiconductor, he was also on Apple's board of directors. In 1995, he was asked by fellow board members to step in as CEO following huge losses and the ouster of CEO Michael Spindler. Amelio had previously rescued National Semiconductor from the brink of failure, and Rockwell International's semiconductor division before that. His track record suggested that he could deliver on the board's mandate to get Apple back on track.

As described in his books, Amelio's approach to managing a company involves a straightforward, rational, team-oriented process of identifying problems, dissecting them, developing

FIGURE 3.1 Former Apple CEO Gil Amelio

Copyright © 1997 The Associated Press. Used by permission.

strategic solutions, and then enacting the solutions. He explained: "My approach to restoring an ailing company back to functional strength does not rely on a series of flamboyant decisions made independently as each new challenge arises, but on a well-defined process."[1] He continued: "The transformation process isn't one that needs to be designed from scratch for every company, but has a group of essential elements in common, which are tailored and reordered to fit the particular set of ailments being faced."[2] He further explained: "At the risk of oversimplifying, . . . the process revolves around financial issues, business practices, and people issues, and includes elements such as achieving financial stability first, creating a vision that defines success, learning what the end customer values and delivering that, and establishing metrics in order to 'measure your way to excellence.'"[3]

ATTEMPTING A TURNAROUND AT APPLE

Amelio envisioned the turnaround process at Apple as collective and collaborative. He stated his initial hopes for the executive team: "We'll think this through together and together we'll reach a decision, and then we'll sign up to make things begin moving the way we agree they should."[4]

As part of the process, Amelio led an early off-site meeting with his executives to discuss the state of the company. At the off-site, he expected a frank discussion of some of the company's obvious problems, some difficult conversations about the causes of the problems, and some tough decisions to develop solutions. Here's what he said happened:

> Everyone arrived at the off-site having been notified of the agenda and the goal, so I expected some heated debate from sharp managers with different viewpoints and different experiences. And 1 had steeled myself for a concerted resistance that would challenge me to earn my leadership stripes. I watched for their openness to each other's ideas. I waited to see a sense of solidarity and togetherness, a sense of a feistiness . . .
>
> None of it happened.
>
> The group met each item on the agenda with a cool distance. The lack of connectedness between the players was both shocking and frustrating. Even on an issue as fundamental as what the core business should be, I had no success in getting them to reach any agreement.[5]

Amelio had run up against Apple's culture, which he said had "always championed the individual and stressed freedom to act unilaterally." The culture drove much behavior. As he explained, "executives made decisions based on what was right for their own operation, not on what was right for the company. And the culture stressed the individual and freedom of action instead of cooperation and working toward a set of common goals." He continued, "At Apple, each manager had run up a pirate flag that was flapping in the breeze: the counterculture at work, independents shunning the rigors and disciplines of tradition and rules."[6]

Amelio came to understand that Apple's culture was preventing people from doing what he wanted them to do. After recognizing this, he realized that he needed to change the culture to grow or pursue anything new. As he explained, "It was becoming evident that without some remaking of Apple attitudes and style, we were not going to get the company onto a healthier course." He used a metaphor: "I found I was trying to steer an out-of-control vehicle that was about to crash. It would be the height of folly to think a crash could be avoided without change." He elaborated: "I wanted Apple people—such very creative people—to enjoy the benefits of working within a disciplined business structure. I never wanted to kill the culture; I wanted to help it grow up to enjoy a richer future."[7]

With great effort, Amelio did make some progress in changing Apple. He cut costs, eliminated unsuccessful products, developed a broad business strategy, opened discussions with Microsoft about sharing software, and reorganized the company into a functional organizational design. He eventually fired lots of the members of his executive team. Some say that the culture started to change a little. But sales continued to drop, and the board failed to develop confidence in Amelio before he

FIGURE 3.2 *Business Week* cover, proclaiming,
"The Fall of an American Icon"

Copyright © 2007 James through Creative Commons
(http://maebmij.org). Used by permission.

could turn things around. *Business Week* predicted the company's imminent demise (figure 3.2).

Accordingly, Amelio was dismissed after fifteen months, and Steve Jobs (figure 3.3) was brought back to be CEO of Apple. Jobs left the existing culture (which he had helped spawn years earlier) in place by most accounts, and he focused on products; and the rest is history, as they say.

At the time, much speculation surfaced about why Amelio failed. Without a doubt, his failure to read the culture and deal with it effectively constituted a big part of it. Amelio himself wrote that many people thought that: "Amelio came in from the outside, didn't understand the Apple culture, and made the

FIGURE 3.3 Steve Jobs

Copyright © 1997 The Associated Press. Used by permission.

mistake of trying to change it." He subsequently recognized that Jobs did not attempt to change the culture when he came back; instead he saw him as "dragging his managers back into the murky quagmire of the Apple culture just after the Big Bang of creation."[8]

Many observers draw the conclusion, from this episode and similar sagas at other companies, that organizational culture is highly inert, it is futile to try to change it, and even if lots of effort is expended, little change will occur. Indeed, cultural inertia—a kind of resistance to change—exists as a popular belief. Many people see organizational culture as next to impossible to change significantly, especially in an intended direction. Most likely, such observers would regard Jennifer Cook's success at GIO in Genentech (described in chapter 2) as minor tweaks of an existing culture, not the substantial departure from their culture that insiders believed they created.

CULTURAL INERTIA EXAMINED

So why do people believe in, and even take comfort in, cultural inertia? Consider what happens when you go on vacation, let's say to Germany. You may know more or less what to expect in terms of how local people will behave, what they will say and do, what they eat and drink, what they care about—in other words, you know and expect culturally prescribed "German" actions. Moreover, chances are that your expectations, and the locals' behaviors, will be pretty similar five years from now, and even ten to fifteen years in the future. Sure, there will be new fads and fashions, some new verbal expressions, and maybe some changes to general life attitudes and plans. But most of the basic cultural apparatus, the behaviors that define "German-ness," will remain pretty much the same. A German does what Germans do, and for any reasonable period of time, we do not anticipate any marked change in that behavior. German culture, like most national cultures, exhibits a high degree of inertia. And, to a certain extent, we (human beings, that is) like that predictability because it makes it easier for us to know what's coming and adjust our own behavior accordingly.

Cultural inertia also characterizes many formal organizations. Think of the Roman Catholic Church, the University of Cambridge, the Sigma Chi college fraternity, JCPenney, and even more modern organizations like Amazon. For decades, and in some cases even centuries, each of these organizations has displayed a well-known and predictable culture. Sure, insiders periodically offer reports of the changes underway and talk about how the organization's behavior looks nothing like it used to. Comparing an organization to its past typically highlights the changes that it has undergone over time. But this approach usually ignores all the many, many aspects of the culture that did *not* change. To outsiders, it is the stability of the culture, its inertia, that strikes them—the comparison made often involves other organizations, which continue to look very different, and the changes, if they see them, look small compared to the stable parts.

The pull of cultural inertia can be so strong that an organization cannot escape it, despite almost everyone knowing that not changing culturally when required will certainly lead to poor performance at best, and failure and bankruptcy ultimately. Consider Eastman Kodak, Blockbuster, Sun Microsystems, Digital Equipment Company, Kmart, and Pan American Airlines (Pan Am). The handwriting was on the wall for these and many other organizations for years, if not decades. Yet efforts to update and change their cultures always fell short. Younger people today often don't even remember the names of these once-prominent companies, let alone what they did.

We can also come up with many examples of business organizations in which the culture did change, often radically. Think of IBM, Microsoft, Uber, Maersk, and Continental Airlines (before its acquisition by United). Each of these companies (and plenty of others) underwent significant cultural change sometime in the last few decades. And others like Netflix, Fuji Film, JPMorgan, and the Ball Corporation have appeared to reinvent themselves, including their cultures, every few years or so.[9]

We challenge you to come up with a comparable example of a national culture that exhibits as much change in the short term as any of these companies. We think that the challenge involves an impossible question. In our view, national cultures show more inertia than business and other organizations—without exception. And, while plenty of organizational cultures show high degrees of inertia, we see enough examples otherwise to know that inertia is not an absolute. Some, maybe even many, organizational cultures do change—and often that change is the result of an intentional effort.

So, what's different? What makes it possible for organizations to change their cultures, but not nation-states? While there are innumerable differences between organizations and nations, we think that three processes explain the greater pliability of organizational culture.[10]

First, organizations and their leaders typically control their members' entry and exit more tightly than do nations. Sure, nation-states control entry by issuing visas and citizenships, but the criteria are usually much looser and enforced bureaucratically, especially on behavioral expectations. The demographic flow of people into and out of an organization almost always represents a greater proportion of the personnel base than it does in a nation-state. Organizational leaders can—and often do—recruit and dismiss people from their organizations based on how well they fit the culture; leaders of nations rarely do this. Think about the unknowing Americans in Germany who break the cultural norm of punctuality by being late. This behavior will earn these Americans the reputation of being deeply disrespectful to others, but they will not be extradited for it.

Second, organizations and their leaders typically control the status order or hierarchy of people more tightly than nations do. The CEO and executive leaders are usually chosen and granted decision rights in a more orderly and predictable fashion than the head of state of a nation and the associated political staff.

Third, organizations and their leaders control the system's incentives—both what people are rewarded and punished for—more tightly than do nation-states. Specific behaviors and certain individuals can be pinpointed for sanctioning in organizations with greater precision, as well as monitored for compliance. Nations use blunter methods like laws to control incentives. Laws are typically more ambiguous, and enforcement is often more inconsistent than in organizational control systems.

ORGANIZATIONS ARE LESS INERTIAL THAN NATIONS . . . BUT STILL INERTIAL

Despite the differences between nations and organizations, social scientists consider organizations inertial, but neither immutable nor absolutely inert. Sociologists Michael Hannan and John Freeman in 1984 wrote a now-classic article on organizational inertia.[11] They theorized that inertia operated most strongly through an organization's stated goals, forms of authority, core technology, and marketing strategy (listed here in order of force). Interestingly, they did not specify culture as a primary inertial force, probably because the field had not yet begun to focus on culture as an organizational property and culture was subsumed under these four dimensions. They went on to claim that "although organizations sometimes manage to change positions on these dimensions, such changes are both rare and costly and seem to subject an organization to greatly increased risks of death."[12] They found ample support for their claim subsequently in empirical research.[13] In many organizations, culture supports and buttresses these core dimensions.

Still, most social scientists believe that a myriad of social and social-psychological forces operate to hold culture in place, to resist any departures from the cultural status quo, and to create tension when some action fails to conform to normative expectations.

Cultural inertia arises from the very same processes that make culture useful to organizations in the first place, coordinating people and focusing them on conforming to collective norms. In the positive scenario, these norms are optimized for the organization's goals. Working in a fast-paced industry in which new product ideas are essential? You'd want to develop cultural norms for spending time on creative endeavors. Or are you operating in an industry that is predicated on being precise and detail oriented, such as public accounting? Then it would be a good idea to develop cultural norms for prioritizing high levels of accuracy and poring over the details. But the negative scenario portrays a picture of organizations that are pursuing unredeeming goals, pushing people to the brink, and demanding loyalty to do things that are harmful to employees and other stakeholders.

HOW CONFORMITY PRODUCES CULTURAL INERTIA

Why are people willing to conform to culture norms? It's straightforward: Once someone internalizes an expected behavior, they come to believe that it is the right or appropriate way to behave in that setting. Their behavior can readily become internalized—and, as such, perceived as intrinsically motivated—through simple psychological processes akin to cognitive dissonance. It typically goes like this: Employees see themselves working hard and taking positions that prioritize the organization's best interests (some of which may diverge from their own personal values), perhaps even beyond what their compensation would justify. To make sense of their efforts and bring their attitudes in line with their demonstrated behavior, they come to see their behavior as evidence of their commitment to the organization and what it stands for. As a result, they shift their own values and normative expectations to fit with their demonstrated (and often organizationally dictated) behaviors. This process occurs even if the behavior is only tacitly expected and reciprocated by others; and, even if it is also associated with extrinsic or material rewards. Because of the psychological need for congruence between attitudes and behaviors, cultural conformity in behavior and attitude often occurs automatically, without any deliberation.

To intensify the cultural inertia process even further, once employees internalize the culture and see others violating cultural expectations, they are typically willing to express swift and personal disapproval. Taken together, this scaled-up process of many people internalizing the organization's cultural values to make sense of their own behavior can make nonconformity costly and even scary. Indeed, research shows that when people violate organizational norms, they are likely to face social exclusion—colleagues whom they work with day in and day out reject them, making it harder for them to get their own work done and making them feel generally uncomfortable. The threat of social ostracism—even exclusion from the organization—is perhaps the most powerful way to enforce norms, often far more powerful than with extrinsic rewards like compensation.[14]

Don't get us wrong, however: Cultural conformity occurs in many organizations because they need their employees to commit and coordinate to accomplish their large-scale strategic goals. This conformity also helps organizations externally. Organizations need environmental resources to operate and survive. An organization's identity—think of this as its external-facing reputation, which typically mirrors the internal culture—leads external stakeholders like customers, regulators, and shareholders to expect certain behaviors and to withdraw resources when those expectations are violated. Withdrawing resources imperils the organization's survival, it's as simple as that.

A culture is ineffective when the norms driving behavior become outmoded or were never particularly well optimized for strategic success in the first place. When cultural norms do align with an effective competitive strategy, observers typically celebrate the company for its powerful culture. But at least some of its cultural norms will not be effective for long periods of time, as the competitive environment changes and aspects of the strategy get adjusted. And here's the big problem: Cultural inertia instigates conformity to past behaviors—the ones that people are more certain of, causing a lag, with people hanging on to the old norms rather than adopting new, more strategically aligned norms.

So this is the inertia challenge of cultural management: How can you change those aspects of the culture that become outdated while allowing other helpful features of the culture to persist? Leaders have a hard time seeing when previously effective (and highly celebrated) norms become ineffective or even counterproductive. And even subtle hints that question these norms and suggest the possibility of changing them often bring impassioned cries of incredulity and disbelief among the faithful, who see them as the bedrock of company success.[15]

Given these operative social and psychological forces at work, it should be no surprise that intentional cultural change typically requires massive effort and multiple points of attack. As we explained in chapter 1, in order to succeed, a cultural change initiative needs to be comprehensive, in that it must use multiple managerial levers, directed at the organization's existing norms, its employment system, its compensation system, and its formal organizational design. In chapter 8, we will describe and explain these levers in detail. For now, to put the popular belief that culture is inert to the test, let's examine one of the best examples that we've seen—a classic case of busting cultural inertia at Ford Motor Company during the illustrative period before and after Alan Mulally's reign as CEO.[16]

CULTURE AT FORD MOTOR COMPANY

Bill Ford (figure 3.4) served as CEO of Ford Motor Company for almost five years, from October 2001 to September 2006. When he took over, the company was losing massive amounts

FIGURE 3.4 Bill Ford

of money and was known in the automobile industry as a non-innovative "fast follower." Ford made deep cuts and returned the company to profitability in 2002, although its stock price remained lackluster. But by 2003, Bill Ford grew weary of running the company and hoped to hire a dynamic CEO while he remained executive chair. His initial efforts to find a successor did not pan out, although in late 2005, he did eventually elevate Mark Fields to head North American sales. Fields developed a plan called "The Way Forward," which called for massive cuts in jobs and material costs while projecting a new image based on increased sales of trucks and sport utility vehicles (SUVs). Meanwhile, gas and other material prices rose, slowing expected sales growth under the plan, which was soon in trouble.

Chaos ensued inside Ford. As described by automotive industry journalist Bryce Hoffman: "As they struggled to go further faster, Fields began running into the same old brick walls that had held back change for so long at Ford. Entrenched executives gave superficial support to his turnaround efforts but often conspired against them whenever his plans ran counter to their own aims. Ford's rigidly regionalized corporate structure made it impossible to address issues globally. Meetings became tense as tempers flared, and the worsening business environment only served to fan the flames."[17]

The board at Ford decided that that was enough. They told Bill Ford to consider radical options, including mergers, buyouts, and even bankruptcy. After spending a summer with board members exploring possibilities, Ford decided that none of the preferred routes was viable; he also calculated that the company would run out of money in less than three years. Rather than sell or give up, Ford went to the board and made an emotional plea to let him find a new CEO for the company. They concurred, however reluctantly.

FIGURE 3.5 Former Ford CEO Alan Mulally

Copyright © 2014 The Associated Press. Used by permission.

Ford eventually found his CEO in Alan Mulally of Boeing (figure 3.5). Mulally was an engineer who had overseen two major plane development projects, the 777 and the 787 (Dreamliner). These planes brought Boeing out of the slump in demand that it was seeing for its aging 747 plane design. Accordingly, Mulally was seen as a star who was destined to be CEO of Boeing. Instead, Ford enticed him to come to Detroit and accept the CEO position at Ford Motor Company.

CULTURAL CHANGE UNDER
ALAN MULALLY

Before accepting the CEO position, Mulally secured two promises from Bill Ford. First, he asked for assurance that Ford really wanted change at the company; and second, he wanted a personal guarantee that Ford would support him when times got tough. Specifically, Mulally told Ford that if he took the job, "I'm not just going to take it [the company] apart. I am going to take it flying." He then said, "I just want to know that that's what you want to do." Ford concurred, saying, "I will back you 100 percent."

Many people, including Bill Ford, expected Mulally to clean house early on, to dismiss or replace many of the key executives at Ford. Board member Irv Hockaday told Mulally, "There are no sacred cows. . . . Any friends of Bill that are in the wrong positions or you conclude are not the right guys, you can get rid of them . . . and Bill will confirm that." Mulally replied, "That's not an issue because I'm not going to have to get rid of many people." He reiterated that view later when asked at a press conference if he planned to bring in his own team, he replied with a smile, "My team is right here."[18]

Still, on the day of his formal introduction to the executive team, Mulally got a cool reception. Some regarded him as outclassed based on the way that he dressed (sport coat instead of suit), others thought he seemed weak, and even others assessed more of a politician than an executive. Hoffman reports that Mulally surmised that "they don't think I can do this."[19]

As he began his tenure as CEO, Mulally announced a few general thoughts about changes that he had in mind, but he also set in motion a set of new processes for executive decision-making. He told the board: "We have a lot of brands. We have a lot of nameplates. We're known in the US as a big truck and SUV company—and for the Mustang. We have very complex product offerings. I think there is a tremendous opportunity to simplify, consolidate, and focus Ford."[20] He stuck to this coherent narrative throughout the transformation.

Mulally also knew that cutting and reorganizing were not enough. He told his colleagues that Ford needed to start making cars that people wanted to buy, restore faith in the "Blue Oval" of Ford, and accordingly, accelerate new product development. To enhance this focus, Mulally subsequently sold off many Ford brands and assets, including Aston Martin, Land Rover, Jaguar, Volvo, and Mazda.

Mulally also thought that Ford executives had way too many meetings. After enduring one cycle of meetings, he proclaimed, "There are too many meetings," provoking people to answer the question, "When do you have time to think about the customer?"

Mulally announced that going forward, Ford would organize only one corporate-level meeting. It would occur weekly at the same time and place, and attendance was mandatory for senior executives (those away on business could teleconference in). Moreover, the meeting would adhere to a standardized format using a prepared template. Mulally called it a "business plan review," or BPR. Each executive would use the template to personally deliver short status reports on their areas, focusing on the progress made toward the company's goals. No one other than the senior executive of the area was allowed to speak, but others could be brought along as guests. The templates were data-oriented and color-coded the status of the area as green (on track), yellow (potential problems), or red (in trouble). There would be no in-depth discussions, but issues that required attention would be put on a list and reviewed in an immediate subsequent meeting called a "special attention review," or SAR. Mulally told his managers to be ready to decide the status of areas at these meetings and to be prepared to act following them. The BPR would prove to be his main process for managing his team and Ford; it would often last for hours. In Mulally's mind, the BPR process made it impossible for people to hide and ensured accountability.

After a month on the job, Mulally laid out more specific rules for people at Ford to follow, including the executives. He posted them on the wall:

- People first.
- Everyone is included.
- Compelling vision.
- Clear performance goals.
- One plan.
- Facts and data.
- Propose a plan, "find a way" attitude.
- Respect, listen, help, and appreciate each other.
- Emotional resilience . . . trust the process.
- Have fun . . . enjoy the journey and each other.

Mulally also explained a few additional minor rules that pertained to BPRs, such as no side conversations, no jokes at others' expense, and no smartphones.

It took the senior executives at Ford several weeks to learn how to prepare for the meetings and perform adequately. Some chafed and even sought to get around Mulally by running to Bill Ford. To his credit, Ford refused to help any of them (even his brother-in-law), telling them that Alan was running the company and he supported him. As Mulally expected, some executives left the company. As Hoffman relates, "Mulally used those early BPR meetings as a bully pulpit to drive accountability, enforce cooperation, and ensure execution. If any of the executives . . . still doubted that he was serious about changing Ford's culture, those sessions quickly dispelled their illusions."[21]

Mulally still had difficulty getting his executives to report honestly about their area's status and progress. The BPR templates were all colored green despite the company losing billions of dollars. "We're going to lose billions of dollars this year," he said. "Is there anything that's not going well?"[22]

Apparently, in Ford's pre-Mulally culture, delivering bad news was very risky: You would be blamed for it and suffer repercussions. Mulally knew that he could not fix Ford unless he first understood the source and location of the problems, so he knew that he needed to shift the culture to one in which identifying problems would be rewarded, not punished. He remained patient and behaved consistently—providing forums for raising problems and addressing them—despite the frustration that he must have experienced.

The big cultural breakthrough came after another month of green templates. Mark Fields, the prominent senior executive in charge of the Americas, was responsible for launching a highly anticipated new car model, the Edge. At the last minute, some problems with the Edge surfaced that would delay its launch. He decided to report that problem honestly at the BPR, half-expecting that he might lose his job as a result. Hoffman describes the moment:

Fields tried to look nonchalant.

"And on the Edge launch, we're red. You can see it there," he said, pointing to the screen. "We're holding the launch."

There was dead silence. Everyone turned toward Fields. So did Mulally, who was sitting next to him.

Dead man walking, thought one of his peers.

I wonder who will get the Americas, another mused.

Suddenly someone started clapping. It was Mulally.

"Mark, that is great visibility," he beamed. "Who can help Mark with this?"[23]

The next week at the BPR, more slides contained red—and yellow too. It looked like a rainbow. At that moment, Mulally said he knew that the company had turned a corner and the culture was changing. He also realized that he, along with everyone else, now knew why they were losing money, where the problems were, and therefore could set about fixing them. Most important, Mulally also realized that his executives now trusted him and the process that he had introduced. This is what he needed to transform the company. As Mulally later commented, "I knew that if we were to be successful with our plan, we had to break through that culture, where there was little sharing and where people were afraid to share how things really were."[24]

Mulally subsequently simplified the leadership structure of the company, eliminating many local "fiefdoms." The new organizational structure comprised the heads of the major geographies and Ford Credit (all profit centers) and the heads of the twelve functional areas. Each had a seat at the BPR table, and their photos were posted on the wall along with the color-coded status templates for their domain of responsibility. Mulally and Bill Ford also raised billions of dollars from Wall Street to finance the reorganization of the company, as well as a thorough redesign of the product portfolio.

Ford went on the rebound in historic ways, not only surviving the Great Recession, but making it through without either bankruptcy or a government bailout. As Mulally stepped down as CEO in 2014, Ford was making money—it reported a profit of $7.2 billion in 2013 (it had lost $17 billion the year that Mulally arrived). When later asked about how Ford did it, Mulally replied, "Culture is most important. It's our culture, and it's ours by design. Our culture is who we are, it's what we do, it's why we do it, and it's how we do it. Our culture is everything from how we will be to how we will do."[25]

BREAKING THROUGH CULTURE INERTIA

What general lessons about cultural change can we learn from Mulally's efforts at Ford?

First, the transformation at Ford shows conclusively that organizational culture can change in intended ways, even quickly. The Ford example offers additional evidence to augment the Genentech GIO culture change case in chapter 2, supporting the idea that, when leaders are deliberate, culture change can occur rapidly. No one who knew Ford Motor Company before and after Mulally's reign as CEO would deny that significant cultural change occurred. Moreover, the Ford case suggests that to combat cultural inertia, major cultural change may require strong-willed determination from leaders, full and unassailable authority to implement needed organizational and personnel moves, the power to influence behavior as Mulally did in the Edge meeting, and access to financial and other resources.

Second, culture change is much more likely to occur if leaders clearly articulate what the intended culture should, and should not, be. This is what social scientists call "cultural content": it includes norms, beliefs, values, and even language. These ideas can be abstract and general, but leaders need to convey their meaning in concrete and specific ways. In the Ford case, it was essential to move people from a culture whose content emphasized being reluctant to share bad news to one in which people felt strong pressure to surface and report problems and accept help in solving those problems. The description and explanation of the culture must be coherent and should relate to the organization's objectives and what it intends to accomplish.

Third, the leader's words and actions should exemplify the intended culture and model the behavior—always. When others see and hear this behavior, they understand what it means, and even what it looks like. They also appreciate that the cultural expectations apply to everyone, meaning that there are no exceptions. In addition, the leader should be diligent and consistent in reminding others in the organization about the cultural expectations and calling out and correcting violations.

Fourth, an honest and affable leader exerts great influence on others and does not need to compromise principles.

Fifth, an effective leader praises others for cultural compliance and ensures that recalcitrant individuals suffer consequences for their behavior.

Sixth, a simplified organizational structure enhances transparency and accountability, allowing the cultural norms to operate with greater force.

Identifying these lessons is not to say that cultural change always needs to follow them to succeed. In some situations, certain activities may not be needed, or even effective. And surely there are other good ideas about how to initiate and guide cultural change in an organization. But still, this is a pretty good and comprehensive list, representing a good starting plan for a leader who is about to drive a cultural change initiative.

RETHINKING AMELIO AT APPLE

With the Ford-Mulally story under our belts, we can now go back to Amelio's situation at Apple to ask the provocative question: "What if Gil Amelio had done the same (or similar) things that Mulally did at Ford during his tenure at Apple? Would things have turned out differently?"

Asking this question makes you realize how few of these things Amelio did at Apple, and how differently he behaved. Rather than come in with a specific, detailed vision of the culture that he wanted to create, Amelio attempted to do it by ignoring the existing culture and trying to address the strategic and operational problems with a collaborative problem-solving process.

We are sure that this seemed like a good idea to him—after all, everyone admires inclusive management. The problem is that the people whom Amelio sought as collaborators were, in many cases, those who helped create the current Apple culture, and in all cases, they were beneficiaries of it. They likely did not see anything wrong with the culture. And surely they could appreciate that the uncertainty and chaos unleashed by trying to define a new future culture could be threatening and harmful to them and their fiefdoms. Change in any form is scary to many people.

It also did not help that Amelio apparently was not very patient, expecting people to jump right into the transformation process. By contrast, Mullaly set up a system (BPR) that called out people regularly to report facts openly and he remained patient and supportive until the system started to take hold.

Lacking a specific and relevant cultural vision, Amelio could not model intended cultural behavior, could not praise those who complied, and could not sanction those who defied it.

Moreover, even if he had come in with a vision, talked about it regularly, modeled it, and doled out rewards and punishments, it is not clear whether he would have succeeded. One huge problem was that Steve Jobs was lurking in the background, talking with board members and senior executives, telling them that Apple had the talent and the culture that it needed to correct its course, and encouraging resistance to change, at least implicitly. Jobs was not at all like Bill Ford, who steadfastly supported the new CEO publicly and privately while refusing to offer a way around the new demands.

Another big problem was that Amelio did not have the financial war chest that Ford had to aid in developing and launching new products. Apple was on the verge of bankruptcy. So Amelio did what he could—mainly eliminating products that were not performing. He also started to develop a broad corporate strategy and initiated software-sharing conversations with Bill Gates at Microsoft.

Perhaps the change that had the most impact was Amelio's reorganization of Apple. He instituted a functional organizational design, something that fosters technical innovation and reins in costs but which is rarely seen in big companies. The functional design shook up the existing tribal territories and instituted a stronger sense of transparency and accountability. It persists to this day. In fact, some leading analysts attribute much of Apple's subsequent innovation and success to this organizational design, which does support its culture.[26]

For these reasons, we find the question of what would have happened if Amelio had been more Mulally-like hard to answer fully. Sure, we think that Amelio would have made more progress faster in transforming Apple if he had arrived with an articulated cultural target and used his actions and authority to inform and guide people. But we doubt that he could have done anything about Jobs's meddling and the resource constraints that he was facing. These facts alone may have doomed his efforts. The case shows how hard cultural change can be and how culture can exert strong inertia for a variety of reasons. It also shows how many things aligned for Mulally to do what he did to transform the culture at Ford. Mulally should get huge credit for his work, and it does seem that he read the situation very well. But he also likely realizes that he got more than a few lucky breaks, and cultural inertia can sometimes foil even great efforts at change.

What about the question of whether culture is inert? Yes, by its very design, culture is inherently inertial. Academic evidence and business experiences such as Ford under Mulally, however, show us there are ways to break inertia, certainly in organizations and perhaps even possibly in nations.

EVEN INERTIA FROM SOCIETAL NORMS CAN BE OVERCOME

Discrimination against women at work remains a difficult problem in Pakistan. Only about 28 percent of women in Pakistan participate in the workforce, placing it in the bottom ten countries around the world. Many Pakistanis hold a strong view that women should shoulder the household and family responsibilities. Even in sectors with high percentages of qualified women, employment rates are low. For example, 63 percent of medical students in the country are women, but only 23 percent of registered doctors are women.

Despite the national context, Farrukh Rehan (figure 3.6) of Roche Pakistan made empowering women a key priority because he felt that there were many women with untapped

FIGURE 3.6 Farrukh Rehan

Copyright © 2024 Farrukh Rehan, used by permission.

talent in Pakistan. His story is fascinating because he used *organizational* culture change to challenge *national* culture, something that consultants have been advising against since culture became faddish.[27] His efforts at Roche show again that despite cultural inertia—even in the form of norms that are embraced at the national level—culture change can prevail.

Previously a managing director at Roche, a multinational pharmaceutical company headquartered in Basel, Switzerland, Rehan was asked to lead Roche Pakistan. He arrived in Pakistan in 2016. Rehan felt that it was important to bring a diversity of thinking, styles, and approaches into the leadership team and the middle ranks. One major initiative was Roche Pakistan's first Women's Forum in May 2016, during which he met with all the women employees at Roche Pakistan and listened to their concerns and needs. The Women's Forum emerged because an employee had told Rehan that she was thinking about leaving due to the challenges of working and having a newborn.

Rehan and his new leadership team learned that women were interested in senior sales positions and becoming commercial leaders at Roche Pakistan. Rehan emphatically said, "Yes." To accommodate women's obligations, the organization implemented flex time, maternity leave, a five-day workweek, and transportation services for those women who did not have cars. Rehan stated: "Our aim is to create an environment where women don't have to make a choice between home and work."

By the second Women's Forum, in February 2017, three women were on the senior leadership team and there was a female sales manager. Rehan reflected, "We sat for an hour-and-a-half, and the women told me that they 'didn't have anything more to ask—the company had done its part and now it was on them to seize opportunities and deliver on their potential.' I was very proud of that."

By June 2017, almost half of the leadership team members were women—the medical head, human resources (HR) head, compliance officer, and the finance director. "This is unusual in the pharma industry in Pakistan and also in Pakistan in general," said Shafaq Kamran, the new HR head. Rehan believed this to be the highest percentage of women in leadership at any pharma organization in Pakistan. By July 2017, about a third of Roche Pakistan's recruits were women. "Now we have to retain and develop them," said Kamran.

Measuring performance improvements also played a part in Rehan's success. He wasn't afraid to conduct internal surveys on his own to examine how he and the leadership team were doing. This allowed him to see where he was successful (with the commercial-facing teams) and where there were still gaps (back-office staff).

Rehan's accomplishments in the short time that he had led the Roche Pakistan organization were impressive. By July 2017, Roche Pakistan had achieved several specific results. The organization met its annual budget for the first time in three years and stopped the decline in sales. It succeeded in its internal audit. It launched its first large-scale Access Program. Initial feedback from doctors was very positive, and they were very supportive of much broader access to Roche's leading drugs for patients. The organization also launched its first new product in many years, and several other products were in advanced stages of approval. Finally, Roche Pakistan had launched a major effort to focus on educating doctors, nurses, and other health-care professionals on the key safety, quality, and efficacy benefits of its reference products and now the field-based employees of Roche were better prepared to compete effectively.

Employees were energized by the culture change too. An anonymous internal survey conducted in January 2017 revealed that a whopping 100 percent of respondents believed that management was listening to them, and 98.6 percent believed that Roche Pakistan was headed in the right direction. Most respondents (77.1 percent) stated that they felt that their current line manager fully displayed the values required in the new Roche Pakistan culture (transparency, humility, collaboration, and employee-centricity). The 2017 Roche-wide Global Employee Opinion Survey (GEOS) also indicated success, with employee engagement growing by 22 percentage points over the previous GEOS for Roche Pakistan. GEOS scores on senior leadership had increased by 30 points, and management effectiveness was up by 23 points. Moreover, in a culture assessment run by Jennifer Chatman, Roche Pakistan had the smallest gap between its current culture and the culture that it needed to execute on its strategy—smaller than any other

Roche country organization in the vast Europe, Middle East, and Africa (EMEA) region.

Rehan inherited deep cultural legacies—some from the national culture and some from the organizational culture—including a hierarchical, top-down culture, a subservient view of women, a weak leadership team, employees with low morale, and a culture that emphasized respect toward seniors. He did not allow those legacies, many of which were deeply rooted in the national culture, to deter him from making organizational cultural changes. Rehan did not create a culture in a vacuum but rather made sure that the culture reinforced and supported the business strategy, as well as honored some aspects of the strongly held national culture. Beyond the forums that he launched, how did Rehan do it? How did he lead the cultural change at Roche Pakistan?

Early on, Rehan quickly identified those who would be potential cultural influencers and those who might defy his cultural changes. Scoping out supporters and anticipating resistors surely accelerated the cultural transformation. He also identified the sales managers as key since each of them managed multiple people within Roche Pakistan. Changing the leadership team and developing new leaders also helped to accelerate the transformation, which was important because Rehan had a limited, three-year contract. He also began with a few smaller initiatives, which led to small but significant behavioral changes that people could see, allowing him to gain trust and credibility and to prove to people that his cultural efforts weren't just lip service.

Rehan made sure to communicate constantly whenever he had the opportunity, particularly during periods where bigger changes had occurred, such as when he appointed new leaders. He also clearly defined the cultural change in presentations during town halls, wrote blog posts, and sent out e-mails. Rehan walked the talk and tried to embody the cultural transformation himself consistently. By Rehan's modeling change, others began to trust him and follow suit.

Equally important, Rehan mixed practices that supported deeply held national cultural beliefs with those that challenged them. For example, he provided funds that had previously been denied for the Pakistan team to celebrate Independence Day, a valued national holiday. But he also broke down the kind of hierarchy supported in the national culture by, for example, eliminating status-based parking (previously leaders could park closer to the office building than lower-level employees). He set up a ping-pong table on the office building's patio so people at different levels of the company could get to know one another in a more informal setting. Rehan seemed to have a natural intuition for doing the small things that really made a difference, such as calling people on New Year's and using their first names. Combining these smaller efforts with larger, more formal efforts was essential for the improvements he implemented.

Rehan's remarkable success at Roche Pakistan offers yet more evidence that organizational culture, and even cultural norms that are nationally embraced, can change; culture inertia is mutable. The secret, if there is one, is employing consistency, comprehensiveness, and coherence when making the case for culture change and implementing multiple approaches that emphasize the new norms.

SUMMARY

In this chapter, we asked the challenging question of whether culture is inert. To many observers, culture certainly appears inert. They think this because they know that you can show up at an organization years after you were there before, say as an employee, a student, or a member, and it looks eerily like little has changed except the names and faces. In other words, even though the people in the organizations have changed, the behaviors, practices, and norms of the members have not changed. Indeed, cultural inertia is a major fact of organizational life. But accepting the inevitability of cultural inertia is risky as many organizations fail because their culture prevents them from adapting in the midst of technological and market changes.

We offer evidence of notable exceptions—organizations that dramatically shift their cultures leaving little resemblance to their earlier form, often accompanied by great success. In this chapter, we discussed one of the most celebrated modern turn-arounds, Ford. This company's recent experiences show clearly that culture can be changed and it is not inevitably inert, even if inertia is the default expectation.

But the Ford-Mullaly story also shows that radical cultural change is not for the faint-hearted. The leader needs to be determined and have the full support of powerful stakeholders. Moreover, as we explained in chapter 1, to succeed, leaders need to act and behave consistently, adopt a comprehensive approach to changing the organization, and offer a coherent narrative about the goals and the path to achieve them. If leaders can do all that, then they have a chance, maybe even a fighting chance. But bringing about cultural change in organizations is so challenging that you probably also need a bit of luck to succeed as well. Some unexpected things might need to fall your way.

MANAGERIAL TAKEAWAYS
FROM THIS CHAPTER

- Cultural inertia can be very strong, which makes it hard to change an organization's culture.

- Changing an inert culture requires leaders to have a clear vision and an ability to communicate it widely.
- Successful cultural change in an organization requires the support of all the top leaders and stakeholders.
- Cultural change can be slow and requires that leaders are patient.
- During cultural change, incremental successful small changes should be identified and celebrated widely.
- Culture change in an organization can occur even in cases in which a nation embraces outmoded norms.

4

CULTURE FROM THE TOP DOWN?

Employees were exceedingly careful about what they spent. Everyone knew that the CEO reviewed and approved all major expenditures despite the company's substantial size. In fact, for years, his approval was required for any expenditure over $1,000. When asked why he did this—did he not trust his employees?—he replied that it's "not because I don't trust our people but because I know if they know I'm watching, they'll be just that much more careful."[1]

The same CEO showed up once during the graveyard shift in the operational bowels of the company. He looked around, asked how things were going. He hung around for a while, watched people work while chatting with them. Within days, the story of his late-night visit to line workers became well known throughout the company.

A micromanaging boss, you may be thinking: Yes. A CEO who shapes the culture from the top down. Certainly. A dominant person who would be frightening to work for.

That's not what his employees thought.

In fact, 16,000 of them raised $60,000 to take out a full-page ad in *USA Today* on Boss's Day in 1994 to express their affection for him.[2] Well, at least it must be a place where you need

FIGURE 4.1 Former Southwest CEO Herb Kelleher

Copyright © 2005 Getty Images. Used by permission.

to watch what you say and do, a company that would be no fun. Nope—the company's culture was widely known for the fun that its employees had at work, as well as the smiles and laughs of its customers.

By now, you may have surmised that these stories are about the CEO Herb Kelleher and the company that he created, Southwest Airlines (figure 4.1). Everyone who knows about organizational culture talks about Kelleher and Southwest. Calling him a legend could almost classify as an understatement.

As a top executive, Kelleher built and managed Southwest's culture from the top down. How typical is that approach? Is top-down management the best (or even a good) way to manage culture? We take on these questions in this chapter.

Popular beliefs suggest that company culture should *only* be driven from the top down. Remarks like, "While it's possible for culture change to be organic and bottom-up, the fastest and most effective way to bring about a culture change is from the top . . . the CEO has a central role to play in defining and shaping a company's culture," are far more common than those touting the successes of bottom-up cultural change.[3] To address this belief, we consider the Southwest example, along with many others that illustrate the impact that CEOs and senior leaders can have on organizational culture. But we also discuss the limits on even the most senior leaders' influence on an organization's culture and note other powerful sources of cultural change.

But first, let's finish the Southwest story—perhaps the poster child for an organization with a strong culture—a story told and retold, and the question is why?

HERB KELLEHER AND SOUTHWEST'S TOP-DOWN CULTURE

Unlike many companies, Southwest uses organizational culture to its competitive advantage in a central way. Starting with the company's founding in 1974, the original disrupter of US air travel, and continuing even now, Southwest offers lessons for anyone who wants to manage culture. And Kelleher's actions offer valuable lessons about how managing culture from the top down can be effective. The longest-reigning Southwest CEO (from 1981–2001), Kelleher represents a true culture champion.

Kelleher recognized that people—employees—comprise the essence of any industry, including the commercial airline business. He said that he learned the background idea early in life: "My mother taught me that your employees come first. If you treat them well, then they treat the customers well and that means your customers come back and your shareholders are happy."[4]

Of course, many executives proclaim that their employees come first. But it is quite unusual for the employees to believe the rhetoric. Kelleher's employees did, in part because his behavior aligned completely with his words. From having an uncanny knack for remembering the name of every single employee he met, to helping load bags on holidays, to letting employees wear shorts and sneakers to work (well before Silicon Valley norms for informal dress had come into existence), to his speeches, annual reports, and one-on-one conversations showering Southwest employees with gratitude, Kelleher's employees perceived his respect, admiration, and love for them as utterly genuine.

Beyond Kelleher's popularity as a leader lie deep insights about culture in business. Kelleher and his leadership team built a culture that led Southwest to be recognized as the most productive airline, offering the best customer service in the industry. Most important, Southwest turned around more planes at the gate than other airlines—faster, with fewer people and better service, contributing significantly to establishing the low-cost business model that disrupted US air travel. This disruption led the industry, which in the 1970s was dominated by wealthy and business travelers willing to pay a premium to fly, to cultivate the diverse and broad flying public that travels today at reasonable fares.

The coherent core insight driving the success: Southwest aligned its culture tightly with its strategy.[5] Strategically, its employee-first culture works because, in the customer-service-oriented world of airline travel, customers' feelings about an airline determine their willingness to fly with that airline. The front-line employees deliver that service. In a business that is based on low costs, customer service is even more important. Depriving customers of the luxury that used to exist when flying requires making up for it with efficient, friendly, and fun service.

Kelleher also emphasized allegiance and fit with the company overall. He was consistent in his treatment of employees. For example, he didn't talk about "labor-management relationships" because he wanted to avoid people having an "us-versus-them mentality," and he often corrected people if they used "tribal" language. Kelleher once said, "A guy said to me the other day, 'In my department . . .' and I said, 'Oh, are you not a part of Southwest Airlines anymore? Excuse me, I didn't realize you'd split off. Have we notified the SEC?"[6]

Southwest's culture doesn't just aim to make employees feel good. Instead, the culture is tuned tightly to Southwest's competitive demands and strategy. In fact, its culture enabled the company to develop its famous twenty-minute turn time (less than half the industry average of closer to forty-five minutes). The short turn time increased equipment utilization rates from nine hours per plane per day (the industry average) to twelve hours per plane per day. Even more astounding, this performance superiority was accomplished in a heavily unionized industry – with nearly 85% of Southwest employees being union members. How did Southwest do that?

As the turn-time story goes, in its early days Southwest flew four jets to the contiguous states around Texas. The company, like many start-ups, found itself pressed for money. Kelleher and his leadership team realized that they couldn't cover their payroll one month. So they went to their employees with a desperate message. They told employees that the company would need to sell one of its airplanes but would still need to fly the same routes, with three rather than four planes.

Employees quickly accepted the challenge and leaped into action with great initiative and ingenuity, figuring out how to do that by turning the planes faster. But what, exactly, did that mean? It meant everyone doing whatever it takes in the moment, regardless of your actual job description, to get that plane off the ground. This strategically advantageous, comprehensive practice persists to this day, something that competitor airlines have been unable to copy. At Southwest gates, you will see flight attendants helping to clean the planes, pilots helping to break up ice to serve sodas to passengers, and gate agents bringing the last bags onto the plane. Each Southwest employee defines their job as *getting the plane off the ground*, rather than as being a pilot or a flight attendant, because they know, from Kelleher telling them, that "the plane doesn't make money sitting on the ground."[7]

The ease of collaboration at Southwest surprises many because of the high proportion of employees who are members of a labor union. Labor unions often put bright lines around job descriptions, making it clear, for example, what tasks pilots (or flight attendants) can do and won't do. Southwest workers' willingness to undertake tasks outside their official job descriptions to turn the planes faster shows their trust in Kelleher and other Southwest leaders. They trust the company to not only avoid exploiting them but, instead, to share the success that turning the planes faster would yield. Accordingly, Southwest has enjoyed superior turn times for decades, with enormous financial benefits.

Herb Kelleher cultivated much of Southwest's culture. His larger-than-life, culturally consistent personality and vivid, salient behavior sustained Southwest's prolonged business success. Many other organizations show similar leader-driven, strong cultures, including Marc Benioff's equitable culture at Salesforce, Chip Wilson's self-actualized culture at lululemon, and Lisa Su's high-performance culture at AMD.

DO ONLY CEOs INFLUENCE CULTURE?

But do you have to be a CEO, top leader, or founder of your organization to affect its culture, to help build and sustain a strategically relevant culture?

The answer is nuanced. CEOs almost always play integral roles in major strategic decisions that later induce culture changes, intentionally or not. For instance, airplane manufacturing giant Boeing was founded and governed initially by engineers who spent lots of time on the shop floor monitoring plane assembly, a task that helped them design planes. But as the company developed into a financial behemoth, its executives decided to merge with McDonnell Douglas, to move its headquarters away from its Seattle factories to Chicago, and to spin off its design and manufacturing processes to a network of partners, including a previously owned plant in Wichita that became Spirit AeroSystems.

Somewhere along the way, Boeing transitioned from an engineering-manufacturing culture to a finance-oriented culture, according to many observers.[8] Analysts consider this long, slow culture transition to be at the core of Boeing's major problems over the last two decades, including plane crashes and other highly visible accidents like a plane's door blowing out in midflight in 2024. Boeing's new CEO, Kelly Ortberg, is working to reacquire and reintegrate the component manufacturer Spirit Aerosystems (at a cost of over $8 billion) to try to shift the culture back toward engineering and manufacturing.[9] The hope is that an integrated organization will align incentives and behavior, as well as facilitate direct monitoring of assembly. So this is an example in which the CEO is putting in significant effort to reorient the strategy and culture, and we will see whether he is able to do so.

Culture erosion also occurred at the Body Shop, the 1976 start-up whose culture was said to embody "the scent of self-care with social justice," when founder-CEO Anita Roddick sold the company in 2006 and stepped down.[10] Likewise, when Unilever purchased Ben & Jerry's Homemade Holdings ice cream company from founders Ben Cohen and Jerry Greenfield in 2001, despite attempts to protect its original zany, progressive culture as an independent subsidiary with a legal covenant, it still eroded over time without their presence. In both cases, when the top leaders exited, the culture dissolved.[11]

What about other kinds of impact, often intentionally, on an organization's culture? Here too, senior leaders control many more levers for cultural influence than do junior leaders, middle managers, and individual contributors. For example, CEOs typically have a better shot at changing the reward system or enacting policies and procedures to promote and highlight certain behaviors over others. CEOs can also often change the content of the culture of a company directly, such as Boeing's decision in 2024 by Ortberg to deemphasize diversity, equity, and inclusion (DEI) in the culture and instead emphasize "integrity, hard work, and technical expertise."[12] And in the wake of high-profile accounting scandals like Enron, the Public Accounting Oversight Board and other regulators now emphasize "Tone from the Top," a message implying that a company's top executives play the primary role in defining and setting its culture.[13]

But do we overinterpret the role that CEOs play in managing culture? Certainly, the media highlights the most dramatic examples of CEOs influencing their companies, possibly leaving a false impression of their reach. Conversely, we often blame leaders for their companies' misfortunes, a practice that overemphasizes leaders' impact on culture.[14]

This chapter addresses the question of how much control top leaders have over their organizations' cultures. The short answer is that top leaders—founders, CEOs, presidents—can and often do have a greater impact on organizational culture than pretty much any other single person in the organization. The formal authority and positional power that these leaders hold affords them this impact. At the same time, other members of the organization, and even external events, often exert significant cultural influence or even drive culture change.

To disentangle the "top-down" popular belief, this chapter proceeds as follows. We first explain why the top-down popular belief exists, looking realistically at the advantages that top leaders possess in shaping culture. Then we consider why it's important to avoid overattributing an organization's culture to a specific leader. Finally, we calibrate how much control leaders possess, balancing their advantages against the other sources of cultural influence. Those other sources of cultural influence include (1) employees and their ability to either get behind culture change or conversely, withhold their commitment, determining whether unilateral leadership decisions will be acted on or implemented; (2) individual influencers who are not the CEO or a senior leader but do have significant informal influence enabling them to change or resist top-down changes to the culture; (3) shareholders who can collectively exert influence through governance votes; (4) CEO and management team succession; and (5) exogenous economic, social, and political events.[15]

HOW LEADERS INFLUENCE CULTURE: THE GOOD AND THE BAD

In Ed Schein's classic book on organizational culture, he emphasizes the significant role that leaders play in establishing and maintaining culture. When referring to founders, Schein says, "If we are talking about culture formation, learning occurs through the leadership of a founder or entrepreneur who uses his or her personal power to demand some new behavior directed toward achieving some purpose."[16] But exactly how do leaders affect culture? What specific actions do they engage in?

THE GOOD

Research consistently shows that a leader's personality and values affect an organization's culture. On the plus side, if a leader is more open, the culture is more likely to emphasize innovation. If the leader is more conscientious, the culture likely emphasizes detail orientation. Interestingly, if the leader is more agreeable, the culture may end up being less results oriented, as agreeable leaders have trouble being decisive.[17]

Why do a leader's personality and values matter? Personality is a way of describing a person's typical tendencies, focusing on consistent behaviors. Values are enduring beliefs that a specific mode of conduct or end state of existence is personally or socially preferable to an opposite or converse mode of conduct or end state of existence.[18] Think about a CEO who always asks questions about new, innovative practices, who expresses enthusiasm and interest in creative ideas, and who frequently funds risky ideas. Over time, based on this CEO's supportive behaviors, people working with the CEO will think of more creative ideas and thus prioritize them in their own work. And the organization may become known as a good place for creative people, attracting people who already prioritize being creative. These tendencies set the stage for a culture that emphasizes innovation.

Leaders also influence culture by using their authority in setting policies, promotions, and rewards.[19] And this logic of leader personality and value systems influencing culture is intensified when the CEO founded the company.[20]

Consider Marc Benioff, CEO and founder of Salesforce (figure 4.2). For years, he claimed that the company embraced

FIGURE 4.2 Salesforce CEO Marc Benioff

Copyright © 2018 Getty Images. Used by permission.

gender equity and emphasized fairness in the culture. He articulated why gender equity was so important: "Holding equality as a value is not just a matter of fairness or doing the right thing. Nor is it about PR or 'optics' or even my own conscience. It's a crucial part of building a good business, plain and simple. And there is an endless amount of research to prove it."[21]

Despite his public statements, in 2018, two of the most senior women in the company told Benioff that women at Salesforce systematically received less pay than men doing the same work. He describes himself as defensive when he received this news. He recalls: "Back in 2015, I knew we still had a long way to go on this issue, but I was utterly convinced that Salesforce belonged to the tiny minority of tech companies that truly valued gender equality. I simply did not believe that pay disparities could be pervasive. 'Impossible,' I told them. 'That's not right. That's not how we operate.'"[22]

Even with his initial disbelief, Benioff did not ignore the information or sit idly waiting for the complaint to pass. Recognizing that the fix could be very costly, he first commissioned an audit, saying, "Let's go from top to bottom, one person at a time . . . We assembled a cross-functional team and developed a methodology with outside experts that analyzed the entire employee population to determine whether there were unexplained differences in pay."[23] To Benioff's dismay, the results came back showing gender pay gaps all over the company, with 6 percent of Salesforce's 16,000 employees—almost 1,000 of them—needing salary increases to achieve parity. Benioff immediately authorized $3 million in pay adjustments.

Yet additional gender-based pay inequities emerged the next year too, fueled by acquisitions and growth. As Benioff recalled, "Realizing that this [issue] had the potential to become a recurring problem, we decided to take more stringent measures.

We devised a new set of job codes and standards and applied them to each newly integrated company, to make sure everyone performing similar work was similarly compensated from day one. From there, the Employee Success team began reviewing merit increases, bonuses, stock grants, and promotions to root out disparities there, too."[24]

Equalizing pay at Salesforce ultimately cost nearly $9 million by their third pay assessment. The company also invested in a variety of new, continuing, comprehensive practices— mentoring programs targeting high-potential women, courses on unconscious bias offered in Salesforce offices around the world, and many others. These efforts formed a coherent message to employees that fairness and gender equity mattered for the business.

Even with all these structural adjustments, in the end, Benioff believed that top leaders' behavior mattered most, proving essential to setting and changing culture. He explains: "The most important thing leaders can do to promote equality is to open themselves up, take an honest inventory, listen to people, and never be too proud or defensive to make corrections."[25] It helps enormously that Benioff behaves consistently in his interactions and actions and takes measures to correct the situation when it looks otherwise.

Benioff tells several stories about his own missteps and openness to feedback, even after he made huge investments in creating gender equity at Salesforce. At a big event celebrating Salesforce's eighteenth anniversary, Benioff introduced the four speakers, three men and a woman, all Salesforce executives. The three men came first, and Benioff introduced them and then shook hands with each of them. But when he introduced the fourth speaker, a woman, instead of shaking her hand, he gave her a hug. He later realized that by treating her differently, he diminished her—a fact that he missed until someone pointed it out.

Benioff's efforts to reset the culture emphasizing fairness required not only significant investments in new policies and programs but also, clearly, his own visible commitment. As a result, Salesforce benefited in the tight tech labor market. The company received accolades such as "Best Company to Work For" in 2018 and 2019 and found itself able to attract top talent. Without Benioff putting in motion policies and practices focused on rooting out and eliminating gender equity as a key form of fairness, and also paying attention to his own actions, Salesforce would not look much different from any other tech company.

Benioff was the founder and a major owner of Salesforce, which gave him more control and influence—it may be a special case. So a reasonable question is whether we can identify other cases where a new leader takes over a poorly performing company and personally leads the charge to transform the culture en route to success. In chapter 3, we reviewed the efforts of Alan Mulally to turn around Ford, but he did have the backing and ongoing support of the company's beloved owner, Bill Ford.

By contrast, let's consider a case where a single top leader ran a cultural transformation from the top down. When Lisa Su (figure 4.3) became CEO of Advanced Micro Devices (AMD) in 2014, the company was close to declaring bankruptcy. Su had been hired by AMD two years earlier as senior vice president and general manager of Global Business Units. When appointed CEO, she had enough knowledge of the company—its strategy and products—to step into the top role, but she could also see clearly what wasn't working.

As CEO, Su has fostered a high-performance culture that is both supportive and diverse. She said, "One of the things I believe is that great leaders can actually have their teams do 120

FIGURE 4.3 AMD CEO Lisa Su

Copyright © 2024 Reuters Pictures. Used by permission.

percent more than what they thought was possible. What we try to do is to really inspire phenomenal and exceptional results." When Su was a student at the Massachusetts Institute of Technology, she chose electrical engineering as her major because she viewed it as the hardest subject. She believes that solving the most important problems is a path to success:

> I like to set very high standards and expectations. What's inspiring to me is working on something that is really, really hard, or really, really important, and then working with the team to figure out how to reach that goal. There's an art to doing that, because sometimes those stretch goals can seem unachievable, and they can make a team less motivated . . . [but] if I use my analogy of we're trying to get 120 percent out of the team, I think you can use that in just about any situation. If the team thinks they can do

something, then they can probably do 20 percent more. The art is showing them that it's possible and being somewhat understanding if we fall a little bit short. Even if you fall a little bit short, you did much more than you thought you could.[26]

Strategically, Su steered AMD toward simplicity in its products and services. She reinforced simplicity in building AMD's new culture. As she tells it, "When I first took over, there was a desire from HR and the communications team to put together a mission, vision, and value statement, and I was thinking at the time we are losing money like crazy."[27] Su said to do that would take six months that the company couldn't afford to spend. So instead, she drafted a straightforward memo that she delivered at her first all-hands meeting. The memo, designed to reorient and focus employees efforts, outlined three objectives: "To build great products, deepen customer relationships, and simplify everything we do." The simplicity of the message stuck more than if she'd written a ten-point value statement, Su contends. Not only did she articulate the importance of simplicity, but she demonstrated it in her own behavior. Again, note that Su crafted a coherent narrative about the transformation and acted consistently with it. The plan associated with the narrative was comprehensive.

Su rapidly turned around the struggling company. AMD is now a leader in high-performance computing, and its microprocessors are used in a wide range of computing devices. In just six years, she created almost $90 billion of value for shareholders. Since her appointment as CEO, AMD's stock has skyrocketed from less than $2/share to $160/share. AMD currently has a market cap of approximately $186 billion and is poised to grow even more due to artificial intelligence. The company employs 28,000 people and has won numerous corporate citizenship and workplace awards under Su.[28]

Su continues to receive credit for AMD's miraculous turn-around. She certainly deserves the credit because she altered the company's strategy and cultivated a relevant and effective culture.

THE BAD

A leader's ability to influence culture also means that unappealing leader qualities can spread through a company. For example, many observers suggest that the unbridled, freewheeling ways of young founder Travis Kalanick fostered Uber's early culture of disrespect, abuse, and misogyny, even if they suggest that aspects of its culture were aligned with its aggressive business strategy and aided in its initial pathbreaking execution.

More generally, research shows that narcissistic leaders—those who demonstrate a pervasive pattern of grandiosity, need admiration from others, but also lack empathy—can affect a culture in counterproductive ways. Specifically, narcissistic leaders create organizational cultures that struggle with collaboration and integrity.[29] They also tend to expose their cultures to greater risk because of their own overconfidence.[30]

These elements of culture—being collaborative, ethical, and taking appropriate amounts of risk—arguably represent the most essential qualities for an organization to survive. Regarding collaboration, the very reason why people organize is so they can do things together that no one person can do alone. Organizations that lack integrity simply fail to fulfill their promises to employees, customers, shareholders, and policy makers limiting their chances of survival. Likewise, organizations that take no risk or too much risk will lack competitiveness. Finally, research suggests that narcissistic leaders create problematic cultures that transcend their own tenures, leaving a residue on the culture that outlasts them.[31]

CHIP WILSON RUBS CUSTOMERS THE WRONG WAY

For more insight into the impact that a narcissistic leader can have on organizational culture, consider Chip Wilson (figure 4.4), who started and ran the women's activewear company lululemon.[32] Wilson is, without question, a high-impact entrepreneur. His product designs helped to disrupt the women's clothing industry,

FIGURE 4.4 Former Lululemon CEO Chip Wilson

pioneering the "athleisure" category with prices five times higher than traditional activewear for fairly generic items like black leggings. He made savvy decisions, including using so-called attractors to establish fashion trends and to demonstrate the clothing in yoga and Pilates studios, while targeting older, more affluent women as the customer base. In just over three years, the company went from a $40 million, privately held Canadian start-up with fewer than 500 employees to a public company located in multiple countries worth $360 million, with 3,000 employees. Within six years, the company was worth over $1 billion.

The company's rapid growth occurred partly because of the strong, strategically aligned culture that Wilson built. He insisted on hiring people who appeared highly self-aware and "egoless," and lululemon screened prospective employees for culture fit. Among other things, the company asked job-seekers to explain as part of their job interview what the lululemon manifesto—written on its coveted bags—meant to them.

Once people joined the organization, Wilson pressured everyone—including his new CEO, Christine Day (hired in 2008)—to attend Landmark, the human effectiveness training that superseded Werner Erhard's 1970–1980 controversial Erhard's Seminar Training (EST) program. The goal was to equip employees to "be present and bring yourself to work." Wilson insisted that each employee be responsible for strong business results and accountable for relationships. Crossing boundaries between work and life, he also asked everyone to articulate their goals, on one-, five-, and ten-year timetables. And, importantly, Wilson required people to articulate what lululemon's core values meant to them "and how they live within your function."

Store managers played a key role in the company. Lululemon recruited entrepreneurial and highly educated people. Managers were held completely responsible for their store's success and exercised wide latitude in how they generated sales. For example, an infamous 2002 marketing strategy in one store offered a free outfit to anyone who would stand naked in the store window for thirty seconds. In addition, lululemon described its sales philosophy as not selling clothes but helping people live "longer, healthier, more fun lives." Accordingly, store employees sought to serve as educators, whose job involved "help[ing] guests understand technical functionality of components." Further, lululemon believed that "education is the highest form of sales," and that the "garment will sell itself if the features are right."

In short, Wilson did a wonderful job in defining and bringing to life a strong culture that aligned well with the company's strategy.

Recognizing that, with growth, the company needed a professional leader with more experience than he had, Wilson hired Day as CEO in 2008, after a brief false start with Bob Meers as CEO. Day had been COO at Starbucks, and her mandate at lululemon was to grow the company to $1 billion in revenue.

But as lululemon grew, and especially after going public, Wilson's narcissistic impulses began to hurt the company and undermine its culture. Through his own actions, he began defying the narrative that he had created.

Consider the incident in which he blamed a failure of the pricey fabric that lululemon had invented (called "luon") on women's bodies. Wilson intimated that women's chubby thighs created too much pressure on the fabric, a debacle aired on Bloomberg TV in March 2013:

LULULEMON FOUNDER CHIP WILSON: Women will wear a seatbelt that won't work, or a purse that doesn't work, or quite frankly, some women's bodies just don't work for it.

BLOOMBERG REPORTER TRISH REGAN: They don't work for the pants?

WILSON: They don't work for certain women's bodies.

REGAN: So the pants might be see-through on some women's bodies, but not on others?

WILSON: No, no. Because even our small sizes would fit an extra-large. It's more about the rubbing through the thighs, how much pressure is there.

Even when Wilson had a chance to apologize for blaming the product failure on customers, he missed the mark. Instead, he offered the following statement:

Hello, I'm Chip Wilson. I'm founder of lululemon athletica. I'd like to talk to you today about the last few days of media that's occurred around the Bloomberg interview.

I'm sad. I'm really sad. I'm sad for the repercussions of my actions. I'm sad for the people at lululemon who I care so much about, that have really had to face the brunt of my actions. I take responsibility for all that has occurred and the impact it has had on you. I'm sorry to have put you all through this . . . For all of you that have made lululemon what it is today, I ask you to stay in a conversation that is above the fray. I ask you to prove that the culture that you have built cannot be chipped away. Thank you.

To us, this statement reads like a failed apology attempt directed at his staff rather than an apology to the public, those customers whom he had insulted.

The fiasco even reached late-night television, with host Stephen Colbert skewering Wilson by summing up his apology: "You hear that, ladies? Chip Wilson is sad that your chafing ham-hocks made him put his employees through this difficult time."

After stepping down as CEO, Wilson stayed on as chair. He interfered so significantly in the company's operations and strategy that Day resigned as CEO in 2013 after growing the company to $1 billion. In December 2013, the board forced Wilson to resign as chair. Inexplicably, he continued to battle the board. In June 2014, he voted against the company strategy that the rest of the board and management wanted to pursue. Wilson eventually agreed to sell half his lululemon stock to a capital management firm. Since then, he has not been connected to the company, aside from holding 9 percent of its stock.

From the start, Wilson said that he aimed to create a culture of self-awareness, low ego, health, empowering women, and positivity toward others. His public missteps directly contradicted many of the values of that intended culture. His actions slowed lululemon's growth and hurt the company financially.

After Day's departure, lululemon recruited Calvin McDonald as CEO. He made the culture less about himself and appeared to double down on the culture that lululemon had aspired to make a reality before Wilson undermined it. Recently, McDonald said:

> The culture at lululemon is one that I fell in love with early on, because there really is this genuine passion to help others achieve their full potential and how we do that is obviously what we do every day. But sometimes the intent didn't line up with the impact. It took self-reflection as an organization on how we can do better to recruit with diversity at the forefront, how we can do better to become more inclusive, and then to ensure that we have equity across all aspects of the organization, not just in pay. This is really the conversation we've been in, the commitments we make, and the role that this team's going to have, part of our Inclusion, Diversity, Equity and Action team, not just in North America, but globally. So, it's really leaning in from an investment standpoint on resources to broaden the team and the conversation ensuring

that we're driving the change that we wanted, to have the outcome that we're all aligned to.[33]

On Glassdoor, McDonald gets a very high (90 percent) approval rating. And under his reign for the past seven years (2018–2025), lululemon appeared on the Glassdoor "Best Places to Work" list.

Again, we see a case in which the CEO or the founder can have significant impact on a company's culture, whether that impact ends up helping or hurting the company.

NARCISSISTIC LEADERS

Sadly, too many leaders come across as narcissistic, and the impact is often catastrophic for the companies that they lead. Think of Adam Neumann (figure 4.5) at WeWork, who professed his

FIGURE 4.5 Former WeWork CEO Adam Neumann

Copyright © 2017 Reuters Pictures. Used by permission.

commitment to building an effective culture, saying, "The right people don't care about a corner office—they care about the culture, if you're mission-driven, what you're going to do to make the world a better place."[34] He founded WeWork with a promise "to create a business that makes a difference in the world."[35] Neumann claimed that his descendants would be running WeWork in three hundred years.

But how did he behave as leader? Not well. WeWork senior executives requesting an in-person meeting might be asked to fly with Neumann from New York to San Francisco at a moment's notice. But he was just as likely to make them wait for hours, leave before they arrived at the airport, or simply have no time to talk to them during the six-and-a-half-hour flight.

He aspired to live forever, be "leader of the world," and be the world's first trillionaire. Instead, the company lost 90 percent of its value, going from a $47 billion valuation to near bankruptcy, even as he walked away with $1.7 billion.

Or consider Elon Musk at Twitter (now X), who said in 2022: "Going forward, to build a breakthrough Twitter 2.0 and succeed in an increasingly competitive world, we will need to be *extremely hardcore*. This will mean working long hours at high intensity. Only exceptional performance will constitute a passing grade. If you are sure that you want to be part of the new Twitter, please click yes on the link below."[36]

Musk then fired two-thirds of the company. He also made confusing requests of employees, such as asking them to print out dozens of pages of code they'd recently written, only to reverse course and tell them to shred it. At least one Twitter (X) employee also tweeted about sleeping on the floor at the office. Musk claims that he has worked as much as 120 hours a week at times and has slept on the floor at a Tesla factory.

Like Su at AMD, Musk had the advantage of avoiding inertia in taking over Twitter. But the decisions that he made initially did not appear to be effective, and the previous culture seemed difficult to sustain. For example, after Musk took over, advertising revenue at Twitter shrunk by 50 percent and the company's valuation stood at only one-third of what Musk paid for it. All the same, Musk's fortune, among the largest in the world, is intact because Tesla and his other companies, like SpaceX and xAI, continue to generate financial returns.

Why do so many CEOs come across as narcissistic? Research shows that people who are high in narcissism seek out positions of power and are disproportionately represented among corporate leaders.[37] To be classified as high in narcissism means that a person meets the criteria for narcissistic personality disorder: They display an inflated sense of their own importance, a view that they are not subject to the normal rules and norms, and a belief that they are superior to others. These people need admiration, carry themselves with extreme self-confidence, exploit others for their own ends, and become hostile toward those who challenge them.

Of course, a reasonable observer would likely think that these attributes would disqualify narcissists from leadership roles in the first place. Unfortunately, reality is more complicated. Narcissists often rise to high-level positions in organizations, in part because their narcissistic dark side may not appear right away, and in part because they have some overlapping qualities with visionary leaders, such as having grandiose aspirations that they can promise to deliver in compelling ways.[38]

But research also shows that narcissists tend to be abusive leaders. They criticize others and blame them for failures; they take the credit for success even if they were not responsible for that success; they blame others for failure even if they themselves were responsible for that failure; and they create cultures with lower integrity and less teamwork.[39] In fact, appointing narcissists to senior leader roles carries great risk, leading researchers studying narcissistic leaders to conclude: "Those we often admire as transformational leaders may also be narcissists. What we see initially as visionary, self-confident, strong-willed, charming, and challenging may—in the extreme—be grandiose, entitled, arrogant, exploitative, impulsive, and aggressive. A failure to understand these differences can be dangerous, putting people and institutions at risk".[40]

Research further suggests that weeding out narcissists requires being vigilant, particularly at the most senior levels of leadership. For example, boards of directors should look for evidence that any leader whom they are considering appointing shows a strong track record of sharing the spotlight with others and developing the leaders with whom they are connected. Sharing credit for success with others is a key differentiator between narcissistic and visionary leaders. If a candidate shows little evidence of developing other leaders and bringing people along with them, alarm bells should go off.

LIMITS ON LEADERS' INFLUENCE OVER CULTURE

Obviously, many founders and CEOs exert tremendous influence over their organization's culture. The examples given in this chapter show us that top leaders can use culture to accelerate their organization's success and infuse industries with new models. But they hold influence regardless of the virtues of their ambitions. Southwest, Salesforce, and AMD all benefited from highly effective founders and leaders and their deliberate actions to build an effective culture. But because holding the power position of CEO is also associated with a loss of impulse control, things can go off the rails as they did at lululemon, WeWork, and apparently, at least as of now, at X.[41]

As influential as founders and CEOs appear, they do not fully control whether a particular culture is created or maintained. This is good news for people other than senior leaders who believe that their culture needs to become more strategically relevant, strong, or adaptive. It is empowering to know that you still can change culture even if you are not the CEO or founder. Further, based on our discussion in chapter 3 about the psychological basis of internalizing cultural norms, we know that the most significant change occurs when many people are involved in creating that change. Accordingly, identifying the other major sources of cultural influence helps inform managerial action by clarifying the limitations that leaders face when trying to influence culture.

So, besides CEOs and senior leaders, what are the other major sources of influence on organizational culture and culture change?

First, research shows that interaction partners (interlocutors)—the people in the organization whom you interact with—influence your perceptions of the culture.[42] Since most people in organizations of any size do not regularly interact with the CEO or other senior leaders, these leaders have less potential influence relative to a person's close network. For example, research shows that as interaction grows between any two people—even by e-mail—their language becomes more similar. Anthropologists and economists have long thought that shared language reflects a significant form of cultural influence.[43]

Second, research shows that shareholder expectations and demands affect a public company's culture.[44] Finance researchers found that firms that closely lose governance elections were subsequently more likely to emphasize being results-oriented in their culture and less likely to emphasize being customer-oriented compared to those who closely win their governance elections. Interestingly, and a little ironically, organizations whose cultures emphasize results more intensely and customers less intensely experience a 1.4 percent decline in firm value over time.

Third, there is evidence that some companies have had short periods of success with "leaderless cultures," suggesting that developing a strong culture does not necessarily require strong leadership. Consider Valve, the software and hardware entertainment company that produces Steam, a digital distribution service and storefront. Valve describes itself as "boss-free since 1996." What does this mean? As it explains, "We believe that the best product decisions are made by the people who are actually doing the work. We take great pride in hiring top talent from a variety of disciplines and bringing people together with one simple directive: Collaborate and create."[45] Although Valve is a private company, it is estimated to be worth well over $7 billion, with just over 1,000 employees. It is a strong culture organization, suggesting that there are other paths to building a strong culture besides the heavy hands of strong leaders and senior leadership teams.

Fourth, the palpable existence of subcultures in most organizations implies that senior leaders do not have total influence over culture. Subcultures consist of relatively small clusters of members who share a set of norms, values, and beliefs.[46] Subcultures can permit an organization to generate varied responses to the competitive environment without necessarily destroying its internal coherence. And organizations benefit from simultaneously managing strong, stable cultures while maintaining the flexibility and adaptability necessary to survive the ebbs and flows of turbulent environments, sometimes referred to as "ambidextrous organizations."[47] Subcultures may provide exactly the kind of flexibility and responsiveness that a unitary culture may limit.

Finally, exogeneous events—events outside a company's control, like a recession or the COVID-19 pandemic—can cause cultural shifts. Research has shown, for example, that cultures changed quickly in response to the pandemic. The typical pattern was that companies backed off on performance expectations and increased their emphasis on supporting employees, at least initially.[48] Relatedly, organizations with certain cultural content may be better able to withstand the challenges of adverse exogeneous events, suggesting that certain types of cultures may buffer against environmental volatility.[49]

LYFT'S BALANCE BETWEEN TOP AND BOTTOM

Lyft, the rideshare company, moved quickly and nimbly to change their culture as the realities of COVID-driven remote work became apparent. Its leaders used the opportunity of the pandemic—an externally driven change well beyond any company's control—to adapt the culture for the longer run. This story illustrates how leaders can use apparently uncontrollable forces to improve their organizational culture—a sophisticated and nuanced version of the popular belief that leaders have control over the culture.

Lyft, the rideshare app company, was deeply affected by the pandemic. When COVID hit, not only did it affect Lyft's ridership, but it also affected work arrangements in the company. As a tech company, Lyft wanted to stay open to the possibility of remote and hybrid work for its nondriver employees.

The question was whether connecting less in person would erode the company's strong, strategically relevant culture.

Lyft's president, Kristin Sverchek (figure 4.6), who was formerly general counsel, was intent on finding a work model that reinforced Lyft's founding principles. Unlike Uber, which started as a "black car" service modeled on limousine service, Lyft started as a long-distance carpool service. Lyft's business strategy

FIGURE 4.6 Kristin Sverchek

was all about connecting with people—two people connecting in a car—just as you would with an old friend or family member.

As a result of these origins, Lyft attracted people who were excited about solving their customers' collaboration challenges. This orientation influences everything at Lyft, including how it thinks about employees, customers, and even regulators—not as enemies but as potential collaborators interested in what's good for consumers.

The company hierarchy is unusually flat, with a strong norm of respecting people and their ideas at all levels. One of Lyft's early values was "Uplift Others," meaning everything from contributing to making other people's ideas successful to respecting and including colleagues.

Lyft's founders, Logan Green and John Zimmer, and subsequent leaders believed that everyone in the company is thinking deeply about its business challenges and, as a result, their voices should be heard and considered. Sverchek remembers being challenged by a much more junior employee on a new idea, and that person's idea was strongly supported in the culture. When she led the legal team before becoming president, Sverchek recalls their intense focus on customer service, both riders and drivers, as well as internal customers, and "being a yes team rather than a no team," which is unusual for many legal teams, who often take a risk-averse stance to protect the firm.

Lyft went public with an initial public offering (IPO) in March 2019, and then of course, like all companies, was forced to grapple with the fallout from the pandemic just a year later. As unpredictable public health mandates from the COVID-19 pandemic made their way through the population, the company kept trying to plan for how and when employees would return to work, producing many false starts. There were return-to-office dates that they couldn't meet, and employees complained that they did not know what even the next six months would bring, making it hard to plan their lives. Employees began to ask for more predictability and clarity around work arrangements. At the same time, employees were asking for more flexible work arrangements, and Lyft did not want to become a "yesteryear" nine-to-five company.

How could Lyft manage this apparent conflict between its culture, which was based on the value of in-person collaboration and connection among and between employees and customers on the one hand, and employees' request for both predictability and flexibility in their work model on the other?

The company experimented with a variety of possibilities from 2020 to 2023. For example, initial Lyft policies included allowing employees who had moved thirty miles or more from the San Francisco headquarters during the pandemic to continue working almost fully remotely, even after the shelter-in-place orders ended, and people were free to return to work. And there were no coordinated days that people had to come into the office, even if they lived close by—work was completely flexible in 2022–2023, and people could come in when they wanted. Svercheck said, "It was a pretty bad period for the business, and we were performing poorly."

Nonetheless, after each change in work models, Lyft surveyed its employees to see what they thought.

When a new CEO, David Risher, arrived in April 2023, he advocated for tightly linking Lyft's business strategy with the culture that they needed to execute on that strategy. To do so, he truly believed that the company worked better together, in person. In fact, he believed that a huge part of Lyft's purpose is to have people come out of their homes and bring them into the physical world together. This purpose, he believed, transcends Lyft's customers and applies to employees too.

Having the CEO's authority, Risher could have mandated that everyone return to the office to work every day. But he and Svercheck tweaked the work-from-home (WFH) policy over time instead. By 2024, the WFH policy required that people come to the office three days a week (even though Risher preferred four days), two of which were coordinated and one was a "choice" day—any day that the employee would like to come in. Mondays and Thursdays were coordinated days, and most people's choice day became Wednesdays. Everyone in the company could also take up to four weeks of remote work, and, like many tech companies, Lyft continued to offer unlimited personal time off (PTO). And, notably, Lyft began hiring locals in all markets in which they had offices (e.g., team members who lived within thirty miles of San Francisco or twenty miles of New York City).

As Sverchek says, "We wanted our in-office culture to mirror the external experience that we wanted people to have."[50] In other words, because the Lyft platform is all about bringing people together, the in-office experience should be similarly oriented around interpersonal connections. Risher's view, similarly, was that making big decisions and developing new ideas required people to be together in person. He stopped just short of saying that Lyft employees were necessarily more productive together; but the underlying value was bringing people together to solve problems, just as the Lyft platform is about bringing people together.

Recognizing that workplace/WFH policies have an enormous impact on people's lives, and the new policy would be a major employment decision, Lyft gave people many months to prepare. And it introduced the new policies with lots of fanfare, believing that it would be an opportunity to double down on its strategically relevant culture. There was a "Homecoming" theme, with themed snacks, company news anchors gave updates on how the back-to-office plans were unfolding, and a variety of other events were held to get people excited about a plan that offered less flexibility than people wanted. Sverchek knew they needed to work to get people on board.

By Q3 2023, employee sentiment about the workplace policies moved from 25 percent support to over 46 percent support among employees. And Lyft's performance steadily improved from there, with a 17 percent increase in gross bookings and a 4 percent increase in revenue ($1.2B) by year end.

Risher and Sverchek used their strategically relevant culture to define Lyft's workplace policy. They set goals and were intentional, getting people together in person, an approach that they believed would ultimately result in better company performance. The goal of the workplace policies was not productivity per se, Sverchek said, but having stronger relationships for difficult moments and hard decisions about a business focused on connecting people.

They also listened to employees and clearly communicated what they were doing, explaining their reasoning, and detailing how they considered employees' views. Of course, they did not incorporate all the requests that employees made, but they did generate many communications to make sure that people understood the decisions.

Risher and Sverchek and their leadership team used the data that they collected regularly from the Lyft employee population to see what they needed. They learned that employees wanted to see coworkers and friends, they wanted snacks, and they wanted easier collaboration, which essentially meant more in-person time together. Risher's preference was to mandate four days in the office, but the data that they collected clearly showed that employees wanted three, so they went with employees on the number of days in the office—and those days turned out to be Mondays, Wednesdays, and Thursdays.

These changes were built into hiring and socialization approaches so new employees could learn the company's norms early on. Lyft also increased its commuting subsidy. The once-significant number of employees who are more than thirty miles away are not penalized for being remote, but there has been natural attrition, and the company has shifted recruiting to find people who live within commutable distances. Indeed, a remaining challenge even after the policies were developed was that employees were still not completely co-located, so in-person collaboration was not perfect.

As you can see, the Lyft case is notable in illustrating how leaders can use a company's culture and strategy to navigate through enormously challenging external shocks. Note how closely Risher and Sverchek monitored the changes that they were implementing, and they did not hesitate to adjust and readjust based on the data that they were collecting about their culture—approaches that likely enabled them to be successful.

SUMMARY

In this chapter, we examined the popular belief that culture is managed effectively only from the top down. What does our analysis show?

First, we recognize that senior leaders—founders, CEOs, senior vice presidents—often exert a strong influence on their organizations' cultures. The influence comes from their formal power but is directed by their highly salient actions and behaviors, which are at least partly influenced by their personalities and values. Leaders can help strengthen an organization's culture as we saw with Kelleher at Southwest, Benioff, at Salesforce and Su at AMD, especially if they tell a coherent narrative about the culture and its impact, support the culture comprehensively with a variety of levers, and act in consistent ways. Or leaders can undermine the culture, as we saw with Wilson at lululemon,

Neumann at WeWork, and Musk at X (Twitter). And, in some cases, leaders' cultural influence persists even after they depart—even if they exerted a negative influence. Sadly, this is more likely to be the case when they hold very senior roles. Perhaps mistaken as visionary leaders at first, narcissistic leaders often create toxic cultures that are low in collaboration and integrity. So boards of directors who select CEOs, and senior leaders appointing other senior leaders, need to be vigilant in distinguishing visionary leaders from narcissists.

Second, we can see that prolonged cultural impact does not just require leaders themselves to behave in ways that are consistent with the culture that they are trying to create, so-called modeling behavior. To make culture stick over the long run, leaders need to also put in place comprehensive policies, practices, and systems that reach well beyond their own behaviors. This point is a theme of this book.

Third, while leaders should be aware of and use the outsized potential influence that they have on culture, they should also recognize that change of greater significance occurs when they involve other people in decision-making and implementation. These other people should feel that the culture incorporates their ideas and preferences. The many others who are not founders or CEOs don't just give up when a leader is not doing a good job in creating a strategically relevant, strong, and adaptive culture. Leaders should also recognize the external pressures on an organization to adopt certain cultural priorities. Being realistic about, and calibrating a leader's influence over culture, focusing on what really matters—consistent and comprehensive practices that transcend any individual are what makes culture effective.

Finally, while highly influential, leaders do not exert unlimited control over company culture. Other important sources of cultural material arise from the networks of interaction within the organization. Culture also can be influenced by shareholders, suppliers, and competitors. For example, research has shown that shareholder governance votes determined whether company cultures emphasized customers or financial results.[51]

On the point that leaders do not have unlimited control, we also saw that events in the larger environment—economic downturns, pandemics—can exert significant influences on organizational cultures, and rather quickly. Further, an organization's culture at the start of such an event (or crisis) can materially affect how an organization fares in terms of financial performance through the event. And finally, we saw through the Lyft case that organizations that use external changes as opportunities to adjust the culture can benefit significantly from that change.

Thus, the validity of the popular belief that you must be a CEO, top leader, or founder of your organization to help build and sustain a strategically relevant culture is, as we promised, nuanced. Yes, leaders have more tools at their disposal to affect culture and culture change, but they are also limited by their ability to influence and gain support from many others in an organization, and they are subject to exogenous events and constituent expectations and demands beyond their control.

MANAGERIAL TAKEAWAYS FROM THIS CHAPTER

- Executives and other top leaders of an organization can (and often do) exert enormous influence over its culture. In many ways, the culture of an organization often reflects its leaders.
- The influence of an executive on an organization's culture can be intentional or unintentional, beneficial or

detrimental. Authority and control over resources typically imbue executives with great influence on an organization's culture, even when they are not aware of it.

- Leaders' influence on their organization's culture is not necessarily monolithic, because employees and transaction partners often matter too. The influence of leaders can be blunted by resistance or negated by others' expertise.

- Organizational culture is also influenced by events beyond an organization's or leader's control. In these cases, leaders can still, to some extent, make deliberate decisions to position their organization's culture and strategy to optimize for the events—for example, by changing the culture to prepare for future work arrangements as Lyft did.

- Effective leaders of an organization's culture behave consistently and explain their actions coherently, and they also comprehensively affect many domains of organizational life.

- Effective leaders of an organization's culture rely heavily on the actions and contributions of others; by harnessing the efforts of others in the organization, culture becomes very powerful.

- Cultural leadership takes many forms and includes the informal actions and feedback of many people without great authority or budgetary control. Informal leaders can carry much of the weight of an organization's culture.

- When aligned, culture and strategy can guide work policies and behaviors, affecting an organization's performance.

5

CULTURE IS SOFT?

National Football League (NFL) All-Pro Deion Sanders was hired in December 2022 as the head coach of the University of Colorado, Boulder football team. When he was hired, Sanders (aka Coach Prime; see figure 5.1) received a strong mandate from the university's administration: to transform the beleaguered team into a winner, a contender for titles and championships. By many accounts, Colorado had become mediocre, with players showing a lack of motivation and limited skills. The beleaguered team limped to a 1–11 record in the 2022 fall season. Many people opined that Colorado's football team and coaching staff needed a culture change to turn things around, and they expected Sanders to deliver it.

I DON'T CARE ABOUT CULTURE

But shortly after being hired, Coach Prime was quoted as saying, "I don't care about culture. I don't care." He continued in a mini-rant of sorts: "I'm not welcoming to that word, culture. That's all I heard when I was in Jackson. Culture, culture, culture, culture, culture. Now culture, culture. What the heck does that mean?

FIGURE 5.1 Coach Prime

Copyright © 2023 The Associated Press. Used by permission.

"I don't care about culture," he proclaimed. "I don't even care if they like each other, I want to win . . . I don't think you got to have unity whatsoever."

Sanders's comments stand out because public expressions that disparage organizational culture rarely appear these days. Leaders and employees seem to sense that, in public discussions, organizational culture deserves respect and reverence, whatever they think about it privately. In this way, culture may be akin to any politically correct flashpoint.

Yet, in private, many people express skepticism—or even disbelief—about the value of managing culture as a key ingredient in successful organizations. Steven L. Blue, CEO of Miller Ingenuity, says that many executives incorrectly believe that culture implies "squishy, beer-for-lunch, feel-good" companies and hot start-ups. Blue says that these executives think that culture "doesn't deserve a place 'at the grown-ups table.'"[1]

Why? What is the problem that people have with culture? Certain cynical views of culture, like those of some of Jennifer Cook's scientist colleagues at Genentech (see chapter 1), come from a person's inherent belief in the nearly exclusive superiority of numerically based financial analyses—focusing on the numbers—especially in business. These people believe that business viability should be assessed through "hard" factors like financial evaluations of growth and profit possibilities; in their view, these are the valid ways to evaluate a business, and nothing "soft," like culture, will do. Indeed, we have personally witnessed plenty of MBA students and executives express this view.

Despite the more recent public self-censoring of critical commentary, culture's softness is definitely a popular belief, in our opinion. Even many of its evangelists would usually categorize culture as a "soft" phenomenon, having only to do with building harmonious interpersonal relationships and "improving" people's attitude about their work and employers. Most people believe that culture involves the softer aspects of work, like putting employees in a good mood by offering amenities and perks. They see cultural management as one of the so-called soft skills that business leaders *might* want to develop but are not as essential as hard skills like financial analyses and accounting.

CULTURE IS HARD AMONG NAVY SEALs

But try telling Brent Gleeson that culture is soft. A former Navy SEAL (see figure 5.2), Gleeson recommends that leaders conduct what he calls "culture diagnostics." According to his terminology, a diagnostic involves "gathering as much valuable intelligence [as] is critical for understanding what you will be dealing with and how you plan the mission." Gleeson says, "If you are trying to evolve a culture and redesign it to fit a strategy for change, then you better find ways to measure progress." Clearly, he believes that culture can be objectively assessed.

Gleeson also thinks the SEAL culture makes these soldiers some of the toughest, most hardened combat troops you can find. He says: "The SEAL Teams embody a culture of teamwork, innovation, and a never-quit attitude. This aligns perfectly with our strategy and vision of maintaining our status as the *most elite warfighters in the world*. Everything we do, every experience, every lesson, supports these beliefs." In short, Gleeson points out that he and fellow SEALS trust their lives to the culture. Would they do this if they thought the culture was soft and unreliable?

Leading CFOs, executives who spend their time watching the numbers and the markets, don't underestimate culture by viewing it as soft either. A survey by finance professors at

FIGURE 5.2 Navy SEALs

Copyright © 2014 Reuters Pictures. Used by permission.

Duke University captures CFOs' views about organizational culture. They asked almost 2,000 executives to respond to a survey question about the impact of their organizational culture on performance. A whopping 66 percent of these executives responded that culture was "very important" at their firms, with 54 percent of the CFOs placing culture as among the *top three* things that make their firms valuable. In addition, the CFOs replied that culture had a "big effect" on firms' value (57 percent), profitability (54 percent) and productivity (62 percent).

In discussions with executives and others, we have discerned that the popular belief that culture is soft can mean at least two different things. The first is that softness is subjective—in other words, not quantifiable or measurable in a valid and reliable way. Holding this view likely originates early in a person's life, perhaps in grade school, where students often perceive subjects like math as hard and those like English as soft. Hard is objective, or black-and-white, while soft is interpretive, or more in a gray zone.

The second meaning holds that culture is warm, fuzzy, and friendly—always uplifting and positive and a way to improve employee attitudes. Holding this view likely originates in the employee-centered cultures of early strong culture organizations like Disney and Hewlett-Packard (HP). More recently, the ubiquity of Silicon Valley tech companies offering perks like free food and personal services perpetuates this view.

In this chapter, we explore both meanings to assess whether culture is in fact soft, and if so, in what ways. We begin in the next section by asking whether culture can be measured quantitatively, with indicators of its relative hardness or softness. We then address questions about the softness of culture arising from the heavy and widespread use of attractive perks in some highly visible strong culture companies.

CAN CULTURE BE MEASURED?

Public awareness about culture emanated from observations of so-called learned men traveling centuries ago with great early explorers and adventurers. Following the model set by natural historians, who traveled to faraway places to document unfamiliar flora and fauna, early anthropologists attempted to document the rituals and social practices of Indigenous peoples in remote places, often minimally disturbed by Western visitors or traders. The first anthropologists compiled data from records and interviewed native informants whom they had summoned to describe and classify their cultures.

Anthropologist Bronislaw Malinowski usually gets credited with taking the study of culture into the field, prompting anthropologists to leave their comfortable veranda armchairs and observe natives directly in their own contexts and interact with them. Malinowski believed that to study a culture, analysts must be in close contact with natives, recording and interpreting regular aspects of their everyday lives. This is really a description of an ethnographer, who uses participant observation as the primary method of study. He famously claimed that the purpose of anthropology and ethnography is "to grasp the native's point of view, his relation to life, to realize his vision of his world."[2]

QUALITATIVE VERSUS QUANTITATIVE ASSESSMENTS OF CULTURE

The approach advocated by Malinowski implies that every culture may be unique, and studying culture using the preconceived concepts and theories that were learned by observing other cultures could lead to serious misunderstandings. Instead, ethnographers should interpret *each* culture by observing and engaging with *that* culture. Anthropologist Clifford Geertz notes that these observations require "extraordinary sensitivity, an almost preternatural capacity to think, feel, and perceive like a native."[3]

Most ethnographers would argue that these qualitative approaches are still deeply scientific. But the goal is to create a theory based on their observations, not to test a theory that already exists. Once they come up with a theory of culture based on their observations, then the theory can be tested more systematically across many organizations. For example, Margaret Mead, another pioneering cultural anthropologist, showed how gender roles are shaped by a group's culture, a theory that has been tested in decades of subsequent research.[4]

The debate that Malinowski raises—about qualitative versus quantitative assessments of culture—still riddles organizational culture research both in academic circles and among businesspeople, even after many decades. The question surely lurks behind the claim that culture is soft and cannot be measured, showing that the belief has serious support among some social scientists.[5]

In the meantime, quantitative approaches to assessing culture have flourished. These approaches to culture sometimes rely on assessments from organizational informants, who are asked to report broad patterns of behavior about members of a target organization.[6] In one review, researchers uncovered seventy culture diagnostic instruments, many of which are used to generate cultural typologies that categorize organizations based on predefined dimensions.[7]

There are, perhaps, four prominent quantitative approaches to assessing organizational culture.[8] We briefly review these approaches in table 5.1. What is notable, and concerning, is that some of these widely used organizational culture surveys were not developed to measure culture, but rather as more general

TABLE 5.1 COMPARISON OF FOUR PROMINENT CULTURE ASSESSMENT TOOLS

Feature Category	Dennison Organizational Culture Survey (DOCS)	Organizational Culture Assessment Instrument (OCAI)	Organizational Culture Inventory (OCI)	OCP
Time Investment				
Completion time	20–25 min	10–15 min	20–30 min	15–20 min
Number of items	60 items	24 items	120 items	54 items
Administration complexity	**	*	***	***
Cultural validity				
Pure culture focus	**	***	***	****
Separates culture from performance	*	**	***	****
Measures cultural content	**	***	***	****
What It Measures				
Cultural elements	Values and practices	Cultural types	Behavioral norms	Cultural norms
Noncultural elements	Effectiveness and mission	Organizational effectiveness	Group expectations	None
Primary focus	Performance outcomes	Culture classification	Behavioral standards	Pure culture

Ease of Use

Quick to complete	***	***	**	**
Easy to administer	***	***	**	**
Simple to interpret	***	****	**	*
Measurement Power				
Depth of analysis	***	*	***	****
Cultural nuance	***	**	***	****
Behavioral focus	***	**	****	*
Performance Link				
Financial performance Evidence	***	**	*	***
Empirical validation	***	**	***	****
Research foundation	***	***	***	****
Strategic Value				
Business alignment	****	***	**	****
Change management	***	****	***	**
Performance link	****	**	***	****

* Basic | ** Enhanced | ***Premium | ****Elite

KEY TAKEAWAYS

Time Efficiency	Performance Link
OCAI: Fastest (10–15 min)	OCP: Strong empirical evidence
OCP: Efficient (15–20 min)	DOCS: Strong effectiveness correlation
DOCS: Moderate (20–25 min)	OCI: Moderate behavioral outcomes
OCI: Longest (20–30 min)	OCAI: Theoretical connection

Cultural Validity	Best Use Case
OCP: Highest (pure culture measurement)	OCP: Comprehensive culture analysis
OCI: Strong (behavioral focus)	DOCS: Strategic alignment
OCAI: Moderate (typology approach)	OCAI: Quick culture typing
DOCS: Lower (mixed with effectiveness)	OCI: Behavioral assessment

assessments of an organization's effectiveness. This is a problem because "effectiveness" is a vague concept involving many organizational elements, while culture is a distinct phenomenon that should be isolated.

A different kind of quantitative research relies on traces of behavior—like the language that people use in e-mails, online reviews, and Slack conversations—to detect and describe an organization's culture. Pioneering culture theorists Ed Schein and William Labov viewed language—the actual words that people use—as an integral part of culture.[9] Researchers view how new members of an organization start to mimic the words and phrases that longtime employees use in e-mails as a measure of "cultural assimilation" over time.[10] In one study, researchers examined more than 10.25 million e-mail exchanges in a single organization among 600 employees over five years.[11]

These and other large-scale methods offer intriguing possibilities for asking and answering key questions about how culture develops and changes over time. The advantage is that these approaches measure culture unobtrusively—that is, without the biases that can emerge from asking a sample of people to report on their culture. What is perhaps most promising is that researchers can learn from huge samples studied over long time periods across many industries, making the data on which they base their conclusions much more reliable. These large language models (LLMs), using e-mails, slack exchanges, and website comments such as those on Glassdoor, can allow culture researchers to do the fine-grained, large sample tests necessary to uncover so many questions with greater accuracy, foremost among them how culture influences organizational performance.

In sum, many expert analysts believe that culture can be measured, and their research clearly demonstrates that it can. So what's the problem—why do many still believe that culture can't be effectively quantified?

Researchers in the qualitative camp question whether trying to view organizations in terms of a single overall culture makes sense—instead, they point to the many subcultures that exist in most organizations. They also worry that standardized surveys gloss over unique cultural characteristics that distinguish organizations from each other. As they see it, standardized surveys obscure the culture because people may resist being candid in responding, particularly when they can't use their own words. There is also the issue of culture dimensions being murky and hard to distinguish from one another. For example, is being collaborative really that different from being people oriented?[12] Other criticisms note that even the best culture assessments may not be comprehensive in assessing all possible culture dimensions.

But many, maybe even most, researchers see some culture assessments as helpful, rigorous, and accurate. These assessments typically display desirable features that social scientists call "predictive validity" and "reliability." Predictive validity reflects how well the assessment predicts relevant outcomes, such as whether certain types of cultures predict financial performance.[13] Cultural studies often provide impressive predictive validity for their measures (e.g., relating their measures to individual and organizational outcome data like job satisfaction, commitment, and financial performance). Reliability is about consistency in measurement; researchers have shown test-retest reliability of the measures, providing assurance that there is measurement consistency over time.

What quantitative culture researchers have not done as well is to offer evidence of what is called "construct validity." In contrast to predictive validity, construct validity is about whether the instrument actually measures what it claims to be measuring. Since a construct like culture is abstract, one way to understand it is by seeing whether the various measures relate to it in ways that the theory would predict. This is *convergent* and *discriminant validity*: showing that the measure is related in logical ways to measures of similar constructs, but also distinct from similar constructs. For example, culture should be distinct from one member's job satisfaction, which is more about how much they like the organization than the broader patterns of norms and behaviors that members display.

Establishing validity is essential to proving that you are in fact measuring culture and that the relationships between culture and various outcomes like financial performance and innovation exist.[14]

Unfortunately, too many researchers either rely on idiosyncratic measures of culture with little validation or opt for easily accessible measures like the Dennison Organizational Culture

Survey (DOCS) and Organizational Culture Assessment Instrument (OCAI), which show questionable construct validity (see table 15.1).[15] As measured by these instruments, even when culture and culture fit are related to outcomes such as job satisfaction, sometimes they are less clearly related to objective outcomes like financial performance and financial growth, especially at the organizational level of analysis.[16] Absent a common definition and a validated culture assessment, these measures end up muddying the waters, making the question about culture's impact on hard outcomes trickier to answer.

So, what should you look for if you want to measure an organization's culture? Our advice is to look for an instrument that does the following:

- Demonstrates construct and predictive validity in underlying academic research (in other words, the instrument actually measures culture and offers evidence of links to key outcomes like financial performance)
- Relies on a comprehensive set of content norms to fully assess all relevant aspects of culture and enable standardized comparisons to other organizations
- Creates a profile of the culture in which different norms are assessed relative to other norms
- Treats respondents as informants of the culture rather than asking them for their own attitudes about the company
- Offers distinct measures of culture content and culture strength
- Enables a comparison between the current culture and the strategically needed culture so that culture gaps can be identified and culture change efforts can be focused and precise

Ultimately, the qualitative and quantitative approaches need not be in conflict. Our view is that two approaches can—and often should—be combined effectively and used to understand

and change culture. A quantitative measure of organizational culture can be augmented with qualitative observations that provide details and illustrations of observable behaviors and deeper assumptions. In fact, even though many consultants focus on either qualitative or quantitative assessments of culture, we advise that both approaches be used in combination.

Jennifer Cook at Genentech Immunology and Ophthalmology (GIO), as described in chapter 2, did exactly this. First, she engaged the Trium Group (a culture consulting company) to conduct qualitative interviews, and then she asked Jennifer Chatman to execute and analyze the quantitative organizational culture profile (OCP). Then the Trium Group created "culture placemats" describing each of the four culture pillars that the OCP identified as being essential to execute on GIO's strategy. Combining the benefits of understanding both the norms that GIO employees prioritized from the quantitative analysis and the deeper meaning and manifestations of those norms from the qualitative analysis enabled Cook and her team to take precise action in changing the culture at GIO.

IS CULTURE ABOUT FREE FOOD AND OTHER "SOFT" PERKS?

In the best-selling novel *The Circle*, the protagonist Mae finds herself employed at what she considers the best company in the world, in large part because of the generous perks that it offers. Her employer, a modern Silicon Valley tech company, provides free food and many on-site amenities including gyms, health centers, recreational facilities, dry cleaning, clubs, sports teams, parties, concerts, and events with celebrities. Dorms are available for those who work late and do not want to commute home.

And the company's health care pays for medical treatment for Mae's father, who has multiple sclerosis.

Mae's employer can be seen as a company with the ultimate soft, perk-laden culture. Although satirical, the over-the-top depiction comes closer than you might imagine to resembling the amenities offered at many Silicon Valley tech companies like Google, Facebook, and Airbnb. Popular employee perks include free food (see figure 5.3), on-site personal services like car washes and haircuts, employee stipends, paid time off, discounts and exclusive shopping opportunities, health benefits and programs, family events, parties, speakers, and family events. Undoubtedly, these offerings become part of the employee experience and to some extent contribute to the organization's culture—the salient norms and behavioral patterns.

FIGURE 5.3 Free food at a tech company

Copyright © 2018 Reuters Pictures. Used by permission.

Perk-laden companies are not limited to the tech sector, of course. Apparel designer and retailer Patagonia is a case in point. Based in Southern California and having over 100 stores worldwide, Patagonia's employees have enjoyed on-site child-care since 1984. Today, they also get full health coverage, college tuition reimbursement, on-site yoga and fitness, an organic café, and plenty of other perks.[17] Perhaps the most unusual perk is the extraordinary flexibility in work scheduling, including unexpect-edly taking time off in the middle of the day when the surf's up.

Generous perks look attractive to outsiders, suggesting that these employees have it very good, that they are treated with kid gloves, and that the work experience is easier than at most tra-ditional employers. But perks are only part of an organization's culture. Social science definitions of culture usually include an organization's symbols, behaviors, norms, values, and languages, many of which have little relationship to amenities or perks.

When it comes to generous perks, a key question to ask is: What is expected, or even demanded, in return? The perks of Silicon Valley tech companies are meant to attract and retain valuable, highly-sought-after employees in a tight competitive labor market. But the work itself is often high stakes and chal-lenging, requiring long hours, significant expertise and educa-tion, and prolonged commitment from employees.

Many observers, including Dave Eggers (author of *The Circle*), cynically believe that the on-site personal services and food are provided to minimize employee distractions from outside life, as well as to keep employees at the office for longer periods of time—outcomes that obviously benefit the organization. Indeed, the all-inclusive nature of work at some of these tech compa-nies edges them close to becoming autocratic "total institutions." According to Erving Goffman, a total institution is "a social hybrid, part residential community, part formal organization."[18]

Strong culture organizations like Proctor & Gamble have long blurred the lines between work and life, encouraging employees to make their careers at the company and even marry one another so they will continue to be devoted to the company. Others, such as Apple under Steve Jobs, Tesla and X under Elon Musk, and WeWork under Adam Neumann, have been known to drive people so hard and expect such long hours that the perks at work become essential.

As Goffman lucidly points out, total institutions spawn concerning behaviors that include the following:

- **Creating isolated privilege systems governed by both formal and informal "house" rules.** Notably, these rules can appear arbitrary and petty in nature, especially long after they have been established and the reasons for developing them are forgotten; their continuance mainly represents tradition, and conformity merely reflects obedience by the staff.
- **People are rewarded (rewards are often small and symbolic) for adherence to the privilege systems and punished for noncompliance,** including visible shaming. Often, these "privileges in the total institution . . . are not the same perquisites, indulgences, or values, but merely the absence of deprivations one ordinarily expects not to have to sustain. The very notions of punishments and privileges are the ones that are cut from civilian cloth."
- **Normal work-payment connections are deemphasized and carry less force than with a traditional employer** (Goffman considers the two systems "incompatible"); employees pay more attention than normal to the privilege system as a substitute for money.
- **Focusing on boring, busywork tasks.** This occurs in dysfunctional total institutions, where managers create work that

employees regard as intrinsically meaningless because the ostensible goals are petty. The arrangement makes managers cynical and employees demoralized.

Goffman's examples of total institutions include asylums, prisons, and boarding schools. Few people would consider life in one of these institutions—or any organization resembling them—as easy or soft, in large part because of their totality. We usually imagine the opposite for these institutions, with a hard-boiled, tough culture where little empathy is shown for others. Think of Nurse Ratched (played by Louise Fletcher) who battled Randle McMurphy (Jack Nicholson) in the movie *One Flew Over the Cuckoo's Nest*. While few modern tech companies let supervisors go as far as Nurse Ratched did, they can sometimes engage in behaviors that many find unsettling and can severely constrain how people behave. In this sense, culture is anything but soft.

TOUGH LOVE CULTURES

Then there are those organizations with hard-nosed, "tough love" cultures. Tough love is frequently seen in many strong culture organizations, where standards are set impossibly high ("only the best in the world"), onboarding and socialization can border on hazing, candid feedback can be soul crushing, and the cold and ruthless dismissal of those who do not fit in can be traumatic. Imagine Reed Hastings at Netflix (figure 5.4) telling you that, despite months of hard work representing your best effort, your performance is good but still falls short of expectations, so you are being relieved of your duties. You have failed the infamous Netflix "keeper test."[19]

Other strong culture organizations use downright despicable practices that endanger members and potentially create permanent

FIGURE 5.4 Former Netflix CEO Reed Hastings

Copyright © 2018 Getty Images. Used by permission.

harm. Many of these secretive organizations resemble cults that few outsiders would defend. Consider Synanon and NXVIM, which have been widely publicized in documentaries and whose leaders were arrested for a range of crimes.[20] At this point, it is also worth restating that strong cultures are not necessarily virtuous or positive; cultures can be strong, regardless of the content of the norms that they emphasize. That certainly is the case for these two organizations, which illustrate that culture, in terms of having profound influence on people's behavior, is anything but soft.

STRONG CULTURE OR CULT?

Synanon started in 1958 as a two-year residential program for drug and alcohol addicts. But the leader, Charles (Chuck) Dederich, decided that because recovery from addiction was never complete, participants should not graduate but instead remain as members forever. People inducted into Synanon got their heads shaved and were required to break with any nonmember partners and form new relationships, exclusively within the group. Some men were forced to undergo vasectomies, and some pregnant women were required to have abortions, just because Chuck said so.

A central practice at Synanon was known as "The Game." Labeled as therapeutic, The Game forced members to talk about themselves and reveal their innermost secrets and weaknesses (see figure 5.5). Others in The Game were then asked to engage in severe, open criticism of the speaker using harsh and vulgar language, a form of attack therapy. Social psychologist Richard Ofshe gives his analysis of the impact:

> The Synanon organization, through the use of the Synanon game, controls the behavior of residents. The control system monitors and shapes both gross behavior (e.g. punctuality, theft, grooming) and verbal behavior. The shaping is done not only through direct punishment by verbal aggression, humiliation and guilt manipulation in the interaction or the game, but also through the communication of information *either suggesting or promising that rewards or punishments will be dispensed in non-game settings.* These rewards or punishments are the usual reinforcers of social life, including access to material goods, housing, money, friendship networks, and the like. For Synanon residents, these reinforcers are under the control of the organization's management.[21]

Synanon recruited members deceptively; while it did help some people overcome addiction, it did not tell recruits that another goal of the organization was to build a self-sustaining, alternative society, and it certainly didn't reveal how much control it would eventually exert over members' personal lives. Members were also required to engage in criminal activities

FIGURE 5.5 "The Game" at Synanon

Copyright © 1968 Shutterstock. Used by permission.

against defectors and critics. Dederich and other leaders were ultimately charged with crimes of attempted murder, terrorism, child abuse, evidence tampering, and financial wrongdoing. Eventually, Dederich was convicted and forbidden to participate in Synanon. The organization had not paid its taxes either, and it went bankrupt and closed in 1991.

NXVIM, a strong culture organization with outwardly virtuous goals as a human potential workshop provider, was, as prosecutors would contend, actually a sex cult. Its leader, Keith Raniere, used many strong culture behavioral practices.[22] He also groomed young women and exploited them for sex, using psychological and physical punishment to force compliance. Some women in the cult were even branded physically. Like Synanon, NXVIM attacked its critics in many ways. Eventually, Raniere and others were charged and convicted of federal crimes including racketeering. He was sentenced to 120 years in prison.

Like most cults, Synanon and NXVIM were managed through social pressures and systems of the kind discussed in this book. And it bears repeating that anyone who understands what transpired in these cults would never call the experiences there "soft."

Of course, Synanon's and NXVIM's leaders often lived outside the law, and their organizations represent extreme cases. But you don't need to look very far to find legitimate, ostensibly law-abiding organizations with harsh practices that are anything but soft.

For instance, Axon Enterprise builds and sells tasers and body-worn cameras to over 18,000 law enforcement agencies in 107 countries across the world. A dominant company in the security-oriented market, it has a market capitalization of $15 billion, annual revenue of over $1 billion, and more than 4,000 employees. Reported practices at Axon include pressuring employees to get tattoos of the company's logo and group events where an employee is tased in front of a cheering crowd of fellow employees yelling "Tase, tase, tase."[23] A lawyer who worked there described the culture of loyalty at Axon as "truly toxic."

Another example is the Navy SEALS training process, a grueling long-term series of tests of physical ability, mental toughness, and persistence. A key component is known as Basic Underwater Demolition/SEALS (BUD/S), a twenty-six-week program. In the fourth week of BUD/S, candidates go through "Hell Week." According to an Associated Press report: "During the five-and-a-half-day test, which involves basic underwater demolition and survival and other combat tactics, sailors are allowed to sleep just twice, and only for two hours. It tests physical, mental and psychological strength along with leadership skills, and is so grueling that at least 50 percent to 60 percent don't finish it."[24] In 2022, a seaman died during Hell Week, marking the eleventh such death at these proceedings.

So, while cultural management in some organizations may involve an abundance of seemingly soft perks, this is far from required. Indeed, many strong culture organizations not only dispense with such perks but engage in harsh and sometimes brutal practices that are based on fear, intimidation, and the threat of violence. And we'll say it again—hardly soft.

But even if we consider only professional business entities, what goes on inside strong culture organizations can be unsettling—even chilling—to some observers (as some of our students remind us). Why? What's so disturbing? We think that these observers recognize that cultural management reflects essentially a *social control system*, by which some people are pressured socially to do what others want them to do even if they'd rather not. As O'Reilly and Chatman explain: "To the extent that we care about others and have some agreement about what constitutes appropriate behavior, then whenever we are in their presence, we are also potentially under their control. Just as we may comply with a budgeting system less our compensation be affected (formal control), we may also comply with the opinions of our colleagues so that they will think well of us (social control)."[25] They go on to describe how social control in a cultural system operates: "While formal control mechanisms are usually codified in the form of rules and procedures, social control emerges in the form of values and norms and is regulated through peer influence and the social construction of reality ... This is an important distinction because . . . the reliance on the opinions of valued others implies that social control may be far more extensive and less expensive than formal systems..."

Social control in culturally managed organizations is not always recognized for what it is because often the focus rests on the cultural content itself, which is typically expressed in aspirational and positive terms. Again, O'Reilly and Chatman are right on point: "The paradox is that strong social control systems often result in positive feelings of solidarity and a greater sense of autonomy among people, rather than . . . psychological reactance . . . Because the internalization of some organizational values such as helping others and contributing to society can result in a perception of intrinsic value (that is, something that the person believes in rather than something imposed-externally and subject to extrinsic justification), it may be accompanied by more positive attitudes and freely chosen behaviors."[26]

By this view, culture is not soft but hard-boiled, potentially manipulative and possibly deceptive. It reflects an organized systematic attempt to control the behavior of some people to achieve the aims of others. Those individuals subject to control are induced with a positive set of messages about togetherness and the collective when the impact could either help the collective— when the objectives are laudable—or be less beneficial to all.

SUMMARY

This chapter examined the popular belief that culture is soft. The meaning of "soft" could be about either whether culture can be measured quantitatively or whether culture reflects mainly an easy life of privileged perks like free food.

Academic research on culture shows plenty of qualitative interpretive ("soft") studies of organizational culture. But it also shows scores, if not hundreds, of studies where culture is measured empirically using systematic data collection and coding techniques. Numerous consulting firms also use quantitative instruments to measure and assess culture along with qualitative techniques. While some social scientists still reject the idea that culture can be effectively quantified, this is an extreme and fading view. Yes, there are debates among social scientists over the quality and reliability of certain quantitative instruments and measures, and some social scientists draw a line when considering how much can be inferred from quantitative culture data. But the scientific consensus holds that measuring culture quantitatively is feasible and insightful, even if it takes attention and care to accurately represent the features of culture—its comprehensiveness, the relative importance of some cultural norms over others, and the separation of the content of the culture from its strength. In these respects, culture does not stand out as an unusual phenomenon—the same can be said of many objects of social scientific interest, such as decision biases or interpersonal influences.

As for the perks issue, the two of us live in Silicon Valley and see many companies that offer way over-the-top amenities to their employees, who often take them for granted. While privilege may be a fact of life in these companies, we would suggest that it represents at most a part of these company cultures: There are still widely shared and strongly held expectations about behavior and performance that have little to do with the perks. Indeed, we do not think that it is wrong to regard these perks, which tend to keep people at work longer, as part of the comprehensive social control system. Even if you are well paid and treated like royalty in some ways, there is no denying that a social world that obligates you to do what others want, rather than what you may prefer, can be hard and certainly not soft.

MANAGERIAL TAKEAWAYS FROM THIS CHAPTER

- When culture is referred to as "soft," usually one of two different meanings is invoked: (1) culture is made of qualitative, interpretative behaviors that are not amenable to quantitative measurement; or (2) culture involves the heavy use of privileged perks such as free food. We suggest that neither meaning accurately describes organizational culture, which can be measured and which typically includes much more than perks; culture is a form of social control that can significantly influence members' behavior.

- Culture can be measured quantitatively, and many social scientists and consultants do so. Quantitative measurement allows the comparison of cultures across time and across firms. The best measures accurately represent culture by profiling cultural norms in terms of their prevalence in the organization.

- Culture might include free food and other apparently luxurious perks at some firms, but these practices constitute but a small—and perhaps trivial—part of the overall organizational culture. Further, these perks can increase employees' willingness to work long hours and develop increasingly strong bonds with their coworkers as a result. This cohesion can be a basis for strengthening culture. That said, many firms with strong cultural orientations do not offer free food and other attractive perks; instead, they use abstinence, punishment, and other harsh tactics routinely, involving behavior that few would characterize as soft.

- Cultural management involves social control by leaders to get people to do what the leaders want. Sometimes what leaders want is virtuous, and culture can harness the power of the collective for good, but these same cultural tools can also be used to generate bad outcomes (e.g., to enrich the leaders in some way and exploit members along the way).

6

ALIGNED PEOPLE DO BEST?

I t was a classic Hollywood story.

Appointed as president of Disney in October 1995, Michael Ovitz (figure 6.1) recognized that he had been granted a great opportunity. Not only would he be a partner with CEO Michael Eisner in running Disney, but Ovitz's appointment was widely viewed as unofficially anointing him to succeed Eisner as CEO.

Prior to joining Disney, Ovitz had been known as the most powerful man in Hollywood. Along with four other agents from the William Morris Agency, Ovitz cofounded Creative Artists Agency (CAA), which grew to become perhaps the most important talent agency in the entertainment business.

Ovitz excelled in leading CAA by developing and marketing package deals of actors, directors, and writers, which he sold to the major studios. His packages were viewed as revolutionizing Hollywood. Among his clients were blockbuster actors Tom Cruise, Barbra Streisand, Dustin Hoffman, Kevin Costner, John Belushi, Michael Douglas, Bill Murray, and Sylvester Stallone, as well as renowned directors Steven Spielberg, Barry Levinson, and Sydney Pollack. Ovitz shunned publicity. But he was so feared in Hollywood because of his power to exact revenge that

FIGURE 6.1 Michael Ovitz

Copyright © 2018 Wall Street Journal. Used by permission.

when *The New York Times* ran a story about him, reporters had a hard time getting anyone to talk about him.

Ovitz took charge of his new job at Disney from the start. According to acclaimed journalist James B. Stewart in *Disney-War*, "Ovitz plunged into his new responsibilities, confident that by sheer dint of hard work and enthusiasm he could carve out a role for himself . . . Ovitz surpassed even [prior top Disney executive Jeffrey] Katzenberg's legendary work habits, arriving early, spending twelve hours at the office each day, including Saturdays and Sundays."[1] He held celebrity parties at his home, sent messages to important customers, traveled extensively to meet current and potential business partners, and proposed an ongoing stream of possible innovative new deals for Disney.

Yet almost all of Ovitz's actions and proposals landed as loud thuds inside Disney.

Other top executives, including Eisner, increasingly viewed him with suspicion. His abrasive behavior rattled his colleagues. "He always seemed to be doing two or three things at once, frequently interrupting meetings to use his cell phone, arriving late or leaving early, canceling appointments at the last minute," Stewart reports.[2] Ovitz also often bought clients and employees expensive gifts and charged them to the company. Accordingly, he was accused regularly of lying and violating Disney's ethics and spending policies. These incidents were diligently reported to Eisner by others, and the tension within the management team became unbearable. After just sixteen months at Disney, Ovitz was out—Eisner and the board dismissed him.[3]

How could this happen? How could the most powerful man in Hollywood, a person who built his career and fortune on his social skills, misread the situation at Disney so badly? How could he behave so incongruously? Many observers believed that the problem was one of alignment—or rather lack of alignment—between Ovitz's behavioral style and Disney's organizational culture. Quite simply, Ovitz was a bad fit to the culture.

FITTING THE CULTURE AT DISNEY

Ovitz was a social broker and behaved the way that successful brokers do. He often played various parties against each other and kept them in the dark about what was going on until the

end. As Stewart explains, "As one of the country's most successful agents, Ovitz was, by nature and experience, a dealmaker."
Inside Disney, Ovitz treated his fellow executives similarly to
how he had treated independent actors, directors, and studio
heads at CAA. The lack of transparency and candor generated
suspicion and resentment.

Eisner tried to get Ovitz to adjust his behavior by explaining
how Disney operated and what it valued. According to Stewart,
he told Ovitz:

> The "deal" is not the essence of Disney. . . . Operations are the
> thing. The deal is a means to an end, to get television series made,
> movies made, theme parks built, consumer licenses awarded, tal-
> ent connected. But the deal cannot take the lead. . . . I feel about
> acquisitions exactly as I feel about everything else. We don't need
> them. We don't need the overly expensive movie or television
> show. We do not need the actor who has priced himself out of the
> market. We do not need the acquisition that, even if we feel it fits
> strategically, is economically ridiculous.[4]

The operations-oriented culture at Disney required top
executives and others to work together harmoniously to get
things done. The official cultural message of the company reads:
"Across Disney, we cultivate, value, and encourage curiosity, collaboration, and creativity from everyone, and we strive to build
supportive environments that inspire optimism and drive innovation." This official stance is backed up by an analysis of almost
4,000 Glassdoor employee reviews showing that Disney's most
valued cultural value is collaboration.[5] As social network analysts
note, brokers like Ovitz are often mistrusted because they are so
opportunistic, which makes fitting into a collaborative culture
like Disney especially challenging, if not impossible.

Ovitz's cultural alignment problem becomes even more obvious when you consider who eventually succeeded Eisner. After serving as Disney CEO for over fifteen years, Robert Iger is almost a household name today. But at the time of the Ovitz breakup, he was known within Disney as the competent but low-key executive who ran the Disney-owned American Broadcasting Companies (ABC). In 2000, Iger was chosen to take over Ovitz's old position of president. In 2005, he was appointed as CEO of Disney and went on to lead the company through a sustained period of growth and success.

Iger and Ovitz couldn't be more different in their personalities and behavioral styles, and importantly, their fit with Disney's culture. As columnist Maureen Dowd of *The New York Times* writes, "Mr. Iger comes across as effortlessly elegant. He is the sort of person who takes the time to talk to hoi polloi's parents at parties and poses graciously for photos with fans at the park. He seems relaxed with the staff when we stop for cocktails."[6] Iger is known as perhaps the nicest guy in Hollywood. Top dealmaker David Geffen is quoted saying, "I have never heard one person say a bad thing about him and I have never seen him be mean." Clearly Iger's behavior is consistent given the broad reputation that he has developed.

And what better reputation to have in a corporate culture that endorses collaboration as its top value? Iger got the CEO position in part because his behavioral style was highly aligned with Disney's collaborative culture, and his subsequent effectiveness as CEO arose from that tight alignment.

These now-classic stories of Ovitz and Iger at Disney demonstrate how important culture fit can be for a person's ability to lead and manage, as well as the ability to perform effectively in an organization. The misaligned Ovitz was quickly spurned by executives steeped in Disney's culture, while the highly aligned

Iger got anointed as CEO and went on to lead the company to unsurpassed growth and success.

The implication seems clear: Aligned people do best. But is that always true? And, if not, what are the limits to alignment-based success? What conditions reward person-culture fit and what, if any, do not? In this chapter, we address these and other questions about cultural alignment. We explore culture fit—what it means, when it is useful, how to select for fit, and how it can run amok.

WHAT IS CULTURE FIT?

Most managers and job candidates regard culture fit as important. Managers believe that when someone fits the culture, that person performs better, stays longer, and works better—more harmoniously—with coworkers. Employees believe that culture fit benefits them too; after all, who wouldn't want to work in a setting that makes you feel comfortable and validates your attitudes and behaviors? Psychologists call the behavioral mechanism driving culture fit the "similarity-attraction bias," the very strong tendency that we have to be attracted to others who have similar preferences and values.

But what does it mean to fit an organization's culture? How do organizations assess fit? What advantages and disadvantages accrue to those seeking and cultivating a workforce based on culture fit?

When people talk about culture fit, they are usually thinking about high levels of cultural fit. But culture fit varies from low to high; it's a way of describing how closely a person and the organization's culture agree about their preferred values or norms. People can be culturally misaligned with an organization, indicating low fit, or they can be closely aligned, reflecting high fit.

VALUE CONGRUENCE AND
PERCEPTUAL CONGRUENCE

To make things even a little more complicated, assessing cultural fit between a person and an organization can relies on two principles: value congruence and perceptual congruence.

Value congruence emerged as a concept from psychology.[7] It reflects the correspondence between a person's own preferred values and those reported by their peers in a group. Value congruence theory implies that the locus of cultural fit resides in the alignment between the values that a person espouses and those that prevail in a group. It turns out that value congruence is fairly stable over time since the underlying values often do not change appreciably. People with high levels of culture fit based on value congruence also tend to identify more with their organization and stay longer as members.

In contrast, perceptual congruence relies not on a person's values but on their perceptions of an organization's culture—what values and norms they *think* the culture emphasizes.[8] Perceptual congruence assesses how closely a person's own reading of the culture matches colleagues' reading of the culture. Rooted in cultural sociology, perceptual congruence views culture as shaping people's behaviors through situational cues or interpretations of "cultural scripts" rather than based on what they value personally. These cultural scripts include an organization's rituals, norms, and routines.[9]

A cultural script could be as simple as how people greet one another at work. Do people make eye contact? Do they say hello? Do they ask how the other person is doing, what they are working on, or how they spent their weekend? These scripts vary significantly from one organization to the next. The match between a person's perceptions of culture and that of peers determines that person's ability to exhibit culturally compliant behavior or not. This behavior can be as simple as whether a person dresses the same as others, adopts similar interests, or even adopts the same coded language.[10]

Organizations establish the two types of person-culture fit in different ways. The classic "make versus buy" question serves as a useful analogy. "Buying" focuses on who gets recruited, selected, and hired. Higher fit occurs by identifying and hiring those people who resonate with the organization's values and norms when they walk in the door. "Making" involves what and whom employees are exposed to—or, more broadly, how the organization socializes new people and develops them over time.

Research shows that person-culture fit based on the buy option—selecting for value congruence at hiring—contributes about 15 percent of how well a person fits an organizational culture. That's a reasonable contribution, but get this: Socializing people once they join the organization accounts for over 40 percent of how well they fit![11] This contrast suggests that investing in a search for people who already fit can help, but if you really want to increase fit among employees, exposing people to key cultural experiences once they join is key. This finding also points to the fact that people are far more flexible than we often give them credit for.

So then, what is the impact—does it actually matter whether people fit? What we can say from the discussion here is that value congruence and perceptual congruence operate simultaneously, but each arises from distinct sources (internal versus social cues), and they influence different outcomes. It turns out that those who have high value congruence are less likely to leave an organization, at least voluntarily. People who develop high perceptual congruence, on the other hand, demonstrate more behavioral alignment to the culture.[12]

ADVANTAGES OF HIGH
PERSON-CULTURE FIT

The value proposition of higher fit seems clear for organizations, but why might someone who is looking for a job care about cultural fit? Aren't compensation and opportunity more important? Maybe not. It turns out that how well a person fits the culture influences how effective they are in an organization. With high cultural fit, people will be better able to understand what the organization expects of them and behave in positively accepted ways. Culturally aligned people also connect better with their coworkers.

These outcomes are backed up by research: People who fit an organization's culture receive about 13 percent more compensation; their voluntary departure rate ticks about 20 percent lower as well. Culturally aligned people also report higher satisfaction levels—a whopping 32 percent higher than those who fit less well.[13] A person's fit to the organizational culture also matters significantly more than their fit with the requirements of their specific job. Quite simply, employees benefit personally when they fit their organization's culture: They get paid more, report higher satisfaction, and stay in the job longer.

Organizations also benefit from hiring based on cultural fit. Employees with high levels of fit see the strategic priorities of their organization more clearly and therefore perform better.[14] Since the organization affirms the values that employees already hold and behaviors that they already exhibit, those who fit the culture show significantly higher levels of commitment to the organization—about 28 percent more.[15] Because they experience work as pleasurable, committed employees are also likely to stay with the organization longer.

Research finds that when more employees fit the culture of an organization, those employees work together seamlessly: They experience less conflict and reach agreement more easily.[16]

It is worth noting that these benefits of high levels of person-culture fit occur primarily when an organization's strategy and culture are stable.[17] Since a strategy shift typically requires the culture to change, adjusting how you recruit and social-ize employees becomes important. This was true at Maersk, the Danish shipping company, when it needed to adapt to its new digital transformation strategy. It meant, for example, that relaxing its formal dress code would be a good idea because going digital required hiring 4,000 people from high tech, who were not interested in, or accustomed to, wearing a suit and tie to work.[18]

ESTABLISHING HIGH PERSON-CULTURE FIT IN ORGANIZATIONS

How do organizations cultivate fit among employees? There are two basic tools that we mentioned earlier when discussing the make versus buy decision: Organizations can select new hires to fit the culture, and they can socialize both their newly hired and existing employees to fit the culture. Most strong culture orga-nizations do both, but usually one or the other method receives pronounced emphasis.

SELECTING FOR PERSON-CULTURE FIT

A few years ago, the billboard shown in figure 6.2 appeared on Highway 101 in the San Francisco Bay area.

FIGURE 6.2 Recruiting billboard

Copyright © 2004 Alamy. Used by permission.

What in the world does the billboard's message mean? One of us (Chatman) saw this billboard and Googled it because it was puzzling, to say the least. So, it's a math problem, and when she inputted it, Google returned the correct numerical answer: 7427466391.com—*and an invitation to interview for a job at Google* for the following Tuesday at 10 a.m.!

Get that—the billboard served as a recruiting tool for Google! And what attribute was Google seeking to filter potential recruits on? Idle *curiosity*, one of the company's implicit core values. It aims to be highly innovative, imagining new products and services that never existed before, often while trying to solve major social or technical problems. Curiosity takes center stage in that strategy and being curious applies across all jobs at Google. Google's recruiting approach cuts to the chase, using a cultural attribute that it views as nonnegotiable by filtering potential recruits based on their curiosity.

Identifying key cultural attributes comprises a first step in hiring for cultural fit. Think about your organization's cultural nonnegotiables. What is regarded as essential? At Goldman Sachs, people in the organization share information so clients are supported by multiple people, and no one employee can take a client with them if they leave the firm.[19] At Netflix, "brilliant jerks" are not hired or tolerated because "the cost to teamwork is too high."[20] At a pharma startup, people focus on results first and timeliness because of tight US Food and Drug Administration (FDA) deadlines. Many of these nonnegotiable factors will likely be part of the organization's coherent cultural narrative, and hiring for these factors is part of their efforts to establish consistency in behavior.

The second step in hiring for fit involves finding people who resonate with the selected attributes. Cisco Systems, the company that produced the lion's share of routers and switches for the internet, exerts significant effort toward finding people who fit its culture. Cisco aspires to hire the top 5 percent of Silicon Valley engineers who are working on the latest and greatest innovations; and it needs a lot of them—up to 1,000 per month when tech booms hit. As a grandparent of Silicon Valley firms founded in the "dark ages" of the 1990s, Cisco finds this a challenge. Top engineers want to work on the latest and greatest innovations, and they don't think that will happen at a big, aging company.

Facing this war for talent, Cisco uses some clever tactics. First, it doesn't spend time or money searching for people at job fairs. Instead, it targets people whom it calls "passive applicants." In its view, these might be the top engineers working at a scrappier competitor or a start-up firm, someone who does not yet realize that they would be a better fit at Cisco.

Given this orientation, Cisco uses a shrewd recruiting tool. As an internet company, it was one of the first movers in online recruiting. It noticed that it got the most hits on the recruiting webpage between 10 a.m. and 2 p.m., SVT—that's *Silicon Valley Time*. Why is that significant? It suggested to Cisco that people were looking for a job at Cisco while they were working at their current company—during the workday.

To make things easier for these potential recruits, Cisco installed a button that someone searching on the site could press. Amid relevant recruiting information, the button said simply, "Tap if your boss walks by." If you tapped the button, a pull-down screen would appear saying, "List of gift ideas for my boss and workmates." This device allowed for plausible deniability—an employee at work at another firm searching on the Cisco website could say, "I'm not looking for another job— I'm buying you a gift!" In fact, this button reveals a deep insight into recruiting, which is to understand the exact circumstances of precisely the people whom you aim to recruit.

Cisco also relies heavily on employee referrals, an effective psychological tool for increasing fit, not just for those who join but for those who do the referring as well. This is standard practice in many organizations, but Cisco goes a step further, rewarding the referring employee both if the person they referred gets hired, and again if that person stays with Cisco for at least a year. This practice increases fit among both recruits and referring employees since referring employees are motivated to find recruits that fit the Cisco culture.

Table 6.1 summarizes how a variety of organizations hire for culture fit and the specific practices that they use. Obviously, the details used vary enormously, driven in part by the organization's cultural content, but also the local labor market.

TABLE 6.1 HIRING FOR CULTURE FIT

Company	Cultural Hiring Process
Atlassian	• Selects value-add interviewers who are trained on biases and structured questions. • Asks questions that assess value congruence. • Has a dedicated team for diversity and inclusion.
Amazon	• Uses its leadership principles for interviews to evaluate culture fit, focusing on real-life questions rather than hypotheticals.
Facebook	• Interviewers take a mandatory unconscious bias training program and are required to provide specific reasons for why they liked or disliked a candidate instead of just saying that someone was a bad culture fit.
Google	• Makes hiring decisions through team consensus and a series of independent team reviews. Unlike the hiring manager, committee members are removed from the urgency of selecting someone and can judge the applicant better on merit. • Values applicants who are problem-solvers and have a general cognitive ability over role-related knowledge because positions are constantly shifting.
Nestlé	• Uses case studies and group interviews so multiple members of the team can judge a person's culture fit.
Netflix	• Hires as much for culture fit as for skill. • The second round is a culture fit interview, where candidates are evaluated on how well they align with the company's core values. • Hires only people who share its vision and philosophy.
Pandora	• Works to attract diverse talent through advertising their diversity statistics and by switching over to a culture-add model and valuing new skills or perspectives that employees can bring in hiring.
Patagonia	• Reads résumés from the bottom up to avoid the "culture-fit trap," looking at people's hobbies and interests rather than their experience. • Looks for people with interests outside environmentalism to avoid a homogenous culture. • Hires highly motivated, unconventional thinkers to join the company's mission.

Salesforce	• Uses a gamified learning platform called Trailhead that potential new hires can play on to learn more about the company's culture.
	• Asks interview questions about the company's products or core values that are taught on Trailhead.
Southwest	• Hires for attitude, looking specifically for a "warrior spirit, servant's heart and fun-LUVing attitude"
	• Believes that if a candidate isn't good enough for your loved ones, they aren't fit to serve Southwest's customers.
	• Prioritizes candidates' ability to demonstrate authenticity and love of service, whether through singing, joking, or simply engaging in a heart-to-heart conversation.
	• Looks for employees who can explicitly contribute to a positive work environment.
Tesla	• Candidates must wow everyone they interacted with during the hiring process because the recruiting team would go to bat only for applicants whom they truly felt strongly about.
	• CEO Elon Musk approves every hire, and everyone interviews directly with him.
Trader Joe's	• Seeks to hire nice, kind, empathetic individuals.
	• The customer service training is pretty simple—it emphasizes being yourself.
	• Prioritizes applicants who express their love for Trader Joe's.
Zappos	• Uses the social test: Candidates will meet with multiple Zappos employees, usually including attending some type of department or company event, which enables the employees who are not interviewing prospective employees to meet them informally.
	• Uses the "nice guy" test: Recruiters circle back to the shuttle driver who brought applicants to the interview to ask how they acted toward the driver. If the shuttle driver wasn't treated well, Zappos won't hire that person.

SOCIALIZING FOR FIT

At best, hiring based on culture fit proves to be an inexact science. The tools for measuring culture fit can be blunt, and bias (implicit or even explicit) can undermine the process, as when employees advocate hiring people they "like" rather than those matching important strategic values.[21] Adding to the challenge, those seeking jobs understandably put their best foot forward when presenting themselves. These and other issues often lead to imperfect hiring. For example, at hedge fund Bridgewater, about one-third of the new employees leave before they've had two years on the job. Bridgewater chalks this churn-up as a cost of doing business. It claims that people either thrive in the firm's "unique culture" or "they dislike it and decide to move on."[22]

People and organizations who manage their impressions effectively bump up their hit rates, securing the offer or the recruit. So real fit can prove elusive.[23] Accordingly, socializing people once they join the organization remains essential. In fact, as we reported above, research suggests that it is a more potent way of establishing person-culture fit than hiring for fit.

Organizations use a wide range of practices to socialize their employees. Many companies like Clorox, Genentech, Mars, and WD-40 set up culture advisory boards, typically made of a cross-cutting set of energized employees distributed across functions, products, levels, and geographies. The board typically attempts to instigate, integrate, and in some cases help implement cultural practices through the entire organization. For example, WD-40's Culture Squad solicited input from all over the organization as the company was increasing its emphasis on innovation and adaptability to address the strategic challenges of globalizing the brand. Clorox's Culture Board identified practices and removed obstacles so it could develop a

"Be Bold" campaign, which ended up helping the company to be nimble when the COVID-19 pandemic hit and its cleaning products were in high demand overnight.

Culture advisory boards can speed up and integrate a company's efforts to strengthen and shift the culture, as the GIO case with Jennifer Cook highlighted in chapter 2 shows. Recall that Genentech created what it called Culture Placemats (recall figure 2.5, depicting one of these placemats), each laying out one of the four desired cultural pillars. The placemats defined the pillars in very specific terms. They also offered specific evidence of behaviors that fit the culture versus those that do not. Employees could study up on the culture by looking over their placemats while eating lunch!

Many organizations offer orientation programs to socialize new employees. At Zappos, a core value involves creating "WOW" customer service experiences. If Zappos hires you, for whatever position, expect to spend the first four weeks in your new job staffing customer service phone lines in their call center and learning how to respond to customer needs.[24]

And, of course, many companies use team-building events and shared activities to increase group cohesion and remind people of the company's cultural values. For instance, Pokémon GO hosts outdoor "All Hands" meetings that include scavenger hunting in teams. These events reinforce the essence of their business values—being together, outdoors, and curious, not to mention playing Pokémon GO.

Axon, maker of tasers, uses a more questionable team-building activity. As described by Jeffrey Dastin at Reuters, one team-building event involved tasing an employee in front of a group:

> The employee let out a guttural scream as darts struck his back. Two men lowered his body to the floor. A crowd of co-workers

howled with laughter and cheered as the account executive, still prostrate, managed to praise the weapon that felled him—a Taser electroshock gun manufactured by his company, Axon Enterprises, Inc. "Oh, that's good," the Axon employee, Ross Blank, heaved into a microphone. Blank later posted a video on his LinkedIn account of the company's January event, held at a Phoenix resort. "Taking one more for the team is Bad Assery," long-time executive Steve Tuttle commented on the post. "Love it!" Axon insists that employees don't feel pressured to engage in activities involving being tased, but when a member of the senior leadership team publicly expresses admiration for the employee who absorbed the Taser, people learn what is rewarded.[25]

Using symbolic rewards and recognition that are not solely compensation based clarifies a culture. One company has a "Golden Toilet Award," recognizing the biggest screw-up that week, which employees proudly display on their desks.

On the flip side, even if you hire and socialize people to fit your culture, sometimes mistakes occur. Strong culture organizations need to be willing to part with the people who do not fit in. At hedge fund Bridgewater, even senior executives can be subjected to a "public hanging" when they break the rules.[26] Netflix uses a "keeper test," a cultural principle that encourages leaders to keep only the people they would fight for if they got an offer elsewhere.[27] The other people, according to Netflix, "should get a generous severance now so we can open a slot and try to find a star for that role." The company regards hiring and retaining stars as critical strategically, as it has a market cap of over $435B, with around 13,000 people. Meanwhile, competitor Disney sports a signficantly lower market cap but employs around 220,000 people. In this sense, Netflix generates a signficantly higher market share than Disney does with fewer than

6 percent of the people. No wonder Netflix is concerned with ensuring that people fit—its business strategy hinges, in part, on being incredibly lean, meaning that every employee needs to be a complete star.

Finally, simple daily interactions can be used as symbols to clarify intended behaviors and socialize employees. What are people talking about? What are they busy doing all day? At Microsoft, where innovation is key, leaders explicitly hold back on commenting about issues until other lower-level employees have had a chance to weigh in so no one feels constrained from expressing their ideas.[28]

When Maersk, the Danish shipping company, dropped its iconic dress code in 2017, employees understood that the

FIGURE 6.3A Maersk dropped its dress code in 2017.

Copyright © 2016–17 Maersk. Used by permission.

FIGURE 6.4B

company was finally modernizing (see figure 6.3).[29] This seems like a trivial change, but it accompanied a major strategic shift toward prioritizing digitizing operations, and it included hiring 3,000 new tech people. As such, the dress code issue was enormously symbolic.[30] People in high-tech industries would never come to a company that required they wear a suit to work.

CAN A *LOWER* PERSON-CULTURE FIT BE ADVANTAGEOUS?

Up to this point, we have focused on establishing high levels of culture fit. In most organizations, high culture fit yields all kinds of advantages. But singularly pursuing candidates with very high person-culture fit can create problems. So can socializing, rewarding, and leading based on fit to the current culture.

Patty McCord, former human resources (HR) head at Netflix, puts it this way: "Making great hires is about recognizing great matches—and often they're not what you'd expect . . . What most people really mean when they say someone is a good fit culturally is that he or she is someone they'd like to have a beer with. But people with all sorts of personalities can be great at the job you need done. This misguided hiring strategy can also contribute to a company's lack of diversity, since very often the people we enjoy hanging out with have backgrounds much like our own."[31]

Katrina Lake, founder and CEO of Stitch Fix, the subscription clothing company, draws similar conclusions:

> Trying to look for more people who fit in is like an anti-diversity [approach] . . . Growth comes from learning . . . and that learning comes from seeing different perspectives and seeing things in a way you didn't see them before. And that can come from the people you surround yourself with. . . . Diversity in terms of backgrounds is important. I also think that diversity of thought is important. A lot of what has made Stitch Fix successful has been data scientists sitting alongside stylists and trying to figure out how a stylist's brain works. Those are two groups of people who don't often have coffee together. We want to be the living breathing example of why diversity is important and how you can build that into a big publicly traded company and serve as an example.[32]

These sentiments are absolutely valid, with research showing that universally high levels of person-culture fit can lead to unwanted forms of homogeneity in an organization. Homogeneity of thought can be associated with lower identity-based diversity, biased behaviors, and the exclusion of entire groups (e.g., by race or gender).[33] This may be why culture fit is so frequently criticized by those supporting diversity, equity, and inclusion (DEI) efforts. Uniformly high fit can also reduce creativity and innovation within organizations.[34] Further, when an organization's strategy changes and there is typically a need to shift cultural norms to execute this new strategy, it can prove difficult to reorient people who were hired and socialized to fit a different culture.

For employees, getting hired into an organization that embraces the culture that they prefer is comfortable and affirming. But it may also limit opportunities to stretch and learn. So it is essential to consider the kind of fit that employees need to function effectively in the organization now and into the future. For this reason, we advise developing a "portfolio" approach to person-culture fit, with a range of fit levels. Maybe there are a few people who support the legacy culture, a few who fit well with the new strategic needs and cultural priorities, and a few who don't fit in apparent ways at all but who can introduce significant innovation into the organization by challenging the status quo.[35]

There are also specific situations in which organizations should consider hiring people who do *not* fit their current culture. One is when the culture is ineffective—when it is not aligned with the strategy and is motivating people to behave in ways that are not helpful for the organization. In this case, hiring people who explicitly do not fit the current culture would be valuable. Ideally, leaders would seek people who fit the intended, not the current culture. These new hires are "future fits"; they fit the strategically needed culture but not the current culture, and they can help create the culture change that aligns the organization with its needed strategy.

A second situation occurs when the organization is seeking growth and innovation. Hiring people who are willing to challenge the status quo and shake things up will be useful to promote creativity. And creative people are less likely to succumb to the pressures of fitting in; they are nonconformists, after all.[36]

MANAGING CULTURALLY HETEROGENEOUS TEAMS

Since most organizations frequently seek growth and innovation, figuring out how to manage employees with varying levels of fit, or fits to different subcultures, becomes important.

For example, it may be important to differentiate among people who show diverse levels of expertise, even if that does not seem politically correct. Researchers studying the cultures of Himalayan expeditions found that when people were overly focused on fitting the collaborative norms of the expedition, differences in expertise were overlooked and, shockingly, more climbers died.[37] Research on personality and emotional expression suggests that variation can be good for leader-team relationships (e.g., an extroverted team needs an introverted leader) and team effectiveness overall.[38]

Some researchers advocate for designing ambidextrous organizations that operate several different business models simultaneously.[39] A common form of ambidexterity involves an organization exploiting a well-developed market—its "cash cow" business—and using that business to fund innovation and growth in new markets. These vastly different strategies typically require different cultures and people who fit one but not necessarily the other culture.

Netflix currently faces a different kind of cultural ambidexterity challenge. With growth, the company integrated backward, expanding its original business model as a distributor of entertainment. Now Netflix produces its own shows and movies in Hollywood (and elsewhere), as well as streaming them online to the world for a subscription fee. A former Netflix HR executive suggested to us that culturally, Hollywood is all about maintaining relationships (with producers, directors, actors, and the like), while the streaming service and its technology expertise embraces "radical candor" culturally. Netflix has worked hard to straddle these vastly different—and sometimes conflicting—cultural orientations between these two different parts of its workforce. Radical candor works well with engineers and the like on the technical side of the business, but it does not enhance relationships on the content production/creative side of the business.

Ambidextrous organizations pursuing very different strategies present difficult cultural challenges: Leaders must design and manage two (perhaps radically) different cultures within a single corporation where many leaders and employees can see the differences in what's favored and allowed in the two cultures, as well as resource differences. Employees and others within the same corporation often seek and demand equal treatment, so internal, intentionally designed cultural differences often generate resentment, anger, and claims of unfairness that may impede its work. In short, managing cultures effectively in an ambidextrous organization takes exceptional skill and attention; many organizations find this trick hard to pull off.

Scoot in Singapore is an example of a successfully developed internal unit that operates with a totally different culture than its parent partner in the ambidextrous corporation, Singapore International Airlines (SIA).[40] As is well known, SIA is one of the best and most luxurious airlines in the world, charging premium prices and catering to the wealthiest customers. Its eponymous brand is being a high-end global passenger airline with a dedication to detail and luxury service matched by few. The culture is fully designed and precise, right down to what is acceptable for employees to wear and how they can do their hair and nails.

Scoot is SIA's wholly owned short to midrange budget brand. Culturally, it can be seen as almost the antithesis of SIA. While maintaining an emphasis on plane safety, Scoot offers few of the perks and luxury amenities found on SIA, including entertainment. The culture is designed to be fun, casual, and breezy while emphasizing frugality. Flight attendants on Scoot enjoy greater freedom in what they can wear. Notably, compensation at Scoot is also significantly lower than at SIA.

Managing these very different brands and cultures presents many challenges for Scoot's leaders, not only in dealing with employees but also customers, who sometimes expect the same service and amenities. Many airlines, including United and American, have tried to build and operate similar internal budget-minded units, only to fail and abandon these efforts after spending considerable amounts of time and money.

SUMMARY

Commonly practiced in many organizations, hiring and socializing employees for culture fit carry many benefits for both employees and companies. That said, fit can bring disadvantages too. This observation suggests that something like culture-fit portfolios—developing organizations that maintain a mix of people who closely fit the current culture and those who closely fit a strategically needed culture.

MANAGERIAL TAKEAWAYS
FROM THIS CHAPTER

- Person-culture fit arises from how congruent people's values are with the organization's values and how aligned people's perceptions of the culture are with those of their coworkers (peers, bosses, and subordinates).
- Many benefits accrue to people who display a high degree of alignment between their behavior and the prevailing dominant beliefs and norms of their organization's culture.
- People who fit the culture tend to perform better, move up in their organizations more rapidly, and stay longer than those who don't fit as well.
- Person-culture fit can be achieved through culturally selective hiring practices.
- Person-culture fit can also be achieved, and more powerfully, through early and intense socialization practices within the organization.
- Under certain circumstances, such as when the strategy changes, when the culture is misaligned with strategy, and when innovation is important, organizations may find it helpful to maintain culturally heterogeneous portfolios of employees and other people.

7

CULTURE AND THE BOTTOM LINE

"We can't afford it. I mean, that's warm and fuzzy stuff. Who cares?"

That's Rick Cronk, when he was president of Dreyer's Grand Ice Cream, which he bought with his business partner and Dreyer's CEO, T. Gary Rogers; and together, they grew Dreyer's from a $1 million company to a $1.5 billion company, making Dreyer's the number one ice cream company in the US. (figure 7.1). Cronk was quoting the secondhand advice offered by some of his fellow executives about what to do with the strong culture at the company that management had nurtured, as they faced a serious financial crisis.[1] According to Cronk, these executives advised decisive action in killing the people-friendly empowerment culture (known as "The Grooves") that management had long promoted:

"Let's just go let people know what the hell has to be done. Let's get the job done, you know, terminate or find jobs for those people we can't afford any more. Let's call a spade a spade and play hardball."

Cronk notes, "There was a lot of that going on . . .we had a VP of sales who firmly believed in that, firmly."

FIGURE 7.1 Former Dreyer's CEO Rick Cronk

Cronk's fellow executive is hardly alone. Although bald pub-lic expressions of disdain for organizational culture are rare these days, in private many people express skepticism, or even disbe-lief, about the value of managed organizational culture in run-ning an organization. Why?

Some cynics of culture, like Jennifer Cook's colleagues at Genentech (see chapter 2), express these views because of their inherent reliance on numbers in science and "hard" factors like finance. They believe that hard factors are the only legitimate way to interpret and evaluate business viability.

Others who are cynical about culture have become so from experience—bad experience. Unfortunately, many employees today have experienced an overly eager manager rolling out an intended culture with grandiose promises that never come true, or an incoherent narrative that doesn't make sense. The fail-ure likely comes from unrealistic expectations about culture's impact, especially in the short term. Or it comes from a faulty implementation or execution of cultural management. Or it may arise because a proposed cultural transformation threatens the status quo that some people benefit from (see chapter 3 regard-ing Apple).

Finally, too many employees express skepticism because they suffer from what might be called "culture fatigue syndrome." Quite simply, they have witnessed many unsuccessful cultural transformation initiatives in their careers and have grown cyni-cal about managed culture as a result. This cynicism arises when people don't believe that the proposed changes are serious, con-sequential, or permanent.

For the skeptics and cynics, a kind-of-positive view says that while culture may be useful in making employees feel satis-fied and even happy by offering a warm atmosphere and pleas-ing perks like free food, it does not really matter much for the bottom line. Less positive views hold that any investments in or expenditures on culture detract attention and drain resources from the organization. In other words, these people believe the bottom line is adversely affected by managed culture.

WHAT EXECUTIVES THINK ABOUT CULTURE

Yet many executives and others believe that culture is powerful and, when managed properly, can have an enormously positive impact on the bottom line. Heidrick & Struggles surveyed 500 global CEOs of multibillion-dollar companies in 2023 and found that 33 percent of them saw "culture as the number one most important influence on financial performance." This was up from 7 percent in 2021. A full 59 percent of the CEOs considered it "very important or crucial to link culture to strategy to see financial benefits."[2] The survey of CFOs by financial economists Graham and colleagues found that "more than 40 percent of executives believe corporate culture has a big effect on whether a firm is compliant with accounting standards, creativity, project risk, productivity, profitability, and firm value. 60 percent of public firms say culture affects their desire to meet or beat EPS targets."[3]

Rick Cronk of Dreyer's would be at the top of that list. When the company experienced its financial crisis and almost went bankrupt in the late 1990s, Cronk's reaction was not to trash the culture and abandon it, but instead to rely on it, even doubling down by investing more in it. Dreyer's was facing a serious cost overrun because of top management's failure to control costs. Cronk and his team went out and met face-to-face with every member of the company and told them the truth about the problems—they also asked them for help in identifying unwarranted costs and reducing or eliminating those costs wherever possible.

Cronk and his team relied on employees' strong commitment to the company and its leaders, generated from the intentional culture that he and Rogers had built up; they were also acting consistently with practices long enshrined formally in the culture. It worked. Within months, costs went down, and continued to drop for a longer period. Dreyer's also found ways to innovate into new products and markets. The transformation was comprehensive. Within four years, the turnaround was complete. Earnings were positive. Then, in 2002, Cronk and Rogers sold 67 percent of the company to Nestlé for $2.4 billion. Top leaders at Nestlé were so impressed with Dreyer's that they placed all their ice cream business worldwide under its management. In Cronk's view, the culture was not soft and fuzzy stuff that the company could not afford—far from it. He believed that the culture had saved the company and fueled its eventual financial success. The experience strengthened the coherent narrative that he and others articulated about Dreyer's culture and became an integral part of the company's cultural training program.

Other executives mentioned in this book would surely agree about the positive impact of culture on the bottom line. We surmise that the list would include Jennifer Cook of Genentech (chapter 2), Alan Mulally of Ford (chapter 3), Kristin Sverchek of Lyft (chapter 4), Marc Benioff of Salesforce (chapter 5), Reed Hastings of Netflix (chapter 6), and many others, including legendary Duke basketball coach Mike Krzyzewski (aka "Coach K"), founder and former CEO Phil Knight of Nike, founder Yvon Chouinard of Patagonia, and more recently CEO Satya Nadella at Microsoft, who turned around the company by transforming its culture and bringing it back to the top of the tech world.[4] They all have their own stories of business success through cultural management and transformation. We suspect that these leaders would join former IBM CEO Lou Gerstner and others in saying: "Culture Is Everything."

On the opposite end of the spectrum are the cases where a toxic culture wreaks havoc, costs a company enormous revenue, and destroys value, directly and indirectly. Recent high-profile culture train wrecks include Uber, Wells Fargo Bank, and Volkswagen.

At Uber, an aggressive culture that was intended to embolden the company to overcome entrenched competitors and feckless regulators knew no bounds. Led by founder and CEO Travis Kalanick, the company spawned a toxic workplace culture where supercompetitive male employees and managers routinely discriminated against and harassed women and abused drivers, male and female. The internal workings of Uber became exposed after a female software engineer described her plight in detail on a public blog. Public outrage followed, and the board dismissed Kalanick, an investigation ensued, and new management was brought in prior to an initial public offering (IPO). Still, by some estimates Uber lost as much as $20 billion in value by the time it went public.[5] More recently, an investigation in France revealed that Kalanick and some of his colleagues engaged in illegal lobbying and bribes to gain access to local markets.[6]

The Wells Fargo story revolved around selling mortgages with higher-than-needed interest rates, generating a fine of $85 million in 2011. Five years later, the bank revealed a phantom accounts practice, whereby incentive-driven bankers, following a culture that over-aggressively endorsed product cross-selling, opened millions of customer accounts that the customers had not approved. The culture also encouraged silencing attempted whistleblowers, leading to a $185 million fine by the Consumer

Financial Protection Bureau (CFPB). As a result of these scandals, 5,300 employees were terminated.[7] In 2023, Wells Fargo settled again with the CFPB for a record $3.7 billion related to illegal practices at the bank involving loan payments, foreclosures, repossessions, fees, and interest of more than 16 million customer accounts.[8] Most observers attribute the problem to executives fostering a culture lax on compliance and overly indexed on profit at all costs.

In 2015, the US Environmental Protection Agency (EPA) found that Volkswagen had engaged in a massive fraud for about eight years of misrepresenting (cheating, really) on the required emissions testing of its automobiles in the United States. The *CPA Journal* wrote, "In 2017, the company was fined $2.8 billion for criminal violations in the United States, and in 2018, it was fined the equivalent of $1.2 billion in Germany. By the end of the second quarter of 2019, Volkswagen's costs associated with the scandal were over $32 billion and mounting as various legal proceedings continued around the world. Pending litigation includes charges filed by the SEC for defrauding bond investors and an unprecedented class action lawsuit in Germany."[9] The company had long prided itself on its strong engineering orientation, where executives were typically drawn from the engineering ranks and were said to know everything about how the cars were made. Although not all facts have been addressed yet, many observers concluded that Volkswagen's culture was to blame: "Volkswagen engaged in a massive fraud with dire consequences for the company and its stakeholders alike. Its corporate culture facilitated both the conception and perpetuation of the charade."[10]

Everyone, it seems, has a culture impact story, positive or negative. But what does all that prove about culture's impact generally? Who to believe? What to believe? Stories are useful but cannot offer the definitive answer about culture's impact on the bottom line. Part of the problem is what is called cherry-picking—stories chosen to support a particular view already decided upon, while other, less confirming stories are ignored. Another problem is that the outcome for any given story is overdetermined—there are too many possible explanations including a variety of idiosyncratic factors.

CAN CULTURE OVERCOME TALENT DIFFERENCES AMONG TEAMS?

Consider the Ryder Cup, the super-high-profile pro golf match pitting a team of twelve American stars against a team of twelve illustrious Europeans played over several days under varying match formats (figure 7.2). Held every two years since 1927, the

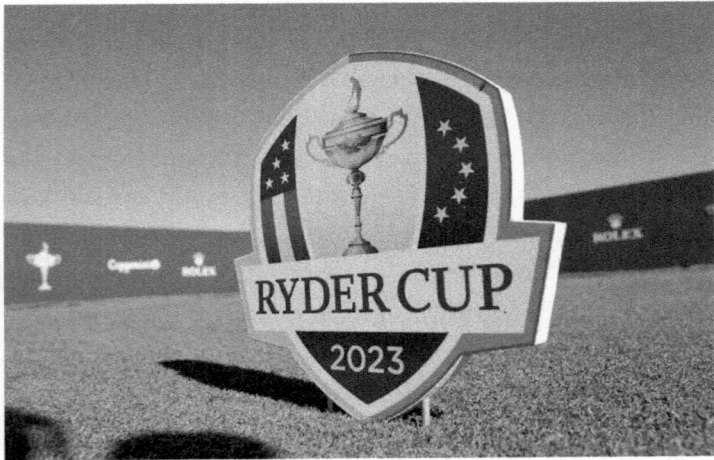

FIGURE 7.2 Ryder Cup logo.
Copyright © 2022 Getty Images. Used by permission.

Americans won twenty-seven times, while the Europeans prevailed only fourteen times. But since 1985, the Europeans have won twelve of eighteen times despite widespread agreement that the American team almost always possesses more sheer golfing ability and talent. Why?

Explanations of European dominance of the Ryder Cup over the last few decades usually center on team cultural issues and player behavior. *Minnesota Star Tribune* columnist Jim Souhan sums up a popular view: "The Americans have entered virtually every Ryder Cup in history with a stronger lineup than Europe, in terms of world rankings and majors won. As Europe has dominated, so has this perception: That the Europeans are better able to transition from the independent-contractor nature of stroke-play tournaments to the emotional cauldron of a match-play tournament that highlights teamwork and unselfishness."[11]

Many players apparently agree. In the runup to the 2023 event, the youngest European player, Ludvig Aberg, expressed his view going into his first event: "what separates us Europeans, the European team a little bit from the American side, where we have that camaraderie." European superstar Jon Rahm focuses on egalitarianism: "You have players that have more experience, but there's no hierarchy." He adds, "On this team, we're all the same. It's all for one and one for all. That's kind of how it is. We are all there to accomplish the same goal. We are all part of the same team, and what you've done before and what you might do after that week doesn't matter at all." Fellow superstar Rory McIlroy (figure 7.3) concurs: "We are all part of a 12-man team, and we are all trying to do our bit, and certainly no one is more important than anyone else."[12]

The Americans often express similar opinions. Consider Dave Stockton, captain of the winning 1991 US team: "If it's between talent and chemistry, I'll take chemistry." Jim Furyk, who played

FIGURE 7.3 Rory McIlroy

Copyright © 2023 The Associated Press. Used by permission.

in nine Ryder Cups for the United States, also believes in the importance of having golfers who complement each other, both on the course and in the meeting rooms. "I think chemistry is extremely important," Furyk said. "I think not only how the players mix together as 12 but how we play together as a team, how the pairings are put together, how those personalities and those styles match up with each other and probably for different formats as well. I think that provides the players the best opportunity to compete and do well."[13]

Others infer the same conclusion from how players behave after the match: "Watch the Euros celebrating after their victories, spraying champagne, mixing with fans. Their camaraderie is as evident as their joy. It's their team, from the captain—this year, it's the Irishman, Paul McGinley—on down."[14]

Meanwhile, the losing Americans often look for someone or something to blame. Culture may or may not enter into the discussion. The coach often gets taken to task, either for his team selections, group pairings, or management style. The course setup or fan behavior also sometimes get blamed.

Golf writer Eamon Lynch thinks that the culture angle is overwrought. He points to plenty of rancor on the European team across the years, citing stars Seve Ballesteros and Nick Faldo as divisive. Lynch attributes the European success to recognition of a common purpose: "What unity there was within Europe's squad was seeded in common purpose, not in cordial relationships. Many of the continent's top stars felt routinely disrespected on the PGA Tour and found solidarity in a shared objective—kicking the enemy's arse. Bonds between players grew organically around that goal; they weren't a prepackaged requirement to make the roster to begin with."[15]

Ryder Cup teams are small. Even if the cohesiveness of social relationships affects the outcome, we are not sure that we'd call it "culture." But we bring up the case to show the plethora of plausible explanations that usually can be offered for the same outcome. Sorting out the effect of culture on the bottom line, or any outcome, is typically challenging, especially if we are examining a single case or story.

Contrast the American Ryder Cup skepticism with Steve Kerr's perspective on culture (figure 7.4). Kerr is the coach of the Golden State Warriors, a team in the National Basketball Association (NBA), which he led to four NBA titles in 2015, 2017, 2018, and 2022—a miraculous string of wins given that the team had not won a championship since 1975. The Warriors are now tied for third place for the most NBA championships and Finals appearances, behind only the Boston Celtics and Los Angeles Lakers.

FIGURE 7.4 Coach Steve Kerr (center) talks about the
Golden State Warriors' culture

Copyright © 2022 U.C. Berkeley Haas. Used by permission.

Kerr is a firm believer in the power of culture to drive successful performance, especially if the culture raises the level of joy in what people are doing. When asked if he would be more inclined to draft a player who is really talented but doesn't fit the team's culture versus one who does fit the team culture, he said, "Do you take a more talented player who doesn't fit into your culture or a less talented player who does? If you are lucky enough to have that cornerstone like we have with Steph (Curry), then you have to go culture across the board. Because that culture is powerful. It's also enjoyable. You have to have talent, but it's harder to build that culture if you don't have the cornerstone."[16]

Kerr's view is consistent with research showing that culture does matter on the bottom line.

STUDIES OF CULTURE'S IMPACT

To understand how culture affects the bottom line, we need to turn to social science. We get deeper into research here than in other parts of the book because it's impossible to gauge the impact of culture on firm performance without looking closely—very closely—at the research findings.

In particular, let's review the studies that look for systematic effects of culture over a sizable sample of firms. Let's try to understand the main effects (the central tendencies, if you will) of how culture affects organizational outcomes. To do so, let's start by looking at studies that take a big-picture view, studying sets of whole firms and comparing them to each other to try to pin down culture's impact on bottom-line variables. As we will see, this is a daunting task, and these studies often leave many questions unanswered.

DOES CULTURE AFFECT FIRM PERFORMANCE?

Answering questions about culture's impact on an organization's bottom line is not a simple or even straightforward task. Every organization has a culture, whether it is intentionally formed or not, just as every person has a personality. When we ask if one's personality affects their life chances, it becomes obvious that we need to be more precise about what we mean. At a basic level, maybe we mean, "Do variations in personality show correlations with life outcomes?" But since there are endless ways to conceptualize personality, a specific finding of no impact using one conceptualization may be highly unsatisfying because variations in other unstudied conceptualizations may indeed matter, and we can never rule out every possibility. So too with culture and organizational performance.

What to do? Rather than try to address the general question about impact in a definitive way, we instead stick to the evidence, focusing on those major studies that have shown (or failed to show, despite trying) specific ways that culture affects organizational outcomes like financial performance. We start by reviewing studies cast at a macro level, where culture for the whole organization is depicted in a particular way and an attempt is made to link this depiction to organizational-level outcomes. As we will see, this is a challenging task, in large part because so many other factors affect organizational outcomes and we cannot usually control for some major ones, let alone all of them. Accordingly, we will also review studies designed to figure out the impact of cultural factors on other specific outcomes, such as managerial intensity (typically defined as how much the organization spends on managing and controlling operations rather than producing goods and services) and employee turnover, which may be the paths through which culture influences performance (sometimes these are referred to in the research world as "mechanisms").

Taken together, what this means is that culture may influence performance both directly, meaning that certain cultures, such as those with strong cultures that emphasize adaptability, perform better; and indirectly, such as by increasing employees' commitment to the organization, which inspires them to work harder to accomplish goals, which in turn leads to better performance.[17]

Our review of the most important studies shows that aspects of culture do affect the bottom line in organizations, although sometimes in surprising and nuanced ways. We also find plenty of evidence that culture shapes many of the mechanisms that, in turn, affect performance. While these findings leave plenty of open questions about culture's impact on the bottom line, we feel confident that there is ample justification for leaders to prioritize managing organizational culture, especially in certain contexts. We also think that it is helpful for managers to know when the scientific evidence supports what they are trying to do and when they are on shakier ground.

HOW CULTURE AFFECTS PERFORMANCE

At a macro level, an organization's culture might affect organizational performance in either of two basic ways. The first is through alignment with the organization's strategy, and the second is through enhanced commitment and coordination among employees.

Let's take strategy alignment first. What exactly needs to be aligned? A business strategy is a general, firmwide orientation that positions an organization in a market relative to its competitors. Executing the strategy successfully requires translating or deriving the general orientation toward specific behaviors for many different functions, products, and situations. For example, a firm following a low-cost strategy needs to specify whether its cost advantage emanates from buying cheaper input materials, paying lower wages, or both.

Organizational culture is often described and communicated by a set of general values or norms. But these too need to be translated or derived into specific behaviors so they drive action on particular tasks. For example, does the cultural dictum "Hire

Smart" mean that you should hire smart people, or that you should run an efficient hiring and recruitment process using artificial intelligence algorithms?

Alignment or congruence between strategy and culture is a master check to see whether the outcomes of the two processes are consistent with each other. Are we driving down two roads or one? Do the two roads lead to the same place? Graphically, the chain of reasoning involved in an alignment check looks like figure 7.5.

Misalignment involves a conflict or contradiction between strategy and culture. There is plenty of room in between—a culture might not be aligned but also might not be conflicting. There may be little congruence, but the culture also may have

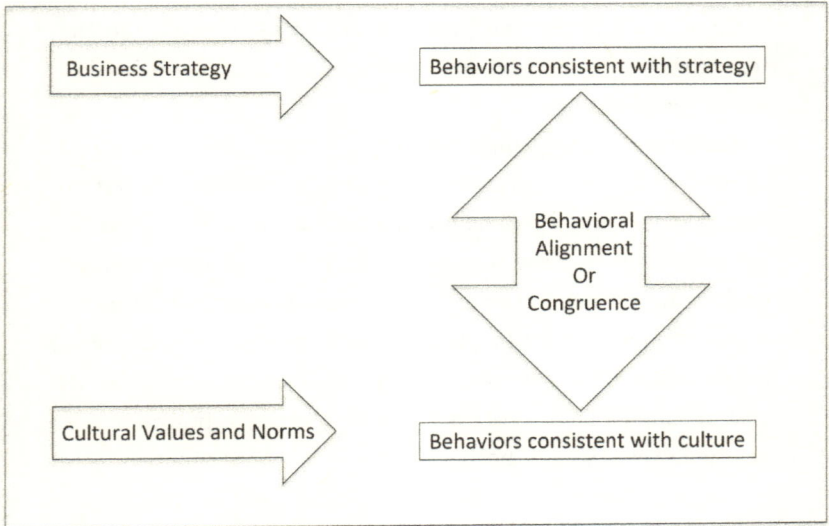

FIGURE 7.5 Strategy-culture alignment

Copyright © 2024 by Jennifer A. Chatman and Glenn R. Carroll. Used by permission.

nothing that undermines or contradicts the strategy. Instead, we think of this situation as more of a missed opportunity.

Enhanced commitment and coordination are different issues. Increasing these is about a potential effect on performance that occurs regardless of cultural content. It is when people work together because they agree on the ideas, and even the assumptions behind them. They understand each other and know what and why the other person is going to do, often without asking or even talking with each other. They also feel strong solidarity with each other. The result is a smoother and more efficient operation.

When economists think of culture, they often invoke the commitment and coordination concept, knowingly or not. The models of organizational culture built by economic theorists such as David Kreps use culture in this way and model it accordingly.[18] It is important to recognize that for this pathway to generate better organizational performance, we at least need to know that the strategy is not misaligned. Misalignment would lead to efficient operation of the wrong or conflicting behaviors, given the strategy.[19] By contrast, if the cultural content is in that in-between territory of not aligned and not misaligned, it likely will have a positive impact on performance since an efficient operation is usually better than an inefficient one.

Of course, an ideal culture is aligned with the strategy while also enhancing commitment and coordination. It's the framework that ensures that the culture has maximal positive impact, the dream of every CEO but the reality of few. In analytical studies, social scientists often try to focus on one or the other causal pathway between culture and performance. We report on both kinds of studies.

STUDIES OF CULTURAL STRENGTH

Perhaps the most common kind of social science study looking for the impact of commitment and coordination on organizational performance compares those organizations with strong cultures with those with less strong cultures. Strong cultures are defined in part as those with high consensus around the norms, values, and beliefs in the organization, although the exact measures vary (see chapter 1). A variety of research studies examine whether the presence of a strong culture is positively associated with organizational performance or highly related outcomes, regardless of the content of the norms, values, and beliefs.

CULTURAL STRENGTH AND MANAGERIAL INTENSITY

If culture constitutes an alternative mode of coordination within a firm, then efficient organizations should find less reason to coordinate in traditional ways, including control by managers and administrators. This insight prompts the empirical question: Do strong culture organizations employ fewer managers and administrators than other similar organizations? The ratio of managerial employees to the total number of employees in an organization is called "managerial intensity" (or "administrative intensity"). Since employee counts are objective and comparable, studies of managerial intensity typically cover many organizations over significant periods of time. Several of them also attempt to measure cultural strength and examine its association with managerial intensity. These studies show time and time again that *strong culture organizations get by with fewer managers (administrators) than comparable other organizations.* That is, managerial intensity is lower for organizations with strong cultures, all other things equal.

Among others, two excellent empirical studies report this finding. The first is a study of about 200 early-stage high-tech start-ups in Silicon Valley. Conducted by sociologists James Baron and Michael Hannan, the Stanford Project on Emerging Companies (SPEC) finds that organizations using what they call a "Commitment blueprint for human relations" (comparable to our definition of strong culture) show significantly less managerial intensity than firms with other blueprints.[20]

The second study, by strategy researchers Adrianna Marchetti, and Phanish Puranam, was intended mainly to examine the impact of digital collaboration technologies on organizations. They studied 3,017 publicly listed US firms from 2010–2019, yielding 20,594 firm-year observations. One component of their analysis examines the relationship between managerial intensity and cultural strength, which they "measure from employees' reviews of their companies posted on the job website Glassdoor.com." In analyzing the relationship between cultural strength and managerial intensity, they report that "an increase in cultural strength is associated with a decrease in managerial intensity."[21]

CULTURAL STRENGTH AND START-UP FAILURE AND IPOS

A couple of notable findings from the SPEC study of Baron and Hannan concern the market outcomes of high-tech start-ups. The first of these involve failure rates. The study shows that high-tech start-ups with strong culture (commitment) models were least likely to fail (compared to all other models) during the observation period. The finding accords with the claim of T. J. Rodgers, founder of Cypress Semiconductor, when he stated, "I believe our Core Values, more than anything else, have kept us alive and well, while three-quarters of 1983's U.S. semiconductor companies have perished."[22]

A second finding from the SPEC study looks at the timing of IPOs. As Baron and Hannan write: "Organization-building and high-commitment [i.e., strong culture] Human Resource Management seems to pay, even in the turbulent 'built to flip' environment of Silicon Valley. In particular, firms founded with Commitment [i.e., strong culture] models were the fastest to go public, relative to otherwise comparable companies whose founders embraced a different model."[23]

Baron and Hannan explain what they think drives this finding: "A number of venture capitalists with whom we have shared our findings tell us that the resilience of the Commitment [i.e., strong culture] model resonates with their experience. They note that the technological and economic uncertainties inherent in high-tech entrepreneurship, combined with the interpersonal stresses involved, put a premium on employees and organizational designs that can cope and adapt. In their judgment, blueprints that manage to capture the hearts and minds of employees up front can better achieve this adaptation."[24]

The SPEC study also finds that strong culture organizations perform second-best (of multiple alternative models) in terms of annual growth following the IPO. Baron and Hannan explain: "By articulating enduring overarching goals from the outset and by creating a powerful sense of belonging, the Commitment [i.e., strong culture] model can help companies avoid or minimize the 'post-partum depression' syndrome that sometimes accompanies an IPO, release of the first product, or achievement of other key corporate milestones."[25]

Taken together, these studies offer evidence for an indirect link, via lower managerial intensity and higher employee commitment, between culture strength and firm performance.

CULTURAL STRENGTH AND FINANCIAL PERFORMANCE

Empirical studies attempting to explain the direct relationship between culture and financial performance remain challenging because so many factors, systematic and random, can affect the bottom line, and it is virtually impossible to control for all of them. Nonetheless, several analysts conducted studies looking for links between the strength of organizational culture and financial performance outcomes. In an early study, Daniel Denison developed a set of hypotheses about traits such as involvement, consistency, adaptability, and mission and their relationship to performance effectiveness.[26] Denison and Aneil Mishra conducted a follow up study of these ideas among Midwestern industrial firms using a survey of C-suite executives.[27] In a sample of 764 firms, they found that these traits, which they considered to be cultural in content, were positively associated with overall performance; they also found that these traits were positively associated with return on assets. The traits mix culture strength (consistency, involvement) with content (adaptability) and include a construct that we consider to be distinct from culture (mission) so the studies remain ambiguous regarding the importance of culture strength and content.

A widely referenced study by John Kotter and James Heskett of the Harvard Business School examined culture strength. They studied a selected sample of 207 firms from twenty-two industries in the United States.[28] Calculating each firm's average performance over a ten-year period, they looked for an association between the perceptions of observers—analysts and others who were familiar with the firm—of the firm's cultural strength, as well as independent measures of the firm's performance. They then used three survey items to measure cultural strength: (1) whether the firm's managers speak of their company's style or way of doing things; (2) whether the firm announces its values with a written creed or credo and attempts to get managers to comply; and (3) whether the firm operates via long-standing policies and practices that preceded those of the current CEO.[29]

One interesting feature of Kotter and Heskett's study is that they also asked the top six officers of each firm to report on their own culture and then compared the insiders' and the outsiders' perceptions of the culture. The correlation between the six internal officers and the outside observers' ratings of the cultures was very high ($r = .77$), suggesting that senior leaders had a realistic view of their company's culture. Kotter and Heskett also used separate measures of the culture's content and developed case study explanations for which culture content attributes seemed to help individual firms. But the headline in their study was the finding that firms that observers regarded as operating with strong cultures emphasizing consistency showed higher levels of market value growth, net income growth, and return on investment. In their words, "we conclude from this study that there is a positive relationship between strength of corporate culture and long-term economic performance, but it is a modest relationship."[30]

George Gordon and Nancy DiTomaso also addressed the financial performance issue using management survey data from eleven insurance companies in 1981.[31] They found a positive association between cultural strength (measured as consistency in responses to survey items about values in 1981) and firm asset and premium growth from 1982–1987.

Overall, the evidence suggests that *cultural strength affects bottom-line financial performance.* But we would also strongly caution that this finding is suggestive and tentative, as many scientists are highly critical of these efforts because of sampling and measurement issues.

CONTINGENT EFFECTS OF CULTURE ON PERFORMANCE

After reviewing the studies attempting to link cultural strength directly and indirectly with organizational performance, some social scientists have balked. They did so because, by their thinking, it is not reasonable to envision a straightforward, directly causal connection between cultural strength and performance in all contexts. Rather, in their view, the relationship between strength and performance should be contingent on specific conditions or contexts, as outlined earlier in this chapter in the discussion of alignment, as well as in figure 7.5.

In what contexts would cultural strength matter most for performance? Ronald Burt and collaborators argued that in industries constrained by strong competition, cultural differences related to efficiency should matter most.[32] To demonstrate this point, they reanalyzed John Kotter and James Heskett's data and showed that strong cultures generate greater performance benefits in highly competitive industries.

Jesper Sørensen made a similar kind of argument about the benefits of cultural strength in stable versus volatile markets. Specifically, he argued that strong cultures generate reliable performance when the environment is stable. But when things get volatile, Sørensen sees strong cultures as becoming liabilities because they severely limit the exploration needed to adapt to changing conditions. Using Kotter and Heskett's data merged with financial performance data (return on investment and cash flow), he shows that, consistent with Burt's analysis, "there is evidence that the reliability benefits of strong cultures are enhanced in more competitive environments." He also finds evidence to support his own argument regarding market stability and cultural strength: "As industry volatility increases, the reliability-enhancing benefits of strong corporate cultures attenuate." Finally, he finds another unconditional effect: "Strong cultures in general lead to reductions in performance variability [over time]."[33]

Other studies show how under specific conditions, certain cultural dimensions may influence financial performance. For example, consistent with Sørensen's argument and adding culture content into the mix, one study shows how companies with both strong cultures and culture content that emphasizes adaptiveness thrive over time.[34]

Another study examined how organizations respond to sudden major changes in their external environment.[35] Researchers examined 1.8 million employee Glassdoor reviews and a sample of 1,068 publicly listed US firms. They used pre-COVID (2019) culture data derived from the Glassdoor reviews to examine whether organizations with certain cultural orientations fared better during the pandemic crisis. Controlling for industry, they tracked financial performance until well after the pandemic and found that firms with cultures with content emphasizing adaptability and deemphasizing collaboration were more resilient, exhibiting higher return on assets and Tobin's Q in subsequent years. These findings offer some additional evidence for the discussion about cultural inertia in chapter 3.

Overall, the evidence from these studies suggests *that cultural strength (possibly combined with specific culture content) affects bottom-line financial performance only (or more forcefully) under certain conditions.* But we would also be quick to say that we are far from being able to list with confidence a full set of the specific conditions under which cultural strength matters most.

CULTURAL VALUES AND PERFORMANCE

Other notable studies look at the relationship between various cultural factors and organizational performance. In a study by financial economists, Luigi Guiso and colleagues collected data on the advertised values that the S&P 500 companies published in 2011 in their annual reports and websites.[36] They grouped the terms used into nine categories or meaning units, including Integrity, Teamwork, Innovation, Respect, Quality, Safety, Community, Communication, and Hard Work.

Guiso and colleagues report that the average company lists four values, although many list fewer and others more. The most common value advertised is Integrity. They analyze these data by estimating associations of advertised values with measures of firm financial performance. They find *"very little evidence that advertised values are correlated with performance;* there is no detectable correlation with firm profitability" (emphasis added).[37]

Of course, advertised values are typically aspirational and do not necessarily reflect behavioral reality. So Guiso and colleagues used another source of data to measure values perceived by employees, the Great Place to Work Survey, which looks at large companies (i.e., over 1,000 employees). From this source, they were able to compile and analyze data on 679 for-profit firms with 410,521 participating full-time employees from 2007–2011. Using employee responses to the following statement "Management's actions match its words" as a measure of integrity, they find a positive correlation with financial performance (Tobin's Q and return on sales).[38] That is, they find an average employee perception of *"integrity is positively correlated with financial performance."*[39]

The empirical components of this study are rigorous and high quality. We do wonder, however, if the answer would differ if the research question were defined more appropriately. To us, it seems a stretch to expect any specific value to affect organizational performance across *all* firm strategies and industry contexts. In our view, a more insightful study would use theory about expected alignments between specific values and firm strategies to look for performance benefits. For instance, we would expect a company making and offering high-quality consumer goods or services like Clorox to benefit from a customer service–oriented culture; we would not expect a company pursuing innovative, technology-oriented products and services like SpaceX to do so to the same extent.

CULTURAL FIT AND PERFORMANCE, COMMITMENT, AND TURNOVER

Of course, financial performance is not the only outcome that organizational leaders are concerned about. So another set of studies examines the relationship between organizational culture and employee turnover. Specifically, these studies consider employees' fit or match with their organization's culture to see whether the degree of fit affects who leaves and who stays. In general, the estimated relationships show that employees who fit well display lower rates of exit and turnover, especially voluntary exit, a finding discussed in chapter 6. Typical reasoning claims that fit produces commitment and motivation, which in turn affect whether people leave. Of course, turnover is not automatically and directly related to organizational performance, but most analysts believe that stability in an organization's workforce (as evidenced by low turnover) is a prerequisite for high performance. Conversely, few contexts with high turnover are associated with high performance.

An important early study of cultural fit and turnover was conducted by Charles O'Reilly and Jenny Chatman.[40] Their study used data on eighty-seven employees who, as a part of an office automation grant to a university, had been given access to new technologies. The analysts examined commitment based on internalization, or similarity of individual and organizational values. They found that commitment was strongly associated with a stated intention to remain with the organization and was negatively related to actual turnover sixteen months later. Attachment based on identification, or pride in affiliation with the university, was also positively associated with tenure intentions and actual turnover.

Revisiting the SPEC study of young high-tech companies that we discussed earlier in this chapter, James Baron and colleagues also studied turnover rates within firms. Surprisingly, when the founder used the commitment (strong culture) human resource (HR) model, turnover was not lowest. When looking at CEO blueprints at the subsequent time of study observation, however, *the commitment model showed the lowest turnover rate.* The SPEC analysts also examined the relationship between turnover and firm performance. They found a significant negative effect of turnover on revenue growth. They concluded that "turnover appears to have adverse consequences for organizational performance, at least in the short run."[41]

The study by Amir Goldberg and colleagues (mentioned in chapter 6) looked at the relationship between cultural alignment and turnover. To do so, they used a dataset from a technology company that included detailed personnel records on employee start dates, exit dates, and nature of exit (voluntary or involuntary), as well as, uniquely, a corpus of e-mails (10.24 million messages spanning over five years, from 601 employees). Analytically, they used the e-mails to calculate a measure of cultural fit based on the language that people use and its level of conformity to the linguistic style of their colleagues. The analysis shows a significant effect of cultural fit—namely, fit reduces the likelihood of involuntary exit by slightly more than 50 percent. The researchers also report a decrease in voluntary exit when employees have higher fit with the culture.[42]

A follow-up study by Richard Lu and colleagues used culture assessment data from the same technology company.[43] Specifically, they used the organizational culture profile (OCP), that we discussed in the Genentech case in chapter 2. They found that similarity in values between the employee and the organization is significantly and negatively related to voluntary exit. In other words, employees with high cultural fit depart voluntarily at much lower rates than those with less fit.

In sum, we see in these studies a consistent and robust pattern: People who fit well with their cultures depart voluntarily at lower rates than those who fit less well. There is also evidence that members with low cultural fit depart involuntarily at a higher rate than those who fit more highly. Because of the many replications under different conditions with different measures, these findings about the organizational culture's impact are among the strongest and most credible in the social sciences.

SUMMARY

The stories and studies that we have reviewed, and many that we haven't, in this book leave little doubt that culture can affect performance. From the regular high performance of Walmart and Southwest Air to the rescues of Ford and Dreyer's from the brink of collapse, many executives and analysts point to culture as the key factor. From the systematic studies of Fortune 500 companies in multiple industries to those of employees and teams in traditional and modern industries, and extending to start-ups, scholars find that culture affects firm performance and individual employment decisions.

Accordingly, we have seen that the impact of culture can be critically important in the ongoing operations of an organization or navigating organizations through crises. The impact, however, is neither simple nor automatic. As we have said all along, to get a positive impact of culture on the bottom line requires thoughtful design and alignment, as well as vigilant leadership and execution. Benefiting from culture also requires updating it when strategy and environments change, since what worked before may not work in the future.

MANAGERIAL TAKEAWAYS
FROM THIS CHAPTER

- Organizational culture can affect the financial performance of a firm in both positive and negative ways.

- Stronger cultures that are also adaptive may enable firms to navigate unexpected shifts in their external environments.
- Evidence for the effect of culture on the bottom line is strongest when it operates through specific mechanisms such as employee commitment and attrition. High levels of fit increase commitment and reduce turnover.
- Culture has also been shown to affect the administrative intensity of an organization—strong culture organizations need fewer managers and administrators.
- In start-ups, research shows that strong culture organizations require less time to go to IPO status and lead to higher valuations.

8

MANAGING CULTURE

In the 1979–80s, I was working in the Accounting Dept. at HP [Hewlett-Packard]Labs. There was a beer bust for the Lab engineers, and I was down in the serving line for the barbeque in the courtyard by the cafeteria. Special black T-shirts were handed out with some kind of event slogan.

Along comes Bill Hewlett, who was wearing his T-shirt, and asked the server next to me for two hamburgers, probably intending to take one back to his secretary, Maddie. The server, a young woman who had just joined HP, told Bill that she was instructed to serve only ONE hamburger or ONE hot dog per person. Naturally I was stunned, but before I could say anything, Bill just said, "Well, that's OK." I immediately told her that this was Bill Hewlett, and so she quickly offered to serve whatever he wanted. But he just was so nice [and attentive] to her embarrassment, [that he] told her he understood and would be pleased to just follow the rules.[1]

That's Jackie Spinozzi, a former employee of Hewlett-Packard (HP). She's talking about her experience with Bill Hewlett, founder and top executive at HP. HP was one of the first prominent US tech companies to be known for having a strong culture.

And Bill Hewlett was known for being around a lot and talking to people. He was also considered a nice person and beloved by many employees.

Dave Packard, Hewlett's partner at HP, was regarded similarly by employees, and similar anecdotes exist about him. For example, HP ex-employee Joe Schoendorf says:

> My first real memory of "THE HP WAY" came about six weeks later in July when I was invited to Palo Alto Hills Country Club for a senior sales seminar reception. I was standing there, and this big guy comes up to me and introduces himself. "Hi," he said, "I am Dave Packard, and I know you have been with us a few weeks. I am sorry that I have not been able to come down and say hello, but we seem to be growing very fast. Welcome to HP.[2]

The HP culture story is a classic. Both Hewlett and Packard (figure 8.1) were known for their consistently empathetic relationships with HP's employees. They spent ample unstructured time with them, talking about both work and life. The now-common phrase "Managing by Walking Around" originated at HP under their tenure.

Packard often articulated the importance of treating people well, as in a speech in the 1960s where he emphasized, "Tolerance is tremendously significant. Unless you are tolerant of the people under you, you really can't do a good job of being a supervisor. You must have understanding—understanding of the little things that affect people. You must have a sense of fairness, and you must know what it is reasonable to expect of your people."[3]

Global bank Citigroup also possesses a notable culture—one that values agility and diversity, which makes sense given that Citi is the most global of the large US banks. Under CEO Jane Fraser (figure 8.2), the company has grown to nearly $72 billion

FIGURE 8.1 Hewlett-Packard founders Dave Packard (left)
and Bill Hewlett

Copyright © 1981 Getty Images. Used by permission.

in revenue, although the company still faces strategic challenges.
Fraser's approach to culture focuses on how to ensure that people make effective decisions. She explains:

> Leadership has changed. Leadership used to be about telling
> people what to do and making sure they did it. Whereas now,
> in a world where data is everywhere, you are usually not the

best person to take the decision. It's deeper in the organization where they've got far more of the data and the information. So as a leader, you set context now. You set context from the culture, tone, values, and broader strategy, and then you get out of the way and make sure that the next generation is able to grow, lead, and engage with clients and customers.[4]

LEADERSHIP STYLES VARY

It is tempting to conclude from the examples of Hewlett, Packard, Fraser, and many similar others that leaders of strong culture organizations must display warmth toward others and be affable and readily accessible. Certainly, plenty of strong culture leaders behave this way, and it typically engenders commitment and

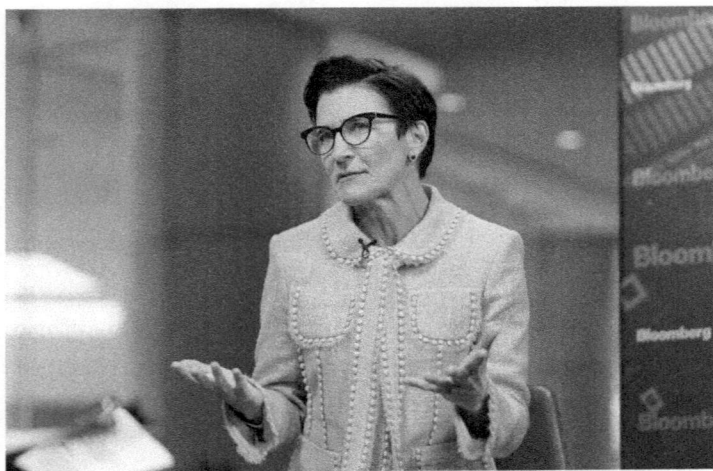

FIGURE 8.2 Citibank CEO Jane Fraser

Copyright © 2022 Getty Images. Used by permission.

loyalty from their employees. But it is hardly the only, or maybe even the most prevalent, way for a top executive to behave effectively when leading a strong culture organization.

To see the other end of the spectrum, consider T. J. Rodgers (figure 8.3), the founder and longtime CEO of Cypress Semiconductor, a strong culture company in Silicon Valley that defied the odds for decades in competing against behemoths like Intel. Known for his demanding and authoritarian-like orders to underlings, Rodgers seems more like a Marine drill sergeant than the CEO of a high-tech company.

An ex-CFO at Cypress remembers Rodgers pounding on his desk, making "near impossible" demands.[5] He did not keep his outbursts private either. Rodgers often took others to task in front of their colleagues, including fellow vice presidents. An ex-CFO is quoted as saying that when angry, Rodgers

FIGURE 8.3 Cypress former CEO T. J. Rodgers

Copyright © 2004 Getty Images. Used by permission.

would get "red in the face and huffy and puffy." Rodgers's former secretary, Valletta Massey, observes that "people think they know how demanding he is. They don't."[6] Moreover, Rodgers demanded everything. Says one journalist: "T. J. expected that management—especially executives—had to sacrifice their personal life to succeed at Cypress."[7]

Perhaps the most prominent example of a tough leader of a strong culture company was Steve Jobs at Apple (see figure 8.4). In his biography of Jobs, Walter Isaacson recounts many incidents of him getting angry, flying off the handle, and berating employees in public.[8]

One of Jobs's more famous blowups came after Apple launched MobileMe (figure 8.5), a remote service tool that claimed to offer continuous web and calendar access across digital devices, in

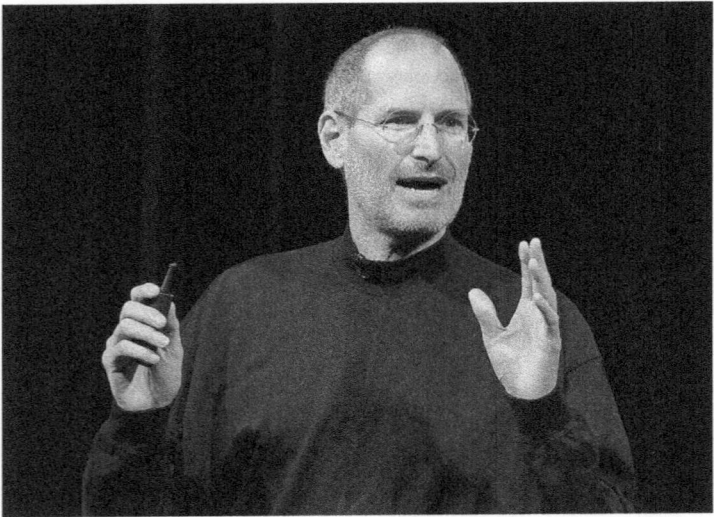

FIGURE 8.4 Steve Jobs

July 2008. But the service suffered technical problems and got bad press reviews, even from usually friendly critics. According to Adam Lashinsky, Jobs assembled the MobileMe team in Apple's auditorium and asked: "Can anyone tell me what MobileMe is supposed to do?"[9] When the team gave their answers, Jobs replied, "Then why the fuck doesn't it do that?" Next, Jobs publicly fired the MobileMe leader on the spot.

Isaacson describes other behaviors that Jobs engaged in that were inconsiderate at best, and perhaps downright disrespectful.

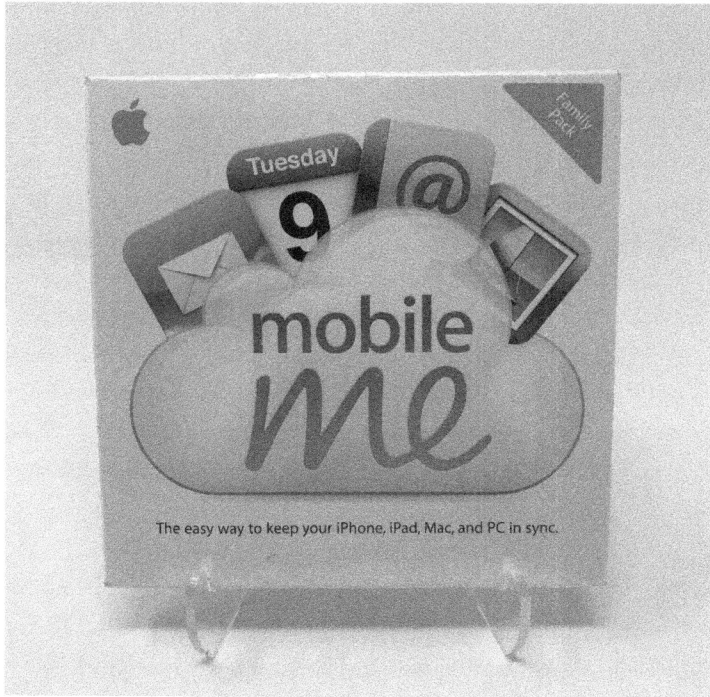

FIGURE 8.5 MobileMe ad

He detested human resources (HR) staff because he said that they had a "mediocre mentality." He routinely told his staff that they "sucked." He would yell at employees he was unhappy with for extended periods of time, often thirty minutes or more. In the Apple cafeteria, he would jump the line in front of other employees. He regularly parked his unlicensed Mercedes-Benz in parking spots reserved for disabled people.

As these examples show, leaders of strong culture organizations do not follow a single model. The range of behavioral styles for strong culture managers is wide. But it is not random. The cases of Hewlett, Packard, Rodgers, Fraser, and Jobs show that despite their wide variations in style, each behaved consistently over time, and with different people and groups. They also never let up, and they comprehensively addressed cultural issues in all contexts of organizational life. And, when asked, each offered a coherent narrative or story of why they did what they did and how the culture helped the company to succeed.

But managing culture is about more than how leaders behave. It is also about the organization itself—how the organization is designed and what routines it practices and processes it operates. Organizations are social systems, with properties and behaviors independent of its individual members. Of course, leaders have more discretion than others to create these policies and practices, but managing culture is about both creating them and ensuring that people are broadly employing them as well.

Which organizational factors prove most important for managing culture? In this chapter, we discuss managerial levers that shape culture—the tools that build a strong culture. These include levers that individual managers can use, as well as those that line up the organization's structural features. Social science theory and research on culture highlights this set of managerial levers over and over again, in all kinds of organizations and for all kinds of strong cultures, ranging from religious cults to terrorist cells to special commando teams to companies that execute with great operational efficiency to innovative high-tech companies. Deciding how many and which levers to use presents a social engineering challenge for managers. Effective impact depends on a comprehensive approach and consistent implementation.

As explained in chapter 1, strong organizational culture involves a combination of a high degree of agreement among participants in their values, beliefs, and norms and high intensity of participants in adherence to these values, beliefs, and norms. It does not rely on content, and any kind of culture can be strong or weak (although as we have noted, aligning culture content with strategic goals is immensely helpful).

Accordingly, any levers that managers use to increase the strength of a culture should either decrease behavioral variations or increase people's intensity in conforming to shared norms. A secondary goal for deciding which levers to use involves eliminating distractions—each lever should help the culture highlight priorities and inform people about which actions they should take. For the most part, each of the levers can be used to develop organizational culture regardless of the specific content of cultural norms. Indeed, we see many of these levers in all kinds of organizations, including business firms, start-ups, mature companies across a number of industries, nonprofits, social movements, religious cults, Himalayan expeditions, Navy SEALS, terrorist cells, and Special Weapons and Tactics (SWAT) teams, among others. Of course, the culture that you cultivate in your organization should align in content with the strategy that you are pursuing. But the value of a culture to your organization depends on people embracing and upholding that culture. That's where the culture levers come in.

MANAGERIAL LEVERS FOR STRONG CULTURE

Hewlett, Packard, Fraser, Rodgers, and Jobs show us how enormously the managerial styles that leaders use can vary. But on other dimensions, their behaviors are surprisingly similar, highlighting, too, that there is significant convergence on the approaches that leaders use to create and manage a strong culture. We identify the most common of these approaches as managerial levers for building a strong culture.

We categorize the levers by general function and activity. Some pertain to recruiting and selecting people, others to training and socialization, still others to communicating through the organization, yet others to the design and structure of the organization, and finally, to managing performance. The strongest culture organizations design processes in all these domains, for maximum comprehensiveness, and they ensure consistency among them.

Levers to Recruit and Select People for Strong Culture

Culturally selective hiring. Culturally selective hiring involves identifying and selecting new members because they hold values, beliefs, and normative orientations that match the organization's intended culture. This lever works because it dramatically reduces heterogeneity in values, beliefs, and norms allowed inside the organization; it intensifies the focus on those that the culture says matter.

Google emphasizes "Googly-ness" in hiring, an example of culture-driven hiring. Google defines "Googly-ness" as behavior embodying intellectual humility, conscientiousness, comfort with ambiguity, and willingness to take a courageous path. Google prioritizes these attributes across all jobs for which it hires; members need to resonate with Googly-ness since they will encounter it across all parts of the organization.

Culturally selective hiring is sometimes criticized these days for encouraging homogeneity and limiting diversity. The rebuttal requires nuance. Yes, culturally selective hiring prunes off people with values and norms that contradict those enshrined by the organization as necessary to execute the strategy—that is the whole point of managing culturally. But those are just a few of the myriad characteristics that make up someone's personality, values, and behavior. In culturally selective hiring, the organization wants to base its hiring on those chosen few characteristics deemed to be critical to success—like curiosity at Google—but at the same time, diversity can be maximized on other characteristics. Because personal characteristics are not randomly distributed in the world, achieving diversity outside the targeted cultural characteristics may require great effort to identify good candidates and recruit them. But research shows that it is clearly worth it in terms of decision-making quality in the organization. When properly implemented, hiring for the kind of "culture add" that Katrina Lake, founder of Stitch Fix, uses to achieve diversity does not conflict with culturally selective hiring.

Recruit and support cultural leaders. Members look to peers and other colleagues for advice and support about how to do work and what is appropriate. Engaging and acknowledging some members to be cultural leaders shows others the way and requires little management effort.

After its merger with Compaq, HP recruited effective cultural leaders to assist in training. The company assembled a cultural integration team that started activities the day that the merger closed. While the merger itself is today considered ill advised, the integration process that the company used, including the "clean room," which allowed the integration team to work out sensitive issues shielded from company politics, is now considered the gold standard.[10]

Other examples include Clorox's 2018 internal "Be Bold" campaign, in which they identified cultural leaders from around the company—about fifteen people total—to instigate and evaluate proposals for areas in which the company could be more innovative. People at Clorox believe that this initiative, which the company was investing in just before the COVID pandemic hit, coincidently increased its effectiveness in meeting the heightened demand for its products during the pandemic.

Finally, the WD-40 company appointed a Culture Squad to define a new strategically relevant culture focused on becoming more seamlessly global and more innovative. The Culture Squad is made up of organizational members from around the globe, up and down the hierarchy, and involving a wide range of functions and products. They surface and vet initiatives, many of which the company has adopted to implement its global strategy.

Agree and align on the intended cultural attributes and connect them to the external brand. For a range of constituents—from potential recruits, customers, and even regulators—to believe that an organization's culture is strong, they need to see that leaders agree about what the values, beliefs, and norms of the organization should be. In other words, agreement, especially among leaders, is the precondition to building a strong culture—it simply will not emerge if leaders disagree about cultural priorities. Alignment means that the culture supports the organization's strategy and facilitates its execution.

Goldman Sachs is a good example of a consistent internal culture that matched closely with its external brand, especially in its early days when it chose and served client firms.

The firm then was known for its almost religious-like attention to providing service to clients (to whom they wanted to allot a full wallet of business with Goldman Sachs); a focus on sharing information (so clients would not leave with departing Goldman Sachs employees); and a marked orientation toward the long term (so clients were loyal). Goldman Sachs's comprehensive culture was as much a feature of their external brand as its internal norms.[11]

Another example of an organization that matches its internal culture to its external brand comes from the Haas School of Business at the University of California, Berkeley. As part of its strategy to differentiate itself from other top business schools, it created four defining leadership principles (DLPs) that uniquely codify the school's culture and brand: Question the Status Quo, Students Always, Beyond Yourself, and Confidence Without Attitude.[12] The school wove the DLPs into everything it did, over 180 different processes, from asking students to write an essay about what one of the DLPs meant to them, to evaluating teaching based on how well faculty demonstrated the DLPs, to recognizing students who excelled in embodying each DLP with awards, to celebrations with alumni that were DLP themed (e.g., the "Beyond Yourself Bash").

These efforts worked well. Focusing on the DLPs internally and externally enabled the Haas School to ramp up giving to the school—eight of the ten biggest gifts in its history were given in the name of one or more DLPs. It also resulted in the school boosting applications and winning more students and faculty from competitor schools. Notably, *Poets & Quants*, the popular online magazine for prospective and current master's of business administration (MBA) students, commented, "There is no doubt that Haas stands alone among business schools in consciously defining and shaping a strong culture to its competitive advantage. The school's defining leadership principles are deeply embedded in the school and the mindset of many of its stakeholders."[13]

Hire people for the long term. Long-term employment means that people who join the organization expect to stay for a long time, if not their entire careers. Intending to cultivate long-term employment reduces heterogeneity by fostering a strong connection to the firm rather than a specific job or occupation.

Examples would include iconic manufacturing companies such as Caterpillar, General Motors, and Ford Motor Company, or the global Japanese companies such as Toyota, Honda, and Mitsubishi. The company Simpson Manufacturing, highlighted in the WorkLife podcast,[14] has always focused on hiring and promoting from within, which has led to a strong, customer-focused culture and a highly motivated workforce.

Flatten the hierarchy. A flat hierarchy means that there are fewer levels and a shorter chain of command, and responsibilities are more decentralized; that is, lower-level employees have significant decision-making responsibility. Reducing hierarchy creates transparency, strengthens accountability, fosters a sense of egalitarianism, and generates high involvement, all of which reduce behavioral variation (which could reduce strategically relevant behaviors), and ramp up intensity.

A good example is the gaming company Valve. According to Ulrich Möller and Matthew McCaffrey, "Valve is a 'flat' company without a management hierarchy or traditional boss roles: instead of top-down organization and management, Valve employees are "free to work on whatever projects they choose and to convince other employees to join collaborative groups. Decision-making is thus 'democratized' rather than centralized in key management positions." This approach helps Valve in generating innovative games in a competitive environment.[15]

Levers to Train and Develop People
for Strong Culture

Intense early socialization. Intense early socialization involves rapid and forceful exposure to the organization's cultural values, beliefs, and norms. It works because organizational newcomers are especially impressionable and eager to please; they either conform or leave. The classic thirteen-week-long boot camp of the Marines at Parris Island, South Carolina, is an extreme example. At boot camp, new recruits are stripped of their personal belongings, isolated socially from outside influences, berated and broken down mentally, and then built back up, piece by piece, in the image of the ideal Marine.

Peer socialization. Coworkers, especially peers, know best what is going on with others in the organization; peers also potentially can significantly influence one another and enhance connectedness. Peer collaboration enhances agreement and places pressure on peers to perform in certain ways to gain respect. An example of this is Google, with its Googler to Googler (g2g) program, in which thousands of employees regularly volunteer to teach and assist others in the company. "Full embeddedness" refers to organizations in which members can access and receive many of their daily needs from inside and do not need to venture out and get exposed to others. Extreme examples include what social scientists call "total institutions"; the classic company town verges on being a total institution.

Contemporary organizations with more embeddedness include Facebook and other high-tech companies that provide free food, day care, dry cleaning, and other services. These appear to be appealing perquisites of employment, but they also have the effect of keeping people at work and blurring the lines between work and life, as discussed in more detail in chapter 5.

Leader modeling. Leaders need to exhibit behaviors that are consistent with the culture and avoid those that are not prioritized in strong culture organizations. Members look to leaders constantly and scrutinize their behaviors to learn and infer what is really important. Leaders need to "walk the walk," not just "talk the talk," because they are so visible and powerful. If a leader's behavior is inconsistent with the culture, or even a little ambiguous in terms of supporting the culture, people will interpret this as meaning that the culture is not that important; they will, consequently, ease up on their adherence to the culture.

As discussed in chapter 4, Herb Kelleher at Southwest Airlines is a good reference point—he exemplified someone having fun at work. What other CEO would show up at a workplace in the middle of the night toting a bottle of whiskey and joking with employees?

Likewise, despite their differences, Hewlett, Packard, Fraser, Rodgers, and Jobs behaved in ways that exemplified core tenets of their organizations' cultures: Hewlett and Packard exuded empathy and understanding of others; Fraser pushed decisions down to the people who have the most data and expertise; Rodgers's style jibed with Cypress's embattled, no-nonsense struggle against giant competitors; and Jobs's behaviors made clear to all that it was OK to dispense with the niceties when seeking beauty and perfection.

And contrary examples are plentiful too. Travis Kalanick at Uber is just one case. The company claimed to prioritize integrity and respect and to consider drivers as valued partners. But in 2017, Kalanick was filmed berating a driver (the film was taken by the driver's dashboard camera) who was worried about how Uber's new fare reductions would hurt his income.[16] Contradictions like this breed cynicism about the culture, and that cynicism, rather than the touted attributes, become the basis of a strong (but toxic) culture.

Making cultural misfits uncomfortable. For those who are not willing or able to learn and adapt to the culture, strong culture organizations consistently make things uncomfortable, sending signals about inappropriate behavior and encouraging misfits to leave. Although this sounds harsh, after being given chances to change, misfits need to be let go if they fail to reorient, as doing otherwise would dilute the culture for those who are embracing it. At the extreme, some companies, including Zappos and Netflix, terminate culture misfits regularly, and often early in their tenure.

Levers to Communicate Strong Culture

Training and communications. Training and messaging about the intended culture are essential to counteract the very real possibility that members misunderstand or are misled about priorities. The narrative around culture should be coherent and consistent. Communication and training tools need to be thoughtfully composed for mass usage—scaled up—in large and complex organizations.[17] Continual and repeated communication of the same message may be tedious to some, but is necessary to reach everyone in the organization. One option is to vary the modality of the message. For example, DaVita, a kidney dialysis company, trains and communicates extensively about its focus on patients and one another. This includes universally known rituals like call-and-respond cheers between the CEO and employees (although anyone in the company can state the calls), including:

"What is this company?"

"You!"

"Whose company is it?"

"Ours!"

"What can it be?"

"Special!"[18]

The Disney Institute runs cultural training programs, as do many companies. Some companies operate internal training units that they call "universities," such as Apple University and Hamburger University at McDonald's. In contrast to outsourcing training and development, this gives a company more control over what people learn about how to get things done in their organization.

Cultural messaging and transparency. Cultural messaging needs to be authentic, aligned, and affective to have an impact. "Authentic" means that the message does not seem generic, no matter how eloquent it is. "Aligned" means that it supports the strategy and is consequential. "Affective" messages tap into emotions and enhance intensity. Similarly, transparency creates an environment of openness and can build trust. It can include structures, policies, and decisions. Transparency allows members to understand organizational decisions and their rationales, even if they disagree.

Developed by founders Larry Page and Sergey Brin, Google's ten original cultural mission principles (see table 8.1) provide a good example.

Another example is Southwest Air's customer service message posted during the COVID pandemic. The message started by proclaiming: "Our commitment to the safety of our employees and customers is our top priority." What is particularly interesting about this sentence? Employees are listed first—and not even in alphabetical order! This very subtle ranking shows how thoughtful and deliberate Southwest is about its communications. Even when a message is targeted to customers, Southwest keeps its employees front and center.

Highlighting transparency, Ray Dalio's hedge fund Bridgewater videotapes and records just about every meeting to be

TABLE 8.1 GOOGLE CULTURE PRINCIPLES

1. Focus on the user and all else will follow.

2. It's best to do one thing really, really well.

3. Fast is better than slow.

4. Democracy on the web works.

5. You don't need to be at your desk to need an answer.

6. You can make money without doing evil.

7. There's always more information out there.

8. The need for information crosses all borders.

9. You can be serious without a suit.

10. Great just isn't good enough.

(Quoted from SEC documents.)

shared with employees. Other examples include Open Book management companies like the travel adventure company Backroads. Open Book is a movement that advocates internal financial transparency in private companies. Private, Berkeley-based Backroads is one of the largest travel adventure companies, hiring dozens of novice travel guides every year to lead affluent groups of travelers to various locations around the world. Prior to adopting Open Book, many guides had been suspicious of the salaries and finances of the office personnel and owner Tom Hale.

Manage emotional reactions. Listen to complaints and take appropriate action, including eliminating nonessential bureaucratic processes that annoy people and explaining the logic behind those that are required. Conversely, activities and events that generate goodwill toward the company and management should be promoted, provided that they are consistent with the culture.[19]

An example would be vacation scheduling at Netflix. Known internally as the "No Vacation Policy," the company actually allows unlimited vacation and leaves it up to the employee to decide how much vacation to take and when. Ironically, or perhaps because of this flexibility, which bolsters Netflix's core cultural value of responsibility for ones actions, Netflix employees generally take less vacation than employees at other companies.

Assess and survey the culture. Taking periodic and systematic snapshots of the culture enables leaders to figure out where change is needed most. Assessments can be qualitative or quantitative, but they need to be objective and comprehensive (capturing the full culture and a representative sample of the organization). An example can be found at Genentech, when Jennifer Cook ran the GIO division using the organizational culture profile (OCP). See chapters 2 and 5 for a discussion of measuring culture. Many other surveys are available for self-use or in conjunction with a consultant.

Levers to Structure an Organization for Strong Culture

The levers described in this section are systemic in nature. They address some aspect of organizational design or a specific routine.[20]

Broad job designs and wide unit groupings. Strong culture firms often work to reduce differences, in a formal sense, within an organization. For example, many people in the organization may hold the same job title and rank, a complementary idea to the flatter hierarchy discussed previously. This lever serves to reduce distinctions among members, reducing heterogeneity.

The autonomy afforded by broad job design also often ramps up commitment and intensity. Similarly, wide unit groupings mean that the average unit or department in the organization has broad scope; it implies that internal structural differentiation is kept low, preventing the buildup of local interests and reducing heterogeneity. Netflix is a good example, with its flat, decentralized organization and three basic divisions—functional, geographical, and products. An extreme example can be found at Zappos, which for a period embraced a design called, "holocracy," an extremely decentralized system with "no job titles, no managers, and no hierarchy."

Job rotations. Another structural lever involves using job rotations, a system where members routinely change jobs every so often. The changes are often planned and expected and can involve changing geographies, divisions, and duties. Job rotation gives members a wide set of perspectives about the organization and its work and serves to decrease behavioral variety by generating a broader view of how various units of the organization are tied together. Among many others, the consulting firms of Deloitte and Bain use systematic job rotation to sustain culture.

Broad decision-making. Structures with broad decision-making approaches get many people involved in decisions. Even if the impact is minimal (say, via a public forum seeking input), involvement helps them understand and implement decisions. Examples include Intel, with its "Disagree and commit" principle, which obligates employees to give their opinions about upcoming decisions but then help implement the decisions once they are made; and of course, Jennifer Cook's message "You choose it" to signify employee involvement in creating the GIO culture at Genentech (see chapter 2).

Levers to Manage Individuals' Performance for Strong Culture

Aligned compensation. To align compensation means that the endorsed cultural traits are consistent with respect to compensation practices and promotion chances. If the culture message is about high performance and accountability, then compensation needs to be aligned so high performers are well rewarded, or else people will disregard the message. Examples include Cypress Semiconductor and Netflix.

Rewarding culturally conforming behavior directly. This lever implies that members who behave according to the culture are rewarded regardless of how their actions affect revenue or performance. Conversely, people who behave in ways that oppose the prevailing norms are penalized. Cultures that encourage things like "taking risks without regard to failure" lack credibility if that behavior is not rewarded directly. At Goldman Sachs, bankers who fail to share information with colleagues and across the company are given negative performance evaluations.

Group-based compensation. Strong culture organizations often tie rewards to group outcomes, teams, divisions, or the entire company. Whether in pay or bonuses, group-based compensation creates a sense of solidarity and enhances agreement within the group (and can do the opposite for those outside the group); it also works against individual efforts that undermine group outcomes, even if they seem beneficial in isolation. An example would be partnerships, as at Deloitte and PWC, where partners share returns equally or based on some set rule such as seniority.

Nonmonetary rewards. These rewards include awards, honors, and acknowledgments. These rewards are often more symbolic than material but because they represent social acceptance and approval, they are often highly valued by employees. Examples can be found at DaVita and Zappos, where employees are publicly recognized for their contributions in sometimes extravagant ceremonies.

Table 8.2 offers an overview of the main levers for each general category. Obviously, some of these are impractical for certain types of organizations, and in other cases, they may not be effective. (Some are even potentially at odds with each other, depending on the implementation.) Leaders need to use good judgment in choosing and implementing these levers.

LEADING CULTURAL CHANGE WITH THE LEVERS

The managerial levers offer a comprehensive set of tools for leaders to use in developing and managing culture. How do you use these levers in practice? Do you need to use each one? Do they need to be sequenced in some way? To address these questions, imagine that you are in charge of culture change in a company whose future business success depends on its culture. What would you do?

Consider what Ulf Hahnemann did (see figure 8.6). He was the chief human resources officer (CHRO) of Maersk, the Danish shipping company founded in 1904. Along with the CEO at the time, Søren Skou and the executive leadership team at Maersk, Hahnemann faced exactly these questions a few years ago.[21] His culture change process effectively reshaped Maersk's

TABLE 8.2 MANAGERIAL LEVERS TO BUILD AND MAINTAIN STRONG CULTURE

Recruiting and Selecting People	Training and Developing People	Communicating to Others	Organizational Structuring	Managing Performance
Culturally selective hiring involving many in the organization	Intense early socialization at onboarding	Training and communications on the culture and norms	Broad job designs and organizational units	Compensation aligned with the strategy and culture
Recruit and support informal cultural leaders	Peer socialization and work guidance and support	Cultural messaging and transparency of information	Regular job rotation	Recognize and reward culturally conforming behavior
Align internal culture and connect it to the strategy and external brand	Leader modeling to set examples for others	Manage emotional reactions of self and others	Flatten hierarchical units and arrangements as much as possible	Group-based compensation rather individual performance–based
Intentionally long-term employment	Deal decisively with cultural misfits, regardless of performance	Survey and assess the organization's culture regularly, make findings public, and discuss them	Broad involvement in decision-making	Nonmonetary rewards such as awards and prizes

FIGURE 8.6 Ulf Hahnemann

culture and aligned it with its new strategic direction, which involved getting the company up to speed digitally. The success of his approach resulted in vastly improved customer feedback and substantial financial growth.

Look at some of the levers that Hahnemann and Maersk's executive team used:

1. *Transferred decision-making to customer-facing employees:* This initiative aimed to decentralize decision-making and empower employees who were closer to the customers. While it caused initial chaos and resistance, it was necessary for supporting customer-centricity. Regional divisions were given the option to establish regional customer experience councils, and those that did received three-day training in customer experience improvement methods. Empowering employees to make decisions locally led to increased positive risk-taking, enhanced responsiveness and customer service, and ultimately, improved customer satisfaction, a critical effort given that Maersk's net promoter score (NPS), a measure of customer satisfaction, was in the *negative* low 30s as Hahnemann and Skou began their work. The result was a significant increase in net promoter score (NPS) for regions that participated, highlighting the positive impact of local decision-making and customer centricity on customer satisfaction. In subsequent years, Maersk's NPS continued to rise, reaching 33 (out of 100) – over a 60 point rise from 2016 -- in 2022.

2. *Created companywide key performance indicators (KPIs) and a bonus program:* By implementing uniform KPIs and a bonus program for all employees, Hahnemann aligned everyone's goals with the company's strategy. This move shifted the focus from individual competition to collective success, encouraging cross-functional collaboration, customer focus, and a

better understanding of individual roles in achieving company objectives.

3. *Implemented leadership training:* Leadership training for senior leaders aimed to transform their styles to be more people-centered and aligned with the desired culture. This was critical for leaders to model the new behaviors.

4. *Founded the Maersk Leadership Academy:* The Maersk Leadership Academy provided leadership training for 9,000 people-managers. The academy offered programs for first-time and frontline leaders, senior leadership teams to implement the Integrator Strategy, and executives to rethink the role of technology. The programs emphasized the importance of establishing personal connections among participants before focusing on content, following Peter Block's principle of "Connection before content. Without relatedness, no work can occur."[22]

5. *Introduced transparent internal communication:* The move toward more open and honest communication helped employees understand the company's strategy better and fostered a less hierarchical relationship between leaders and employees across various organizational levels.

6. *Eliminated the dress code:* Dropping its strict dress code was symbolic of Maersk's willingness to let go of outdated cultural norms. While the policy faced resistance from senior executives, it promoted a more relaxed, inclusive, and open work environment, where new tech hires would feel more comfortable.

7. *Made visible commitments to diversity:* Joining the Copenhagen Pride Parade and creating rainbow containers demonstrated the company's newfound commitment to diversity and inclusion, signaling a progressive stance (see figure 8.7).

8. *Removed the testing regime for hiring:* By removing cognitive and personality assessments for job applicants, Hahnemann

aimed to shift the focus from IQ scores to broader skills and competencies. This move was aligned with fostering a more diverse and inclusive workforce.

9. *Installed ombudsmen:* Establishing ombudsmen provided employees with a formal channel to voice their grievances, promoting transparency, agency, engagement, empathy, and conflict resolution.

10. *Introduced Gallup Q12 as a leadership accountability tool:* The Gallup Q12 engagement survey served as a valuable tool for assessing and improving employee engagement, which was a crucial element of the company's cultural transformation process. It provided data-driven insights that supported Maersk's efforts to create a more engaged, motivated, and empowered workforce.

In our view, the magic in Hahnemann's approach—the reason why he was able to move an old, inertial company so quickly—is not the sequencing of levers but more about the sheer number of levers that he used. In other words, the culture change was comprehensive, coherent, and consistent.

FIGURE 8.7 Maersk rainbow container

Copyright © 2022 Maersk. Used by permission.

SUMMARY

Managing organizational culture is not an intellectual mystery—the levers used are based on well-understood social and psychological processes of influence, motivation, and commitment. Nonetheless, simply understanding social science does not imply that you can easily manage culture. The historical record shows just the opposite, in fact: companies and managers are attracted to leading through culture because of its potential power, but more often than not they fail to deliver fully on the promise, and if they do deliver, rarely is it sustained over long periods of time. These failures often emanate from a lack of consistency in managerial actions and organizational structures.

Managers could use more levers than they typically do. During discussions with managers across the years, we have routinely asked them whether their organization's culture needed to change and if so, what are the first things they would do to make it happen? Answers to these questions have remained the same across many different groups and years. Astoundingly, about 80 percent of managers state (often emphatically) that their organization's culture does need to change. And, eerily, the same three things always rise to the top of their to-do lists: (1) to get top management to agree on the needed behavioral norms and values, (2) to align compensation to reward the intended outcomes, and (3) to communicate to and train people in the agreed-upon features of the intended culture.

While these three levers are very powerful, they also represent just a few of the more comprehensive set available. Moreover, these levers might be considered somewhat unimaginative because they involve activities that are perhaps the most familiar and comfortable to managers. Each of these levers typically involves something under the direct control of a manager and entails activities that they often do on a regular basis: "Let's call a meeting and talk," or "Tweak the reward system," or "Send out communications," or "Ask people to enroll in a training program." Managers tend to stay in their comfort zones, so to speak, when contemplating cultural change efforts. On the other hand, employees become weary when hearing about a new cultural change effort that uses the same techniques that the last one did, only the words in the slide deck have changed, or so it seems at times.

The three top-cited levers might work in building and sustaining a strong culture, but they are not necessarily the strongest in terms of instigating behavioral change. Also, why would managers want to limit the powerful tools at their disposal? Effective cultural management requires a comprehensive and consistent approach across a full set of levers, many of which are structural or architectural in nature. The systemic effects from these design-based levers may not be attributable to any specific managerial action, but because of their consistency and comprehensiveness, their impact is often powerful and lasting. The essence of cultural management is to design a system that runs as expected, without direct control or intervention or relying on a specific leader. Managing indirectly by design is hard for many managers to do, as it involves giving up control; it is especially hard to do when an organization is in crisis or disarray. Likewise, full consistency is hard to achieve but is critical for cultural acceptance, as exceptions to the norms are quickly spotted and interpreted as meaningful, even if everything else points in a different direction.

MANAGERIAL TAKEAWAYS FROM THIS CHAPTER

- Managers have multiple levers at their disposal to develop and manage organizational culture. These levers are well studied and understood by social scientists.

- The managerial levers show up time and time again at strong culture organizations, although few organizations use all of them.

- Many managers think of only three managerial levers directly under their control when it comes to managing culture: (1) get agreement on cultural values and norms, (2) communicate the culture and offer associated training programs, and (3) align the organization's incentives with its strategy and culture. While effective and important, these three levers represent but a subset of the tools available for managing culture.

- To shape and develop culture, managers should use multiple managerial levers simultaneously because, for people to believe in the culture, they must be surrounded by it. They must believe that behaving consistently with the desired culture is valued and consequential. And the organization's design and systems need to synchronize with the culture and induce social behaviors that support it.

- The managerial levers for developing strong culture are multifaceted. They emerge from and need to correspond to the employment system in place, the incentive system, and the structural arrangements of the organization, which should all serve the business or market strategy.

9

CONCLUDING REMARKS

In this book, we have taken on five popular beliefs about culture, attempting to clarify their accuracy and relevance for executives and others. The premise behind this exercise holds that developing a scientifically informed perspective about organizational culture—its basis, how it works, and its consequences—will provide leaders with sound ideas about how to use their culture for strategic success and how to approach emerging cultural issues. We hope that our efforts here have provided you with a more informed view of these popular beliefs, using both classic and new examples and cases, as well as weaving in insights from academic research.

So where do things stand with these popular beliefs after our discussion? If pressed to render summary judgments on the validity of each popular belief, we would highlight the following observations, organized by book chapter and illustrating each one by further articulating Jennifer Cook's work at Genentech (discussed in chapter 2) and the impact it had on her organization, as a focal point.

From chapter 3, we see that culture can change, but leaders need to be deliberate and follow a plan to disrupt the inevitable inertia that can form in organizations. Relating this insight to Jennifer Cook's efforts, she and her leadership team were incredibly deliberate, from asking her senior leaders what they needed to systematically assessing the culture at Genentech Immunology and Ophthalmology (GIO), cascading the findings to various groups of employees, engaging teams directly in surfacing cultural initiatives, identifying ways of reinforcing these new practices, tracking progress on the new initiatives, walking the talk herself, and finally following up by continuing to measure and support cultural change. These efforts resulted in measurable cultural change at GIO—and impressive financial and strategic gains.

Chapter 4 demonstrates that culture can be created and strengthened by people and forces other than the CEO or senior leaders, but typically, CEOs and senior leaders can (and should) contribute significantly to cultivating and maintaining such cultures. Again, Jennifer Cook's approach is instructive. She began her culture change effort, as discussed in chapter 2, with her observations that GIO could not achieve its ambitious business goals without integrating its teams. She did take a risk in assessing the culture—what if the results had indicated that the desired culture was very discrepant from GIO's strategy? What if the gaps that people identified were simply untenable? But Cook knew that without making employees accountable for results, without her challenge of "You choose it," the change would not have been as swift or powerful.

Chapter 5 shows that culture is not just soft, it can have an enormous impact on financial performance and people's behavior, and it reflects regular patterns of interaction among members. Here, the comparison to Jennifer Cook's work was her awareness of the power of culture to influence people's behavior, realizing that no matter what she did or didn't do, a GIO culture would form. She would have a better chance of harnessing the power of culture by developing an authentic culture that helped GIO achieve business results. Her view was that "culture is made up of all the choices individuals within it make every day," so even seemingly small changes—starting meetings with patient stories and renaming the vials of medicine to count them as the number of patients that GIO helped—had an enormous impact on people's behavior and perceptions within the division and what really mattered. By using culture to energize and engage employees, GIO became one of the best divisions to work in at Genentech.

In chapter 6, we saw that lower levels of cultural fit, at least among a subset of members, can instigate innovation and culture change, although high person-culture fit offers distinct advantages to organizations and employees. Relating this insight to the Genentech case, Jennifer Cook was challenged by skeptics who "had seen this movie before" and criticized the early culture change efforts. Their challenges pushed her to directly acknowledge doubts and cynicism, knowing that the only way to convince people was to demonstrate the changes and their benefits. Note that a set of cultural levers pertained to making the more newly created GIO culture more accessible to outsiders, who perceived that GIO's values were congruent with them and, as a result, were selected into the division from other divisions within Genentech. Further, because of the comprehensive set of culture levers, including Jennifer Cook's discipline in "walking the talk" and serving as a model of the culture, it was very easy for people to see and understand the culture, enabling them to increase their own perceptual congruence.

From chapter 7, we learned that culture matters to the bottom line of a business, but its impact can be nuanced and indirect. In considering how this insight played out at Genentech, Cook's GIO division achieved its ambitious business goals, essentially tripling the business, four years earlier than its five-year strategic plan, in large part because of the culture change that Cook enacted. Do we know for sure that its culture drove these spectacular business results at GIO? We don't. But we do know from survey results eighteen months after the culture change efforts began that employees responded with a collectively strongly positive response to the division's culture: "The GIO culture helps to guide my business decisions." We also know that because of the focus on innovation and people in the GIO culture, people shared effective go-to market approaches more broadly, which surely contributed to the rapid increase in revenue at the division. The effect of culture was at least partially direct, and it surely operated through employees' actions.

Chapter 8 offers a comprehensive set of levers or tools for managing culture effectively. Applying these levers to the GIO context, Jennifer Cook viewed managing culture as an ongoing leadership priority. She continued to evaluate the connection between GIO's vision, strategy, and culture, collecting data and supporting the development of new relevant culture levers, including who were hired and how, how they were onboarded, how communications worked internally, how people were rewarded formally and informally, and how leaders behaved. Initiatives such as the Culture Advisory Board, job rotations, and the Development Center (to name only a few that employees suggested and GIO implemented) show the value of comprehensiveness. And, importantly, Cook did all the culture work in the context of the work that GIO was doing anyway—it was not an add-on. Managing culture was not an afterthought; it was central to strategy execution at GIO.

With the advent of artificial intelligence tools revealing the desire and possibility of a revolution in how, where, and when people work, as well as the inevitability of significantly more remote work in countless organizations, ensuring that your culture is contributing to organizational success rather than eroding it is essential. Our hope is that this book offers insights derived from social science about organizational culture and how it works. Armed with these insights, we know that you will be better prepared to develop, align, manage, and change your organization's culture. It will be strategically relevant, strong, and adaptive over time. When we are confronted with new challenges—harnessing artificial intelligence, digital transformation, diversity, equity, and inclusion (DEI), and new approaches to work—culture will assist and enable how we handle them.

We expect that you, like us, will draw the conclusion from reading this book that using culture is neither as hard nor as easy as it sometimes appears. The hardest part about using culture is often being deliberate, comprehensive, and consistent. Think about the level of deliberativeness that Southwest Airlines maintained to send a message directed at customers during the COVID-19 crisis that listed employees before customers. Such intentionality over long periods of time and across many, many messages, tasks, and even the smallest organizational details is what leads to culture-induced organizational success. Using culture is not rocket science, but it does require a kind of persistence that many leaders and organizations find elusive.

Finally, remember the three Cs of culture: develop a *coherent* narrative about the culture and its importance, manage it with a *comprehensive* set of levers, and behave *consistently* over time and in front of various stakeholders and others. We believe that, armed with these cultural insights, your people, groups, and organizations will be better able to accomplish collective goals more effectively.

NOTES

1. POPULAR BELIEFS ABOUT CULTURE

1. PwC, "Global Culture Survey 2021," 2021, https://www.pwc.com/gx/en/issues/upskilling/global-culture-survey-2021.html.
2. Deloitte, "Core Beliefs and Culture Chairman's Survey Findings," 2012, https://www2.deloitte.com/content/dam/Deloitte/global/Documents/About-Deloitte/gx-core-beliefs-and-culture.pdf.
3. Korn Ferry, "Build a Strong Organizational Culture That Reflects Your Vision and Goals," accessed July 28, 2025, https://www.kornferry.com/capabilities/organization-strategy/change-culture-comms/cultural-transformation.
4. Heidrick & Struggles, "Aligning Culture with the Bottom Line: How Companies Can Accelerate Progress," 2021, https://www.heidrick.com/en/insights/culture-shaping/aligning-culture-with-the-bottom-line-how-companies-can-accelerate-progress.
5. J. R. Graham, J. Grennan, C. R. Harvey, and S. Rajgopal, "Corporate Culture: Evidence from the Field," *Journal of Financial Economics* 146, no. 2 (2022): 552–593.
6. Glenn R. Carroll and Lara Yang, "Gender and Culture in Organizations: Perceptions, Beliefs and Experiences" (November 2022), Working Paper No. 4212, Stanford Graduate School of Business.
7. Gallup, "Organizational Culture Indicators," 2024, https://www.gallup.com/471521/indicator-organizational-culture.aspx.

8. E. H. Schein, "Defining Organizational Culture," in J. M. Shafritz & J. S. Ott, ed., *Classics of Organizational Theory* (2nd ed.) (Dorsey Press, 1987).

9. For other approaches to explaining how to manage organizational culture, see Boris Groysberg, Jeremiah Lee, Jesse Price, and J. Cheng, "The Leader's Guide to Corporate Culture," *Harvard Business Review* 96, no. 1 (2018): 44–52; and James Heskett, *Win from Within: Build Organizational Culture for Competitive Advantage* (Columbia University Press, 2022).

2. COOKING UP CULTURE

1. Charles O'Reilly and Jennifer Chatman, "Culture as Social Control: Corporations, Cults and Commitment," in B. Staw and L. Cummings, ed., *Research in Organizational Behavior*, vol. 18 (JAI, 1996), 157–200, https://psycnet.apa.org/record/1996-98665-004.

2. This chapter draws heavily from Jennifer Chatman, "Culture Change at Genentech: Accelerating Strategic and Financial Accomplishments," *California Management Review* 56, no. 2 (2014): 113–29, https://doi.org/10.1525/cmr.2014.56.2.113. See also related business cases. All the quotes and figures regarding Genentech are from these documents and are used by permission.

3. John R. Graham, Jillian Grennan, Campbell R. Harvey, and Shivaram Rajgopal, "Corporate Culture: Evidence from the Field," *Journal of Financial Economics* 146, no. 2 (2022): 552–93, https://doi.org/10.1016/j.jfineco.2022.07.008.

3. IS CULTURE INERT?

1. Gil Amelio and William L. Simon, *On the Firing Line: My 500 Days at Apple* (HarperPerennial, 1999), 48.

2. Amelio and Simon, *On the Firing Line*, 48.

3. Amelio and Simon, *On the Firing Line*, 48.

4. Amelio and Simon, *On the Firing Line*, 48.

5. Amelio and Simon, *On the Firing Line*, 49.

6. Amelio and Simon, *On the Firing Line*, 228, 271, 81.

7. Amelio and Simon, *On the Firing Line*, 278, 279.

8. Amelio and Simon, *On the Firing Line*, 278.

9. Andrew Binns, Charles A. O'Reilly, and Michael L. Tushman, *Corporate Explorer: How Corporations Can Beat Startups at the Innovation Game* (Wiley, 2022).

10. For all three of these processes, some of the greater control that leaders hold in their organizations emanates from the smaller size of the systems—few, if any, organizations have the size of even small nation-states.

11. Michael T. Hannan and John Freeman, "Structural Inertia and Organizational Change," *American Sociological Review* 49, no. 2 (1984): 149–64, https://doi.org/10.2307/2095567.

12. Hannan and Freeman, "Structural Inertia and Organizational Change," 156.

13. G. R. Carroll and M. T. Hannan, *The Demography of Corporations and Industries* (Princeton University Press, 2000).

14. Matthew Feinberg, Robb Willer, and Michael Schultz, "Gossip and Ostracism Promote Cooperation in Groups," *Psychological Science* 25, no. 3 (March 1, 2014): 656–64, https://doi.org/10.1177/0956797613510184; Jennifer A. Whitson et al., "How, When, and Why Recipients and Observers Reward Good Deeds and Punish Bad Deeds," *Organizational Behavior and Human Decision Processes* 128 (2015): 84–95, https://doi.org/10.1016/j.obhdp.2015.03.006.

15. Jack A. Goncalo, "Past Success and Convergent Thinking in Groups: The Role of Group-Focused Attributions," *European Journal of Social Psychology, 34*, no. 4 (2004), 385–95. https://doi.org/10.1002/ejsp.203.

16. Much of the narrative about cultural change at Ford draws from the excellent book by Bryce G. Hoffman, *American Icon: Alan Mulally and the Fight to Save Ford Motor Company* (Crown Business, 2012).

17. Hoffman, *American Icon*, 49.

18. Hoffman, *American Icon*, 72, 93.

19. Hoffman, *American Icon*, 88.

20. Mullay, cited in Hoffman, *American Icon*, 98.

21. Hoffman, *American Icon*, 121.

22. Mullay, cited in Hoffman, *American Icon*, 122.

23. Hoffman, *American Icon*, 124.

24. Theo Leggett, "How Ford's Alan Mulally Turned Around Its Fortunes," *BBC News*, July 1, 2014, https://www.bbc.com/news/business-28087325.

25. This quote is from Dan Pontefract, "Former CEO Alan Mulally Is Who CEOs Need to Be Today," *Forbes*, July 11, 2022, https://www .forbes.com/sites/danpontefract/2022/07/11/former-ceo-alan-mulally -is-who-ceos-need-to-be-today/?sh=3916e6b66490. The specifics of the turnaround are fascinating and could not have been done without the cultural change that Mulally started and drove at the BPR meetings. But this longer story is also about strategy and execution. Continued modeling and enforcement aside, the basics of the Mulally cultural initiative had been set by the actions described. For readers interested in the larger transformation, we suggest Hoffman's *American Icon*.

26. See Joel M. Podolny and Morten T. Hansen, "How Apple Is Organized for Innovation," *Harvard Business Review*, November–December 2020, https://hbr.org/2020/11/how-apple-is-organized-for-innovation. They attribute the design to Steve Jobs, but Amelio and Simon's book makes clear that they had been working on it earlier.

27. This section was excerpted from the full case described in Jennifer A. Chatman, "Roche Pakistan (A) and (B): Turning Around a Crisis Through Cultural Transformation," *Berkeley Haas Case Series*, October 2017.

For advice on assimilating to national cultures, see, for example, Erin Meyer, *The Culture Map: Breaking Through the Invisible Boundaries of Global Business* (Public Affairs, 2014), https://erinmeyer.com/books/the -culture-map/; and Tsedal Neeley, "How to Successfully Work Across Countries, Languages, and Cultures," *Harvard Business Review*, August 29, 2017, https://hbr.org/2017/08/how-to-successfully-work-across -countries-languages-and-cultures.

4. CULTURE FROM THE TOP DOWN?

1. Matt Schudel, "Herb Kelleher, Visionary Co-founder and Chief Executive of Southwest Airlines, Dies at 87," *The Washington Post*, January 6, 2019, https://www.washingtonpost.com/local/obituaries/herb-kelleher -visionary-co-founder-and-chief-executive-of-southwest-airlines-dies -at-87/2019/01/04/7d3160e2-1031-11e9-84fc-d58c33d6c8c7_story.html.

2. Karen Schwartz, "Tangy Touch in the Sky," *SouthCoastToday*, November 16, 1995, https://www.southcoasttoday.com/story/business/1996/11/17 /tangy-touch-in-sky/50619361007/.

3. Scott A. Scanlon, Dale M. Zupsansky, and Stephen Sawicki, "The Importance of Culture on Today's Businesses," *Hunt Scanlon Media*, March 16, 2023, https://huntscanlon.com/the-importance-of-culture-on -todays-businesses/.

4. Kevin and Jackie Freiberg, "20 Reasons Why Herb Kelleher Was One of the Most Beloved Leaders of Our Time," *Forbes*, January 4, 2019, https:// www.forbes.com/sites/kevinandjackiefreiberg/2019/01/04/20-reasons -why-herb-kelleher-was-one-of-the-most-beloved-leaders-of-our-time/.

5. See chapter 6 for more information on strategy-culture alignment and its impact on performance. It is worth noting that after much deliberation and pressure from investors, Southwest announced in 2024 that it was going to change some of its basic operations, moving to fixed seating and charging for certain amenities. It remains to be seen whether these changes will affect the airline's ability to conduct fast turnarounds (Southwest claims that it will not) or its culture. See Alison Sider, "Southwest Airlines Is Ditching Open Seating on Flights," *The Wall Street Journal*, July 25, 2024, https://www.wsj.com/business/airlines /southwest-airlines-is-ditching-open-seating-on-flights-25bb30fd.

6. Kevin and Jackie Freiberg, "20 Reasons Why Herb Kelleher Was One of the Most Beloved Leaders of Our Time."

7. "The Excellence Files: Southwest Airlines Segment," Enterprise Media, 2002 (video), Accessed October 8, 2025, https://www.trainingrightnow .com/course/ENT422/the-excellence-files---southwest-airlines.

8. Jerry Useem, "The Long-Forgotten Flight That Sent Boeing Off Course: A Company Once Driven by Engineers Became Driven by Finance," *The Atlantic*, November 20, 2019, https://www.theatlantic.com/ideas /archive/2019/11/how-boeing-lost-its-bearings/602188/; James Surowiecki, "What's Gone Wrong at Boeing?" *The Atlantic*, January 15, 2024; Jerry Useem, "Boeing and the Dark Age of American Manufacturing," *The Atlantic*, April 20, 2024, https://www.theatlantic.com/ideas /archive/2024/04/boeing-corporate-america-manufacturing/678137/.

9. Eric Brothers, "Boeing to Acquire Spirit AeroSystems in $8.3B Deal," *Aerospace*, July 2, 2024, https://www.aerospacemanufacturinganddesign .com/news/boeing-acquire-spirit-aerosystems-8-3b-deal/; Clare Bushey, "Boeing Chief Outlines Overhaul of Plane Maker to Halt 'Serious Performance Lapses,'" *Financial Times*, October 23, 2024, https://www .ft.com/content/f3eebcfc-f0af-4d43-8305-04c54f199ef7.

10. Richard Taylor, "The Body Shop Brand Can Be Revived, But It Can't Coast on Goodwill Forever," *The Drum*, February 13, 2024. https://www.thedrum.com/opinion/2024/02/13/the-body-shop-brand-can-be-revived-it-cant-coast-goodwill-forever.

11. Peter Carlin, "Pure Profit—For Small Companies That Stress Social Values as Much as the Bottom Line, Growing Up Hasn't Been an Easy Task. Just Ask Ben & Jerry's, Patagonia and Starbucks," *Los Angeles Times*, February 5, 1995, https://www.latimes.com/archives/la-xpm-1995-02-05-tm-28412-story.html.

12. Christopher F. Rufo, "Why Boeing Killed DEI," *City Journal*, November 12, 2024, https://www.city-journal.org/article/why-boeing-killed-dei.

13. For example, see CFI Team, "Tone at the Top," Corporate Finance Institute (CFI), accessed April 23, 2024, https://corporatefinanceinstitute.com/resources/management/tone-at-the-top/.

14. Jeffrey Pfeffer, *Power in Organizations* (Ballinger, 1981).

15. Wenzhi Ding et al., "Corporate Immunity to the COVID-19 Pandemic," *Journal of Financial Economics* 141, no. 2 (August 2021): 802–30, https://doi.org/10.1016/j.jfineco.2021.03.005.

16. Edgar H. Schein, *Organizational Culture and Leadership*, 5th ed. (Wiley, 2017), 237.

17. Charles A. O'Reilly III, David F. Caldwell, Jennifer A. Chatman, and Bernadette Doerr, "The Promise and Problems of Organizational Culture: CEO Personality, Culture, and Firm Performance," *Group & Organization Management* 39, no. 6 (2014): 595–625, https://doi.org/10.1177/1059601114550713.

18. Milton Rokeach, *The Nature of Human Values* (Free, 1973), 5.

19. Charles A. O'Reilly III, Jennifer A. Chatman, and Bernadette Doerr, "When 'Me' Trumps 'We': Narcissistic Leaders and the Cultures They Create," *Academy of Management Discoveries* 7, no. 3 (September 2021): 419–50, https://doi.org/10.5465/amd.2019.0163.

20. Diana C. Kyser, "Through the Looking Glass: Company Culture as a Reflection of Founder Personality in Entrepreneurial Organizations," dissertation submitted to Temple University Graduate Board, May 2017; Paul X. McCarthy, Xian Gong, Fabian Braesemann, Fabian Stephany, Marian-Andrei Rizoiu, and Margaret L. Kern, "The Impact

of Founder Personalities on Startup Success," *Scientific Reports*, *13*(1), (2023) 17200, https://www.nature.com/articles/s41598-023-41980-y.

21. Monica Langley and Marc Benioff, "How Salesforce Closed the Pay Gap Between Men and Women," *Wired*, October 15, 2019, https://www.wired.com/story/how-salesforce-closed-pay-gap-between-men -women/; Marc R. Benioff and Monica Langley, *Trailblazer: The Power of Business as the Greatest Platform for Change* (Currency, 2019).

22. Langley and Benioff, "How Salesforce Closed the Pay Gap Between Men and Women."

23. Advanced Micro Devices (AMD), "Corporate Responsibility at AMD," accessed April 23, 2024, https://www.amd.com/en/corporate/corporate -responsibility.html.

24. Langley and Benioff, "How Salesforce Closed the Pay Gap Between Men and Women."

25. Langley and Benioff, "How Salesforce Closed the Pay Gap Between Men and Women."

26. Langley and Benioff, "How Salesforce Closed the Pay Gap Between Men and Women."

27. Adam Bryant, "Lisa Su on the Art of Setting Ambitious Goals," *New York Times*, May 19, 2017.

28. Bryant, "Lisa Su on the Art of Setting Ambitious Goals."

29. O'Reilly et al., "When 'Me' Trumps 'We'."

30. Ulrike Malmendier and Geoffrey Tate, "Behavioral CEOs: The Role of Managerial Overconfidence," *Journal of Economic Perspectives* 29, no. 4 (November 2015): 37–60, https://doi.org/10.1257/jep.29.4.37; Charles A. O'Reilly III, Bernadette Doerr, and Jennifer A. Chatman, "'See You in Court': How CEO Narcissism Increases Firms' Vulnerability to Lawsuits," *Leadership Quarterly* 29, no. 3 (June 1, 2018): 365–78, https://doi.org /10.1016/j.leaqua.2017.08.001.

31. O'Reilly et al., "When 'Me' Trumps 'We'."

32. Much of the following discussion of lululemon is drawn from the case by Michael Tushman, Ruth Page, and Tom Ryder, "Leadership, Culture, and Transition at lululemon," *Harvard Business School Multimedia/ Video Case 410–705*, December 2010, https://www.hbs.edu/faculty /Pages/item.aspx?num=39817#:~:text=Citation,410%2D705%2C %20December%202010.

33. Marielle Leon, "How ululemon's CEO, Calvin McDonald, Has Navigated the Pandemic to Date," *Glassdoor for Employers*, October 6, 2020,https://www.glassdoor.com/employers/blog/lululemon-ceo-navigated -pandemic/.

34. Nicholas Carlson, "WeWork Cofounders Explained the Future of the Office at IGNITION 2016," *Business Insider India*, April 3, 2017, https:// www.businessinsider.in/wework-cofounders-explained-the-future-of -the-office-at-ignition-2016/articleshow/57993401.cms.

35. Samantha Sharf, "3 Startup Lessons from WeWork Founder Adam Neumann," *Forbes*, October 2, 2017, https://www.businessinsider.in /wework-cofounders-explained-the-future-of-the-office-at-ignition -2016/articleshow/57993401.cms.

36. Prarthana Prakash, "Elon Musk Sends Middle-of-the-Night Demand-ing 'Extremely Hardcore' Work Culture at Twitter with 'Long Hours at High Intensity'," *Fortune*, November 16, 2022, https://fortune.com /2022/11/16/elon-musk-email-twitter-extremely-hardcore-long-hours -high-intensity/.

37. Charles A. O'Reilly III, Bernadette Doerr, David F. Caldwell, and Jennifer A. Chatman, "Narcissistic CEOs and Executive Compen-sation," *Leadership Quarterly* 25, no. 2 (April 1, 2014): 218–31, https:// doi.org/10.1016/j.leaqua.2013.08.002; Charles A. O'Reilly III and Ber-nadette Doerr, "Conceit and Deceit: Lying, Cheating, and Stealing Among Grandiose Narcissists," *Personality and Individual Differences* 154 (February 1, 2020): 109627, https://doi.org/10.1016/j.paid.2019.109627.

38. O'Reilly et al., "Narcissistic CEOs and Executive Compensation"; Charles A. O'Reilly III and Jennifer A. Chatman, "Transformational Leader or Narcissist? How Grandiose Narcissists Can Create and Destroy Organizations and Institutions," *California Management Review* 62, no. 3 (May 1, 2020): 1–23, https://doi.org/10.1177/0008125620914989.

39. O'Reilly and Doerr, "Conceit and Deceit."

40. O'Reilly and Chatman, "Transformational Leader or Narcissist?": 4.

41. Dacher Keltner, Deborah H. Gruenfeld, and Cameron Anderson, "Power, Approach, and Inhibition," *Psychological Review* 110, no. 2 (2003): 265, https://psycnet.apa.org/fulltext/2003-00307-004.html.

42. Richard Lu, Jennifer A. Chatman, Amir Goldberg, and Sameer Sriv-astava, "Two-Sided Cultural Fit: The Differing Behavioral Conse-quences of Cultural Congruence Based on Values Versus Perceptions,"

Organization Science 35, no. 1 (April 2023): 71–91, https://doi.org/10.1287/orsc.2023.1659.

43. Alessandro Duranti, "Language as Culture in U.S. Anthropology: Three Paradigms," *Current Anthropology* 44, no. 3 (2003): 323–47, https://doi.org/10.1086/368118; Edward P. Lazear, "Culture and Language," *Journal of Political Economy* 107, no. S6 (1999): S95–S126, https://doi.org/10.1086/250105.

44. John R. Graham, Jillian Grennan, Campbell R. Harvey, and Shivaram Rajgopal, "Corporate Culture: Evidence from the Field," *Journal of Financial Economics* 146, no. 2 (2022): 552–93, https://doi.org/10.1016/j.jfineco.2022.07.008.

45. Valve, "Boss-Free Since 1996." https://www.valvesoftware.com/en/people#:~:text=We%20believe%20that%20the%20best,Valve%20who%20do%20just%20that.

46. Alicia Boisnier and Jennifer A. Chatman, "The Role of Subcultures in Agile Organizations," in *Leading and Managing People in the Dynamic Organization*, ed. Randall S. Peterson and Elizabeth A. Mannix (Lawrence Erlbaum Associates Publishers, 2003), 87–112.

47. Michael L. Tushman and Charles A. O'Reilly III, "Ambidextrous Organizations: Managing Evolutionary and Revolutionary Change," *California Management Review* 38, no. 4 (July 1, 1996): 8–29, https://doi.org/10.2307/41165852; Michael Tushman and Wendy Smith, "Organizational Technology: Technological Change, Ambidextrous Organizations and Organizational Evolution," in *Blackwell Companion to Organizations*, ed. J. A. C. Baum (Blackwell, 2002), 386–414.

48. Derek N. Brown et al., "How Have Organizational Cultures Shifted During the COVID-19 Pandemic . . . and What Might Need to Change Back?" *California Management Review* (2021), https://cmr.berkeley.edu/assets/documents/pdf/2021-07-how-have-organizational-cultures-shifted.pdf.

49. Jennifer A. Chatman, Yixi Chen, Virginia Choi, and Michele Gelfand, "Organizational Culture Moderates the Relationship Between Environmental Volatility and Firm Performance: The Case of the COVID-19 Pandemic," forthcoming in *Academy of Management Discoveries* (2026).

50. Jennifer Chatman, Sameer Srivastava, and David Rocklin, "How Lyft's Strategy Informed Their Return to Work Approach," University of California, Berkeley Case Series, 2024.

51. Jillian Grennan, "A Corporate Culture Channel: How Increased Share-holder Governance Reduces Firm Value," 2019, SSRN, *2345384*. https:// papers.ssrn.com/sol3/papers.cfm?abstract_id=2345384.

5. CULTURE IS SOFT?

1. Steven L. Blue is quoted in Rieva Lesonsky, "It's National Mom & Pop Business Owners Day, Entrepreneurs Are Optimistic, Why Culture Is a 4-Letter Word and Other Things Entrepreneurs Need to Know,"*smallbizdaily*, March 29, 2017, https://www.smallbizdaily.com /national-mom-pop-business-owners-day-entrepreneurs-optimistic -culture-4-letter-word-things-entrepreneurs-need-know/. See also Steven L. Blue,*American Manufacturing 2.0: What Went Wrong and How to Make It Right*" (Productivity, 2016).

2. Bronislaw Malinowski, *Argonauts of the Western Pacific* (Routledge, 1922), 25.

3. Clifford Geertz, *Local Knowledge: Further Essays in Interpretive Anthropology* (Basic Books, 1983), 86.

4. Margaret Mead, *Coming of Age in Samoa: A Psychological Study of Primitive Youth for Western Civilization* (William Morrow, 1928).

5. Edgar H. Schein, *Organizational Culture and Leadership*, 5th ed. (Wiley, 2017).

6. Jennifer A. Chatman, "Improving Interactional Organizational Research: A Model of Person-Organization Fit," *Academy of Management Review* 14, no. 3 (July 1989): 333–49, https://doi.org/10.5465/amr.1989.4279063; Jennifer A. Chatman and Charles A. O'Reilly, "Paradigm Lost: Reinvigorating the Study of Organizational Culture," *Research in Organizational Behavior* 36 (January 1, 2016): 199–224, https://doi.org/10.1016/j .riob.2016.11.004.

7. Tobias Jung et al., "Instruments for Exploring Organizational Culture: A Review of the Literature," *Public Administration Review* 69, no. 6 (2009): 1087–96, https://onlinelibrary.wiley.com/doi/full/10.1111/j.1540 -6210.2009.02066.x; Neal M. Ashkanasy, Lyndelle E. Broadfoot, and Sarah Falkus, "Questionnaire Measures of Organizational Culture," in *Handbook of Organizational Culture and Climate*, ed. Neal M. Ashkanasy, Celeste P. M. Wilderom, and Mark F. Peterson (SAGE, 2000), 131–45.

8. Jennifer A. Chatman and Charles A. O'Reilly, "Paradigm Lost: Reinvigorating the Study of Organizational Culture," *Research in Organizational Behavior* 36 (January 1, 2016): 199–224, https://doi.org/10.1016/j.riob.2016.11.004.

9. Edgar H. Schein, *Organizational Culture and Leadership* (Jossey-Bass Publishers, 1985); William Labov, "The Intersection of Sex and Social Class in the Course of Linguistic Change," *Language Variation and Change* 2, no. 2 (July 1990): 205–54, https://doi.org/10.1017/S0954394500000338.

10. Sameer B. Srivastava et al., "Enculturation Trajectories and Individual Attainment: An Interactional Language Use Model of Cultural Dynamics in Organizations," University of California, Berkeley: Institute for Research on Labor and Employment (2016), eScholarship, https://escholarship.org/uc/item/8bq4q6d5; Amir Goldberg et al., "Fitting In or Standing Out? The Tradeoffs of Structural and Cultural Embeddedness," *American Sociological Review* 81, no. 6 (December 1, 2016): 1190–222, https://doi.org/10.1177/0003122416671873.

11. Richard Lu et al., "Two-Sided Cultural Fit: The Differing Behavioral Consequences of Cultural Congruence Based on Values Versus Perceptions," *Organization Science* 35, no. 1 (April 2023): 71–91, https://doi.org/10.1287/orsc.2023.1659.

12. Susan T. Fiske et al., "A Model of (Often Mixed) Stereotype Content: Competence and Warmth Respectively Follow from Perceived Status and Competition," *Journal of Personality and Social Psychology* 82, no. 6 (2002): 878–902, https://doi.org/10.1037/0022-3514.82.6.878.

13. Jennifer A. Chatman et al., "Parsing Organizational Culture: How the Norm for Adaptability Influences the Relationship Between Culture Consensus and Financial Performance in High-Technology Firms," *Journal of Organizational Behavior* 35, no. 6 (April 11, 2014): 785–808, https://doi.org/10.1002/job.1928.

14. Schein, *Organizational Culture and Leadership*.

15. Yair Berson, Shaul Oreg, and Taly Dvir, "CEO Values, Organizational Culture and Firm Outcomes," *Journal of Organizational Behavior* 29, no. 5 (2008): 615–33, https://doi.org/10.1002/job.499; Suellen J. Hogan and Leonard V. Coote, "Organizational Culture, Innovation, and Performance: A Test of Schein's Model," *Journal of Business Research* 67, no. 8 (August 1, 2014): 1609–21, https://doi.org/10.1016/j.jbusres.2013.09.007.

16. Chad A. Hartnell, Amy Yi Ou, and Angelo Kinicki, "Organizational Culture and Organizational Effectiveness: A Meta-analytic Investigation of the Competing Values Framework's Theoretical Suppositions," *Journal of Applied Psychology* 96, no. 4 (2011): 677–94, https://doi .org/10.1037/a0021987; Amy L. Kristof-Brown, Ryan D. Zimmerman, and Erin C. Johnson, "Consequences of Individuals' Fit at Work: A Meta-analysis of Person–Job, Person–Organization, Person–Group, and Person–Supervisor Fit," *Personnel Psychology* 58, no. 2 (2005): 281–342, https://doi.org/10.1111/j.1744-6570.2005.00672.x.

17. Kristen Castillo, "Inside Patagonia's Corporate Culture That Prioritizes Flexibility and Work-Life Balance," MediaPlanet, accessed August 11, 2025, https://www.futureofbusinessandtech.com/employee-wellbeing /inside-patagonias-corporate-culture-that-prioritizes-flexibility-and -work-life-balance/.

18. Erving Goffman, *Asylums: Essays on the Social Situation of Mental Patients and Other Inmates* (Doubleday, 1990), 12.

19. Netflix has recently revised its culture to emphasize "people over process." One specific aspect of this update attempts to soften the keeper test to make it less "scary." See Nicole Sperling, "Responsibility over Freedom: How Netflix's Culture Has Changed," *The New York Times*, June 24, 2024.

20. Sarah Berman, *Don't Call It a Cult: The Shocking Story of Keith Raniere and the Women of NXIVM* (Steerforth, 2021).

21. Richard Ofshe, "The Social Development of the Synanon Cult: The Managerial Strategy of Organizational Transformation," *Sociological Analysis* 41, no. 2 (1980): 119, https://doi.org/10.2307/3709903.

22. Berman, *Don't Call It a Cult.*

23. Jeffrey Dastin, "At Taser Maker Axon, Ex-staff Say Loyalty Meant Being Tased, Tattooed," Reuters, August 30, 2023, https://www.reuters .com/investigates/special-report/axon-taser-exposures/.

24. Lolita Baldor, "Navy SEALs Training Plagued by Pervasive Problems, According to Investigation After Death of Sailor," *AP News*, May 25, 2023, "Washington News" section, https://apnews.com/article/navy-seal -death-steroids-medical-failures-e49b76593ca884cc521d48a9b0b4a8ef.

25. Charles O'Reilly and Jennifer Chatman, "Culture as Social Control: Corporations, Cults and Commitment," in B. Staw and L. Cummings, ed.,

Research in Organizational Behavior, vol. 18 (JAI, 1996), 164, https://psycnet.apa.org/record/1996-98665-004.

26. O'Reilly and Chatman, "Culture as Social Control," 165.

6. ALIGNED PEOPLE DO BEST?

1. James B. Stewart, *DisneyWar: Intrigue, Treachery and Deceit in the Magic Kingdom* (Simon & Schuster, 2005).

2. Stewart, *DisneyWar*.

3. Ovitz's severance package amounted to over $100 million—by some estimates, it was as much as $140 million.

4. Stewart, *DisneyWar*, 225.

5. Charles A. O'Reilly, Xubo Cao, and Don Sull, "CEO Personality: The Cornerstone of Organizational Culture?" *Academy of Management Proceedings* 2022, no. 1 (August 2022), https://doi.org/10.5465/ambpp .2022.12573abstract.

6. Maureen Dowd, "The Slow-Burning Success of Disney's Bob Iger," *The New York Times*, September 22, 2019, https://www.nytimes.com /2019/09/22/style/disney-bob-iger-book.html.

7. Charles A. O'Reilly III, Jennifer Chatman, and David F. Caldwell, "People and Organizational Culture: A Profile Comparison Approach to Assessing Person-Organization Fit," *Academy of Management Journal* 34, no. 3 (September 1991): 487–516, https://doi.org/10.5465/256404.

8. For a related distinction, see Özgecan Koçak and Phanish Puranam. "Decoding Culture: Tools for Behavioral Strategists," *Strategy Science* 9, no. 1 (2024): 18–37, https://pubsonline.informs.org/doi/10.1287/stsc.2022 .0008.

9. Ann Swidler, "Culture in Action: Symbols and Strategies," *American Sociological Review* 51, no. 2 (April 1986): 273, https://doi.org/10.2307 /2095521.

10. Anat Rafaeli and Robert I. Sutton, "Busy Stores and Demanding Customers: How Do They Affect the Display of Positive Emotion?" *Academy of Management Journal* 33, no. 3 (September 1990): 623–37, https://doi .org/10.5465/256584; Lauren A. Rivera, "Hiring as Cultural Matching," *American Sociological Review* 77, no. 6 (November 28, 2012): 999–1022, https://doi.org/10.1177/0003122412463213; Edward P. Lazear, "Culture

and Language," *Journal of Political Economy* 107, no. S6 (December 1999): S95–S126, https://doi.org/https://doi.org/10.1086/250105.

11. O'Reilly et al., "People and Organizational Culture."

12. Richard Lu, Jennifer A. Chatman, Amir Goldberg, and Sameer Srivastava, "Two-Sided Cultural Fit: The Differing Behavioral Consequences of Cultural Congruence Based on Values Versus Perceptions," *Organization Science* 35, no. 1 (April 2023): 71–91, https://doi.org/10.1287/orsc.2023.1659.

13. O'Reilly et al., "People and Organizational Culture"; Amir Goldberg, Sameer B. Srivastava, V. Govind Manian, William Monroe, and Christopher Potts, "Fitting In or Standing Out? The Tradeoffs of Structural and Cultural Embeddedness," *American Sociological Review* 81, no. 6 (November 2016): 1190–1222, https://doi.org/10.1177/0003122416671873; Lu et al., "Two-Sided Cultural Fit."

14. Jennifer A. Chatman, "Improving Interactional Organizational Research: A Model of Person-Organization Fit," *Academy of Management Review* 14, no. 3 (July 1989): 333–49, https://doi.org/10.5465/amr.1989.4279063.

15. O'Reilly et al., "People and Organizational Culture."

16. Jennifer A. Chatman and Francis J. Flynn, "The Influence of Demographic Heterogeneity on the Emergence and Consequences of Cooperative Norms in Work Teams," *Academy of Management Journal* 44, no. 5 (October 2001): 956–74, https://doi.org/10.5465/3069440.

17. Jesper B. Sørensen, "The Strength of Corporate Culture and the Reliability of Firm Performance," *Administrative Science Quarterly* 47, no. 1 (March 2002), 70–91, https://doi.org/10.2307/3094891.

18. Jennifer A. Chatman, "Maersk: Driving Culture Change at a Century-Old Company to Achieve Measurable Results," *Berkeley Haas Case Series*, April 1, 2024, https://cases.haas.berkeley.edu/2024/04/maersk/.

19. Richard K. Lyons, Jennifer A. Chatman, and Caneel K. Joyce, "Innovation in Services: Corporate Culture and Investment Banking," *California Management Review* 50, no. 1 (October 2007): 174–91, https://doi.org/10.2307/41166422.

20. N. Derek Brown et al., "How Have Organizational Cultures Shifted During the COVID-19 Pandemic," *California Management Review*, July 31, 2021, https://cmr.berkeley.edu/2021/07/how-have-organizational-cultures-shifted/.

21. Lauren A. Rivera, "Hiring as Cultural Matching," *American Sociological Review* 77, no. 6 (November 2012): 999–1022, https://doi.org/10.1177/0003122412463213.

22. Alexandra Stevenson and Matthew Goldstein, "Bridgewater's Ray Dalio Spreads His Gospel of 'Radical Transparency'," *The New York Times*, September 8, 2017, https://www.nytimes.com/2017/09/08/business/dealbook/bridgewaters-ray-dalio-spreads-his-gospel-of-radical-transparency.html.

23. Jennifer A. Chatman and Francis J. Flynn, "The Influence of Demographic Heterogeneity on the Emergence and Consequences of Cooperative Norms in Work Teams," *Academy of Management Journal* 44, no. 5 (October 2001): 956–74, https://doi.org/10.5465/3069440; Susan G. Cohen and Diane E. Bailey, "What Makes Teams Work: Group Effectiveness Research from the Shop Floor to the Executive Suite," *Journal of Management* 23, no. 3 (June 1997): 239–290, https://doi.org/10.1177/014920639702300303.

24. Bernadette Eichner, "Zappos—Hiring for Culture and the Bizarre Things They Do," *Zippia*, May 11, 2023, https://www.zippia.com/employer/zappos-hiring-for-culture-and-the-bizarre-things-they-do/.

25. Jeffrey Dastin, "At Taser Maker Axon, Ex-staffers Say Loyalty Meant Being Tased or Tattooed," *Reuters*, August 30, 2023, https://www.reuters.com/investigates/special-report/axon-taser-exposures/.

26. Stevenson and Goldstein, "Bridgewater's Ray Dalio Spreads His Gospel of 'Radical Transparency'".

27. Netflix has recently revised its culture and now aims to soften its keeper test to make it less "scary." See Nicole Sperling," Responsibility over Freedom: How Netflix's Culture Has Changed," *The New York Times*, June 24, 2024, https://www.nytimes.com/2024/06/24/business/media/netflix-corporate-culture.html.

28. Herminia Ibarra and Aneeta Rattan, "Microsoft: Instilling a Growth Mindset," *London Business School Review* 29, no. 3 (October 2018): 50–53, https://doi.org/10.1111/2057-1615.12262.

29. Herminia Ibarra, "Take a Wrecking Ball to Your Company's Iconic Practices," *MIT Sloan Management Review* 61, no. 1 (October 2019): 1–5, https://sloanreview.mit.edu/article/take-a-wrecking-ball-to-your-companys-iconic-practices/.

30. Chatman, "Maersk: Driving Culture Change at a Century-Old Company."

31. Patty McCord, "Stop Hiring for Culture Fit," *Harvard Business Review*, December 21, 2017, https://hbr.org/2018/01/how-to-hire.

32. "Katrina Lake: Hiring People Who Fit Your Company Culture Isn't Working for Diversity | Code 2018," YouTube, May 30, 2018, https://www.youtube.com/watch?v=dx40NdSz5Pc.

33. Lauren Rivera, "Hiring as Cultural Matching: The Case of Elite Professional Service Firms," *American Sociological Review* (December 2012): 77(6): 999–1022, https://doi.org/10.3389/fpsyt.2023.1243657.

34. Charles A. O'Reilly III, Katherine Y. Williams, and Sigal Barsade, "The Impact of Relational Demography on Teamwork: When Differences Make a Difference," *Academy of Management Proceedings* 1999, no. 1 (August 1999), https://doi.org/10.5465/apbpp.1999.27622078.

35. S. H. Kim, L. C. Vincent, and J. A. Goncalo, "Outside Advantage: Can Social Rejection Fuel Creative Thought?" *Journal of Experimental Psychology: General*, 142, no. 3 (2013): 605–11, https://doi.org/10.1037/a0029728.

36. Jack A. Goncalo and Michelle M. Duguid, "Follow the Crowd in a New Direction: When Conformity Pressure Facilitates Group Creativity (and When It Does Not)," *Organizational Behavior and Human Decision Processes* 118, no. 1 (May 2012): 14–23, https://doi.org/10.1016/j.obhdp.2011.12.004.

37. Jennifer A. Chatman et al., "Blurred Lines: How the Collectivism Norm Operates Through Perceived Group Diversity to Boost or Harm Group Performance in Himalayan Mountain Climbing," *Organization Science* 30, no. 2 (2019): 235–59, https://doi.org/10.1287/orsc.2018.1268.

38. Carmen Nobel, "Introverts: The Best Leaders for Proactive Employees," *Harvard Business School Working Knowledge*, October 4, 2010, https://hbswk.hbs.edu/item/introverts-the-best-leaders-for-proactive-employees; Elizabeth Mannix and Margaret A. Neale, "What Differences Make a Difference?" *Psychological Science in the Public Interest* 6, no. 2 (October 2005): 31–55, https://doi.org/10.1111/j.1529-1006.2005.00022.x.

39. Michael L. Tushman and Charles A. O'Reilly III, "Ambidextrous Organizations: Managing Evolutionary and Revolutionary Change," *California Management Review* 38, no. 4 (July 1996): 8–29, https://doi.org/10.2307/41165852.

40. See the case study in Debra Schifrin, Glenn Carroll, and Jesper Sørensen, "Scoot: Singapore Airlines' Low Cost Carrier Strategy," Stanford GSB Case SM-321, February 28, 2020.

7. CULTURE AND THE BOTTOM LINE

1. For details about Dreyer's crisis and recovery, see the case by Victoria Change, Jennifer A. Chatman, and Glenn R. Carroll, "Dreyer's Grand Ice Cream (Abridged)," Stanford Graduate School of Business, Case OB-53 (A), 2005, https://www.gsb.stanford.edu/faculty-research/case-studies/dreyers-grand-ice-cream-abridged.

   Despite the heated discussions about terminating the culture, Cronk and his fellow executives eventually decided to double down on it: They behaved consistently according to the culture's tenets by collaboratively consulting with employees throughout the company about how to respond to the crisis and enact budget cuts.

2. Rose Gailey, Ian Johnston, and Holly McLeod, "Aligning Culture with the Bottom Line: Putting People First," Heidrick & Struggles, 2023, https://www.heidrick.com/-/media/heidrickcom/publications-and-reports/aligning-culture-with-the-bottom-line_putting-people-first.pdf.

3. J. Graham, J. Grennan, C. Harvey, and S. Rajgopal, "Corporate Culture: Evidence from the Field," *Journal of Financial Economics* 146, no. 2 (2022): 560.

4. For an overview of this transformation, see Charles O'Reilly, "How Microsoft Transformed Its Culture: Five Levers for Organizational Cultural Change," *Management and Business Review*, Winter 2024, https://journals.sagepub.com/doi/pdf/10.1177/26941058202404O1006.

5. Elizabeth Knight, "Uber Pays a $26 Billion Price for Its Toxic Corporate Culture," *Sydney Morning Herald*, June 30, 2017, https://www.smh.com.au/business/uber-pays-a-26-billion-price-for-its-toxic-corporate-culture-20170630-gx1x3w.html.

6. Joanna Robin, "Uber Chief Tells French Lobbying Inquiry Company's Culture Has Been Transformed," International Consortium of Investigative Journalists (ICIJ), June 14, 2023, https://www.icij.org/investigations/uber-files/uber-chief-tells-french-lobbying-inquiry-companys-culture-has-been-transformed/.

7. Emily Glazer, "Wells Fargo to Pay $185 Million Fine over Account Openings," *The Wall Street Journal*, September 8, 2016, https://www .wsj.com/articles/wells-fargo-to-pay-185-million-fine-over-account -openings-1473352548.

8. Trudy Knockless and Greg Andrews, "'The Fish Rots from the Head': Why Fixing Wells Fargo's Culture Is Taking So Long," *ThinkAdvisor*, January 31, 2023, https://www.thinkadvisor.com/2023/01/31/the-fish-rots -from-the-head-backward-why-fixing-wells-fargos-culture-is-taking -so-long-415-484357/.

9. Daniel Jacobs and Lawrence P. Kalbers, "The Volkswagen Diesel Emissions Scandal and Accountability," *The CPA Journal*, July 2019, https:// www.cpajournal.com/2019/07/22/9187/.

10. Jacobs and Kalbers, "The Volkswagen Diesel Emissions Scandal and Accountability."

11. Jim Souhan, "Americans Have Better Ryder Cup Team, but Europe Always Has Better Teamwork," *The Minnesota Star Tribune*, September 24, 2021, https://www.startribune.com/ryder-cup-americans-better-team -europe-better-teamwork-jim-souhan/600100306.

12. Alex Miceli, "'That's What Separates Us:' European Ryder Cup Team Believes Its Camaraderie Is an Edge over U.S.," *Sports Illustrated*, September 13, 2023, https://www.si.com/golf/news/european-ryder-cup -team-feels-camaraderie-remains-an-edge.

13. Art Spander, "Why Has Team Europe Dominated Team USA at the Ryder Cup?" *Bleacher Report*, July 26, 2017, https://bleacherreport.com /articles/2209679-why-has-team-europe-dominated-team-usa-at -the-ryder-cup.

14. Spander, "Why Has Team Europe Dominated Team USA at the Ryder Cup?"

15. Eamon Lynch, "Lynch: Team USA Is Trying to Mimic Europe's Ryder Cup Magic, but Missing the Point," *USA Today*, September 1, 2023, https://golfweek.usatoday.com/2023/09/01/eamon-lynch-team-usa -mimic-europe-ryder-cup-magic/.

16. Steve Kerr interview at the Berkeley Center for Workplace Culture and Innovation 2019 conference, University of California, Berkeley, January 2019, 12:28, https://www.youtube.com/watch?v=1HqEYqyZnqM.

17. Jennifer A. Chatman et al., "Parsing Organizational Culture: How the Norm for Adaptability Influences the Relationship Between Culture

Consensus and Financial Performance in High-Technology Firms," *Journal of Organizational Behavior* 35, no. 6 (April 11, 2014): 785–808, https://doi.org/10.1002/job.1928.

18. David M. Kreps, "Corporate Culture and Economic Theory," in *Perspectives on Positive Political Economy*, ed. James E. Alt (Cambridge University Press, 1990), 90–142. Also see Colin Camerer and Ari Vepsalainen, "The Economic Efficiency of Corporate Culture," *Strategic Management Journal* 9, no. S1 (1988): 115–26. https://doi.org/10.1002/smj.4250090712; Jacques Cremer, "Corporate Culture and Shared Knowledge," *Industrial and Corporate Change* 2, no. 3 (1993): 351–86, https://doi.org/10.1093/icc/2.3.351; Roberto A. Weber and Colin F. Camerer, "Cultural Conflict and Merger Failure: An Experimental Approach," *Management Science* 49, no. 4 (April 2003): 400–415, https://doi.org/10.1287/mnsc.49.4.400.14430.

19. Jay B. Barney, "Organizational Culture: Can It Be a Source of Sustained Competitive Advantage?" *Academy of Management Review* 11, no.1 (July 1986): 656–65.

20. James N. Baron and Michael T. Hannan, "Organizational Blueprints for Success in High-Tech Start-ups: Lessons from the Stanford Project on Emerging Companies," *IEEE Engineering Management Review* 31, no. 1 (2003): 8–36, https://doi.org/10.1109/emr.2003.1201438.

21. Arianna Marchetti and Phanish Puranam, "Organizational Cultural Strength as the Negative Cross-Entropy of Mindshare: A Measure Based on Descriptive Text," *Humanities and Social Sciences Communications* 9, no. 1 (April 19, 2022): 32, https://doi.org/10.1057/s41599-022-01152-1. The study reports a negative correlation between managerial intensity and cultural strength in Glassdoor data from approximately 3,017 firms, measured from employees' reviews, "as the negative cross-entropy of an organization's members' mindshare distributions defined on firm-specific cultural elements." For a similar measure of culture, see Matthew Corritore, Amir Goldberg, and Sameer B. Srivastava, "Duality in Diversity: How Intrapersonal and Interpersonal Cultural Heterogeneity Relate to Firm Performance," *Administrative Science Quarterly* 65, no. 2 (2020): 359–94, https://doi.org/10.1177/0001839219844175.

22. Baron and Hannan, "Organizational Blueprints for Success in High-Tech Start-ups."

23. Baron and Hannan, "Organizational Blueprints for Success in High -Tech Start-ups": 23–24.

24. Baron and Hannan, "Organizational Blueprints for Success in High-Tech Start-ups": 26.

25. Baron and Hannan, "Organizational Blueprints for Success in High-Tech Start-ups": 26.

26. Daniel R. Denison, *Corporate Culture and Organizational Effectiveness* (John Wiley & Sons, 1990).

27. Daniel R. Denison and Aneil K. Mishra, "Toward a Theory of Organizational Culture and Effectiveness," *Organization Science* 6, no. 2 (April 1995): 204–23, https://doi.org/10.1287/orsc.6.2.204.

28. John P. Kotter and James L. Heskett, *Corporate Culture and Performance* (Free, 1992).

29. Their definition of strong culture differs from the definition that we use throughout this book. See chapter 1.

30. Kotter and Heskett, *Corporate Culture and Performance*, 21.

31. George G. Gordon and Nancy DiTomaso, "Predicting Corporate Performance from Organizational Culture," *Journal of Management Studies* 29, no. 6 (November 1992): 783–98, https://doi.org/10.1111/j.1467-6486.1992.tb00689.x.

32. Ronald S. Burt, Shaul M. Gabbay, Gerhard Holt, and Peter Moran, "Contingent Organization as a Network Theory: The Culture-Performance Contingency Function," *Acta Sociologica* 37, no. 4 (1994): 345–70, https://doi.org/10.1177/000169939403700404.

33. Jesper B. Sørensen, "The Strength of Corporate Culture and the Reliability of Firm Performance," *Administrative Science Quarterly* 47, no. 1 (March 2002): 70–79, https://doi.org/10.2307/3094891.

34. Chatman et al., "Parsing Organizational Culture."

35. Jennifer Chatman, Yixi Chen, Virginia Choi, and Michele Gelfand, "Organizational Culture Moderates the Relationship Between Environmental Volatility and Firm Performance: The Case of the COVID-19 Pandemic." Conditionally accepted at *Academy of Management Discoveries* 2026.

36. Luigi Guiso, Paola Sapienza, and Luigi Zingales, "The Value of Corporate Culture," *Journal of Financial Economics* 117, no. 1 (July 2015): 60–76, https://doi.org/https://doi.org/10.1016/j.jfineco.2014.05.010.

37. Guiso et al., "The Value of Corporate Culture," 65 (emphasis added).

38. According to Guiso et al., "The Value of Corporate Culture," "Tobin's Q is calculated as [(Total Assets-Shareholder's Equity + Market Value of Equity) / TotalAssets] where Market Value of Equity is the sum of the total market value of each security issued by the company. The market value is calculated as price of the share at the end of the fiscal year times the number of outstanding shares at the end of the fiscal year.". Return on sales is calculated as net income/sales.

39. Guiso et al., "The Value of Corporate Culture": 75 (emphasis added).

40. Charles A. Reilly and Jennifer A. Chatman, "Organizational Commitment and Psychological Attachment: The Effects of Compliance, Identification, and Internalization on Prosocial Behavior," *Journal of Applied Psychology* 71, no. 3 (1986): 492–99, https://doi.org/10.1037//0021-9010.71.3.492.

41. Baron and Hannan, "Organizational Blueprints for Success in High-Tech Start-ups."

42. Amir Goldberg et al., "Fitting In or Standing Out? The Tradeoffs of Structural and Cultural Embeddedness," *American Sociological Review* 81, no. 6 (November 1, 2016): 1190–222, https://doi.org/10.1177/0003122416671873.

43. Richard Lu, Jennifer A. Chatman, Amir Goldberg, and Sameer Srivastava, "Two-Sided Cultural Fit: The Differing Behavioral Consequences of Cultural Congruence Based on Values Versus Perceptions," *Organization Science* 35, no. 1 (2023): 71–91, https://doi.org/10.1287/orsc.2023.1659.

8. MANAGING CULTURE

1. "Bill & Dave Stories," *HP People Stories*, accessed May 2, 2024, https://www.hpmemoryproject.org/timeline/stories/bill_and_dave_00.htm.

2. "Bill & Dave Stories."

3. Packard was no pushover, however. HP ex-employee Dave Kirby relates that in 1965, a manager wanted to revise HP's internal accounting system. He wrote a memo to Packard explaining his ideas. He received a reply from Packard the next day in a handwritten note that stated baldly, "This is manifestly absurd and evidence of total stupidity." "This Is Manifestly Absurd," *MEASURE Magazine*, May–June 1996, 7, https://www.hp.com/hpinfo/abouthp/histnfacts/publications/measure/pdf/1996_05-06.pdf.

4. "Leadership Is More Setting Context Than Taking Decisions, Says Citigroup CEO Jane Fraser," *YouTube CNA*, October 23, 2023, https://www.youtube.com/watch?v=a8_tEN88P64.

5. Richard Brandt, "The Bad Boy of Silicon Valley," *Bloomberg*, December 9, 1991, https://www.bloomberg.com/news/articles/1991-12-08/the-bad-boy-of-silicon-valley.

6. Massey remembers a time when Rodgers gave her some hand-drawn charts and asked her to use software to turn them into slides for a presentation. After five exhausting days of trying to do this task, she told him through tears that she could not do it. He replied: "I don't need a crybaby, I need a secretary." Brandt, "The Bad Boy of Silicon Valley."

7. Erach Desai, "Where Have All the Leaders Gone—a Profile of T. J. Rodgers," LinkedIn, February 27, 2020, https://www.linkedin.com/pulse/where-have-all-leaders-gone-profile-tj-rodgers-erach-desai/.

8. Walter Isaacson, *Steve Jobs* (Simon & Schuster, 2011).

9. Adam Lashinsky, "How Apple Works: Inside the World's Biggest Startup," *Fortune*, May 9, 2011, https://fortune.com/article/inside-apple/; Jay Yarow, "What It's Like When Steve Jobs Chews You out for a Product Failure," *Business Insider*, May 7, 2011, https://www.businessinsider.com/steve-jobs-mobileme-failure-2011-5.

10. Leslie A. Perlow and Liz Kind, "New HP: The Clean Room and Beyond," *Harvard Business School Case Series*, February 22, 2004.

11. Charles D. Ellis, *The Partnership: The Making of Goldman Sachs* (Penguin, 2008).

12. Jennifer Chatman and Richard Lyons, "The Haas Defining Principles: Creating a Business School Culture (A) and (B) case," University of California, Haas School of Business, *Berkeley Haas Case Series*. October 1, 2017 (A case) and April 1, 2019 (B case).

13. John A. Byrne, "Where Culture Really Matters: Berkeley's Haas School," *Poets & Quants*, June 13, 2018, https://poetsandquants.com/2018/06/13/where-culture-really-matters-berkeleys-haas-school/.

14. Adam Grant, "The 4 Deadly Sins of Work Culture," *WorkLife with Adam Grant*, June 21, 2022, https://open.spotify.com/episode/03LoKfw87AxqczjqXi7ET8.

15. Ulrich Möller and Matthew McCaffrey, "Levels Without Bosses? Entrepreneurship and Valve's Organizational Design," in *The Invisible Hand in Virtual Worlds: The Economic Order of Video Games*, edited by Matthew McCaffrey (Cambridge University Press, 2021), 1.

16. Fawzi Kamel, "Uber CEO Kalanick Argues with Driver over Falling Fares," 3:55–6:10, YouTube (February 5, 2017), https://youtu.be/gTEDY CkNqns?si=nKWy3MvgYwIGkCSx&t=235.

17. Robert I. Sutton and Huggy Rao, *Scaling up Excellence: Getting to More Without Settling for Less* (Random House, 2016).

18. Stanford Graduate School of Business, "DaVita CEO Kent Thiry on Building a Signature Company Culture," YouTube, November 23, 2015, https://www.youtube.com/watch?v=9CN85CFllME.

19. Omar Lizardo, "Cultural Symbols and Cultural Power," *Qualitative Sociology* 39 (April 2016): 199–204, https://doi.org/10.1007/s11133-016 -9329-4.

20. Omar Lizardo and Isaac Jilbert, "Organizations and the Structure of Culture," *Sociology Compass* 17, no. 4 (December 2022): e13063, https:// doi.org/10.1111/soc4.13063.

21. Jennifer A. Chatman, "Maersk: Driving Culture Change at a Century-Old Company to Achieve Measurable Results," *Berkeley Haas Case Series*, April 1, 2024, https://cases.haas.berkeley.edu/2024/04/maersk/.

22. David Gurteen, "Peter Block: Author, Consultant, and Speaker," in *Conversational Leadership* Peter Block, *Community: The Structure of Belonging* (Berrett-Koehler, 2018).

REFERENCES

Advanced Micro Devices (AMD). "Corporate Responsibility at AMD." Accessed April 23, 2024. https://www.amd.com/en/corporate/corporate-responsibility.html.

Amelio, Gil, and William L. Simon. *On the Firing Line: My 500 Days at Apple.* HarperPerennial, 1999.

Ashkanasy, Neal M., Lyndelle E. Broadfoot, and Sarah Falkus. "Questionnaire Measures of Organizational Culture." In *Handbook of Organizational Culture and Climate*, ed. Neal M. Ashkanasy, Celeste P. M. Wilderom, and Mark F. Peterson. SAGE, 2000.

Baldor, Lolita. "Navy SEALs Training Plagued by Pervasive Problems, According to Investigation After Death of Sailor." *AP News*, May 25, 2023. https://apnews.com/article/navy-seal-death-steroids-medical-failures-e49b76593ca884cc521d48a9b0b4a8ef.

Barney, Jay B. "Organizational Culture: Can It Be a Source of Sustained Competitive Advantage?" *Academy of Management Review* 11, no. 1 (July 1986): 656–65.

Baron, James N., and Michael T. Hannan. "Organizational Blueprints for Success in High-Tech Start-ups: Lessons from the Stanford Project on Emerging Companies." *IEEE Engineering Management Review* 31, no. 1 (2003): 8–36. https://doi.org/10.1109/emr.2003.1201438.

Benioff, Marc R., and Monica Langley. *Trailblazer: The Power of Business as the Greatest Platform for Change.* Currency, 2019.

Berman, Sarah. *Don't Call It a Cult: The Shocking Story of Keith Raniere and the Women of NXIVM.* Steerforth, 2021.

Berson, Yair, Shaul Oreg, and Taly Dvir. "CEO Values, Organizational Culture and Firm Outcomes." *Journal of Organizational Behavior* 29, no. 5 (2008): 615–33. https://doi.org/10.1002/job.499.

"Bill & Dave Stories." HP People Stories. Accessed May 2, 2024. https://www.hpmemoryproject.org/timeline/stories/bill_and_dave_00.htm.

Binns, Andrew, Charles A. O'Reilly III, and Michael L. Tushman. *Corporate Explorer: How Corporations Can Beat Startups at the Innovation Game.* Wiley, 2022.

Block, Jack. *The Q-Sort Method in Personality Assessment and Psychiatric Research.* Consulting Psychologists, 1978.

Block, Peter. *Community: The Structure of Belonging.* Berrett-Koehler, 2018.

Boisnier, Alicia, and Jennifer A. Chatman. "The Role of Subcultures in Agile Organizations." In *Leading and Managing People in the Dynamic Organization*, ed. Randall S. Peterson and Elizabeth A. Mannix. Lawrence Erlbaum Associates, 2003.

Brandt, Richard. "The Bad Boy of Silicon Valley." *Bloomberg*, December 8, 1991. https://www.bloomberg.com/news/articles/1991-12-08/the-bad-boy-of-silicon-valley.

Brothers, Eric. "Boeing to Acquire Spirit AeroSystems in $8.3B Deal," *Aerospace*, July 2, 2024. https://www.aerospacemanufacturinganddesign.com/news/boeing-acquire-spirit-aerosystems-8-3b-deal/.

Brown, Derek N., Yixi Chen, Hope Harrington, Paul Vicinanza, Jennifer A. Chatman, Amir Goldberg, and Sameer Srivastava. "How Have Organizational Cultures Shifted During the COVID-19 Pandemic . . . and What Might Need to Change Back?" *California Management Review* (2021). https://cmr.berkeley.edu/assets/documents/pdf/2021-07-how-have-organizational-cultures-shifted.pdf.

Burt, Ronald S., S. M. Gabbay, G. Holt, and P. Moran. *Acta Sociologica* 37, no. 4 (1994), 345–70. https://doi.org/10.1177/000169939403700404.

Bushey, Clare. "Boeing Chief Outlines Overhaul of Plane Maker to Halt 'Serious Performance Lapses'," *Financial Times*, October 23, 2024. https://www.ft.com/content/9ec5638f-eea1-4b9a-be56-e72cfa06f018#post-6177cf2d-6821-49b2-a754-68fac9866a6a.

Byrne, John A. "Where Culture Really Matters: Berkeley's Haas School." *Poets & Quants*, June 13, 2018. https://poetsandquants.com/2018/06/13/where-culture-really-matters-berkeleys-haas-school/.

Caldwell, David F., Jennifer A. Chatman, and Charles A. O'Reilly III. "Profile Comparison Methods for Assessing Person-Situation Fit." In *Perspectives on Organizational Fit*, ed. Cheri Ostroff and Timothy A. Judge. Lawrence Erlbaum Associates, 2007.

Camerer, Colin, and Ari Vepsalainen. "The Economic Efficiency of Corporate Culture." *Strategic Management Journal* 9, no. S1 (1988): 115–26. https://doi.org/10.1002/smj.4250090712.

Carlin, Peter. "Pure Profit—For Small Companies That Stress Social Values as Much as the Bottom Line, Growing Up Hasn't Been an Easy Task. Just Ask Ben & Jerry's, Patagonia and Starbucks." *Los Angeles Times*, February 5, 1995. https://www.latimes.com/archives/la-xpm-1995-02-05-tm-28412-story.html.

Carlson, Nicholas. "WeWork Cofounders Explained the Future of the Office at IGNITION 2016." *Business Insider India*, April 3, 2017. https://www.businessinsider.in/wework-cofounders-explained-the-future-of-the-office-at-ignition-2016/articleshow/57993401.cms.

Carroll, G. R., and M. T. Hannan. *The Demography of Corporations and Industries*. Princeton University Press, 2000.

Carroll, Glenn R., and J. Richard Harrison. "Organizational Demography and Culture: Insights from a Formal Model and Simulation." *Administrative Science Quarterly* 43, no. 3 (1998): 637–67. https://doi.org/10.2307/2393678.

Castillo, Kristen. "Inside Patagonia's Corporate Culture That Prioritizes Flexibility and Work-Life Balance." https://www.futureofbusinessandtech.com/employee-wellbeing/inside-patagonias-corporate-culture-that-prioritizes-flexibility-and-work-life-balance/.

CFI Team. "Tone at the Top." Accessed April 23, 2024. https://corporatefinanceinstitute.com/resources/management/tone-at-the-top/.

Chang, Victoria, Jennifer A. Chatman, and Glenn R. Carroll. "Dreyer's Grand Ice Cream (Abridged)." Stanford Graduate School of Business. Case OB-53 (A), 2005. https://www.gsb.stanford.edu/faculty-research/case-studies/dreyers-grand-ice-cream-abridged.

Chatman, Jennifer A. "Culture Change at Genentech: Accelerating Strategic and Financial Accomplishments." *California Management Review* 56, no. 2 (2014): 113–29. https://doi.org/10.1525/cmr.2014.56.2.113.

Chatman, Jennifer A. "Improving Interactional Organizational Research: A Model of Person-Organization Fit." *Academy of Management Review* 14, no. 3 (1989): 333–49. https://doi.org/10.5465/amr.1989.4279063.

Chatman, Jennifer A. "Maersk: Driving Culture Change at a Century-Old Company to Achieve Measurable Results." *Berkeley Haas Case Series*, April 2024. https://cases.haas.berkeley.edu/2024/04/maersk/.

Chatman, Jennifer A. "Matching People and Organizations: Selection and Socialization in Public Accounting Firms." *Administrative Science Quarterly* 36, no. 3 (1991): 459–84. https://doi.org/10.2307/2393204.

Chatman, Jennifer A. "Roche Pakistan (A) and (B): Turning Around a Crisis Through Cultural Transformation." *Berkeley Haas Case Series*, October 2017. https://doi.org/10.4135/9781526450401.

Chatman, Jennifer A., David F. Caldwell, Charles A. O'Reilly III, and Bernadette Doerr. "Parsing Organizational Culture: How the Norm for Adaptability Influences the Relationship Between Culture Consensus and Financial Performance in High-Technology Firms." *Journal of Organizational Behavior* 35, no. 6 (2014): 785–808. https://doi.org/10.1002/job.1928.

Chatman, Jennifer A., Yixi Chen, Virginia Choi, and Michele Gelfand. "Organizational Culture Moderates the Relationship Between Environmental Volatility and Firm Performance: The Case of the COVID-19 Pandemic." Conditionally accepted at *Academy of Management Discoveries*.

Chatman, Jennifer A., and Francis J. Flynn. "The Influence of Demographic Heterogeneity on the Emergence and Consequences of Cooperative Norms in Work Teams." *Academy of Management Journal* 44, no. 5 (2001): 956–74. https://doi.org/10.5465/3069440.

Chatman, Jennifer A., Lindred L. Greer, Eliot Sherman, and Bernadette Doerr. "Blurred Lines: How the Collectivism Norm Operates Through Perceived Group Diversity to Boost or Harm Group Performance in Himalayan Mountain Climbing." *Organization Science* 30, no. 2 (2019): 235–59. https://doi.org/10.1287/orsc.2018.1268.

Chatman, Jennifer A., and Richard Lyons. "The Haas Defining Principles: Creating a Business School Culture (A) and (B)." *Haas School of Business, California Management Review,* and *Harvard Business School Case Series,* 2017, 2019.

Chatman, Jennifer A., and Charles A. O'Reilly III. "Paradigm Lost: Reinvigorating the Study of Organizational Culture." *Research in Organizational Behavior* 36 (2016): 199–224. https://doi.org/10.1016/j.riob.2016.11.004.

Chatman, Jennifer A., Sameer Srivastava, and David Rocklin, "How Lyft's Strategy Informed Their Return-to-Work Approach." *Berkeley Haas Case Series,* 2024.

CNA. "Leadership Is More Setting Context Than Taking Decisions, Says Citigroup CEO Jane Fraser." YouTube. October 23, 2023. Video, 5:23. https://www.youtube.com/watch?v=a8_tEN88P64.

Corritore, Matthew, Amir Goldberg, and Sameer B. Srivastava. "Duality in Diversity: How Intrapersonal and Interpersonal Cultural Heterogeneity Relate to Firm Performance." *Administrative Science Quarterly* 65, no. 2 (2020): 359–94. https://doi.org/10.1177/0001839219844175.

Crawford, Krysten. "New Case Study Examines How Haas Can Sustain Its Culture." *Berkeley Haas Newsroom*, January 3, 2018. https://newsroom .haas.berkeley.edu/new-case-study-examines-how-haas-can-sustain-its -culture/.

Crémer, Jacques. "Corporate Culture and Shared Knowledge." *Industrial and Corporate Change* 2, no. 3 (1993): 351–86. https://doi.org/10.1093/icc /2.3.351.

Dastin, Jeffrey. "At Taser Maker Axon, Ex-staff Say Loyalty Meant Being Tased, Tattooed." Reuters, August 30, 2023. https://www.reuters.com /investigates/special-report/axon-taser-exposures/.

Deloitte. "Core Beliefs and Culture Chairman's Survey Findings." 2012. https://www2.deloitte.com/content/dam/Deloitte/global/Documents /About-Deloitte/gx-core-beliefs-and-culture.pdf.

Denison, Daniel R. "Corporate Culture and Organizational Effectiveness." *Choice Reviews Online* 27, no. 11 (1990). http://dx.doi.org/10.2307/258613.

Denison, Daniel R., and Aneil K. Mishra. "Toward a Theory of Organizational Culture and Effectiveness." *Organization Science* 6, no. 2 (1995): 204–23. https://doi.org/10.1287/orsc.6.2.204.

Desai, Erach. "Where Have All the Leaders Gone—a Profile of T. J. Rodgers." LinkedIn, February 27, 2020. https://www.linkedin.com/pulse/where-have -all-leaders-gone-profile-tj-rodgers-erach-desai/.

Ding, Wenzhi, Ross Levine, Chen Lin, and Wensi Xie. "Corporate Immunity to the COVID-19 Pandemic." *Journal of Financial Economics* 141, no. 2 (2021): 802–30. https://doi.org/10.1016/j.jfineco.2021.03.005.

Dowd, Maureen. "The Slow-Burning Success of Disney's Bob Iger." *The New York Times*, September 22, 2019. https://www.nytimes.com/2019/09/22/style /disney-bob-iger-book.html.

Duranti, Alessandro. "Language as Culture in U.S. Anthropology: Three Paradigms." *Current Anthropology* 44, no. 3 (2003): 323–47. https://doi.org /10.1086/368118.

Eichner, Bernadette. "Zappos—Hiring for Culture and the Bizarre Things They Do." *Zippia*, December 16, 2022. https://www.zippia.com/employer /zappos-hiring-for-culture-and-the-bizarre-things-they-do/.

Ellis, Charles D. *The Partnership: The Making of Goldman Sachs*. Penguin, 2008.

Feinberg, Matthew, Robb Willer, and Michael Schultz. "Gossip and Ostracism Promote Cooperation in Groups." *Psychological Science* 25, no. 3 (2014): 656–64. https://doi.org/10.1177/0956797613510184.

Fiske, Susan T., Amy J. C. Cuddy, Peter Glick, and Jun Xu. "A Model of (Often Mixed) Stereotype Content: Competence and Warmth Respectively Follow from Perceived Status and Competition." *Journal of Personality and Social Psychology* 82, no. 6 (2002): 878–902. https://doi.org /10.1037/0022-3514.82.6.878.

Freiberg, Kevin, and Jackie Freiberg. "20 Reasons Why Herb Kelleher Was One of the Most Beloved Leaders of Our Time." *Forbes*, January 4, 2019. https://www.forbes.com/sites/kevinandjackiefreiberg/2019/01/04/20-reasons -why-herb-kelleher-was-one-of-the-most-beloved-leaders-of-our-time/.

Gailey, Rose, Ian Johnston, and Holly McLeod. "Aligning Culture with the Bottom Line: Putting People First." *Heidrick & Struggles International*. Accessed May 2, 2024. https://www.heidrick.com/-/media/heidrickcom /publications-and-reports/aligning-culture-with-the-bottom-line_putting -people-first.pdf.

Gallup. "Organizational Culture Indicators." 2024. https://www.gallup.com /471521/indicator-organizational-culture.aspx.

Geertz, Clifford. *Local Knowledge: Further Essays in Interpretive Anthropology*. Basic Books, 1983.

Glazer, Emily. "Wells Fargo to Pay $185 Million Fine over Account Openings." *The Wall Street Journal*, September 8, 2016. https://www.wsj.com/articles /wells-fargo-to-pay-185-million-fine-over-account-openings-1473352548.

Goffman, Erving. *Asylums: Essays on the Social Situation of Mental Patients and Other Inmates*. Doubleday, 1990.

Goldberg, Amir, Sameer B. Srivastava, V. Govind Manian, William Monroe, and Christopher Potts. "Fitting In or Standing Out? The Tradeoffs of Structural and Cultural Embeddedness." *American Sociological Review* 81, no. 6 (2016): 1190–222. https://doi.org/10.1177/0003122416671873.

Goncalo, Jack A. "Past Success and Convergent Thinking in Groups: The Role of Group-Focused Attributions." *European Journal of Social Psychology*, *34*, no. 4 (2004), 385–95. https://doi.org/10.1002/ejsp.203.

Goncalo, Jack A., and Michelle M. Duguid. "Follow the Crowd in a New Direction: When Conformity Pressure Facilitates Group Creativity (and When It Does Not)." *Organizational Behavior and Human Decision Processes* 118, no. 1 (2012): 14–23. https://doi.org/10.1016/j.obhdp.2011.12.004.

Gordon, George G., and Nancy DiTomaso. "Predicting Corporate Performance from Organizational Culture." *Journal of Management Studies* 29, no. 6 (1992): 783–98. https://doi.org/10.1111/j.1467-6486.1992.tb00689.x.

Graham, John R., Jillian Grennan, Campbell R. Harvey, and Shivaram Rajgopal. "Corporate Culture: Evidence from the Field." *Journal of Financial Economics* 146, no. 2 (2022): 552–93. https://doi.org/10.1016/j.jfineco.2022.07.008.

Grant, Adam. "The 4 Deadly Sins of Work Culture." *WorkLife with Adam Grant.* June 21, 2022. Podcast, Spotify, 41:46. https://open.spotify.com/episode/03LoKfw87AxqczjqXi7ET8.

Grennan, Jillian. "A Corporate Culture Channel: How Increased Shareholder Governance Reduces Firm Value." 2019. SSRN. https://papers.ssrn.com/sol3/papers.cfm?abstract_id=2345384.

Groth, Aimee. "Zappos Has Quietly Backed Away from Holacracy." *Quartz,* January 29, 2020. https://qz.com/work/1776841/zappos-has-quietly-backed-away-from-holacracy.

Groysberg, Boris, Jeremiah Lee, Jesse Price, and J. Cheng. "The Leader's Guide to Corporate Culture." *Harvard Business Review* 96, no. 1 (2018): 44–52. https://hbr.org/2018/01/the-leaders-guide-to-corporate-culture.

Guiso, Luigi, Paola Sapienza, and Luigi Zingales. "The Value of Corporate Culture." *Journal of Financial Economics* 117, no. 1 (2015): 60–76. https://doi.org/https://doi.org/10.1016/j.jfineco.2014.05.010.

Hannan, Michael T., and John Freeman. "Structural Inertia and Organizational Change." *American Sociological Review* 49, no. 2 (1984): 149–64. https://doi.org/10.2307/2095567.

Harrison, J. Richard, and Glenn R. Carroll. *Culture and Demography in Organizations.* Princeton University Press, 2006.

Harrison, J. Richard, and Glenn R. Carroll. "Keeping the Faith: A Model of Cultural Transmission in Formal Organizations." *Administrative Science Quarterly* 36, no. 4 (1991): 552–82. https://doi.org/10.2307/2393274.

Hartnell, Chad A., Amy Yi Ou, and Angelo Kinicki. "Organizational Culture and Organizational Effectiveness: A Meta-analytic Investigation of the Competing Values Framework's Theoretical Suppositions." *Journal of Applied Psychology* 96, no. 4 (2011): 677–94. https://doi.org/10.1037/a0021987.

Hastings, Reed, and Erin Meyer. *No Rules Rules: Netflix and the Culture of Reinvention.* Random House, 2020.

Heidrick & Struggles. "Aligning Culture with the Bottom Line: How Companies Can Accelerate Progress." 2021. https://www.heidrick.com/en/insights /culture-shaping/aligning-culture-with-the-bottom-line-how-companies -can-accelerate-progress.

Heskett, James. *Win from Within: Build Organizational Culture for Competitive Advantage.* Columbia University Press, 2022.

Hoffman, Bryce G. *American Icon: Alan Mulally and the Fight to Save Ford Motor Company.* Crown Business, 2012.

Ibarra, Herminia. "Take a Wrecking Ball to Your Company's Iconic Practices." *MIT Sloan Management Review* 61, no. 1 (2019): 1–5. https://www.proquest .com/docview/2335159128?pq-origsite=gscholar&fromopenview=true &sourcetype=Scholarly%20Journals.

Ibarra, Herminia, and Aneeta Rattan. "Microsoft: Instilling a Growth Mindset." *London Business School Review* 29, no. 3 (2018): 50–53. https://doi.org /10.1111/2057-1615.12262.

Jacobs, Daniel, and Lawrence P. Kalbers. "The Volkswagen Diesel Emissions Scandal and Accountability." *The CPA Journal*, July 2019. https://www .cpajournal.com/2019/07/22/9187/.

Jung, Tobias, Tim Scott, Huw T. O. Davies, Peter Bower, Diane Whalley, Rosalind McNally, and Russell Mannion. "Instruments for Exploring Organizational Culture: A Review of the Literature." *Public Administration Review* 69, no. 6 (2009): 1087–96. https://doi.org/10.1111/j.1540-6210.2009.02066.x.

Kamel, Fawzi. "Uber CEO Kalanick Argues with Driver over Falling Fares." 3:55–6:10. YouTube (February 5, 2017), https://youtu.be/gTEDYCkNqns? si=nKWy3MvgYwIGkCSx&t=235.

Keltner, Dacher, Deborah H. Gruenfeld, and Cameron Anderson. "Power, Approach, and Inhibition." *Psychological Review* 110, no. 2 (2003): 265. https://psycnet.apa.org/fulltext/2003-00307-004.html.

Kim, S. H., L.C. Vincent, and J.A. Goncalo. "Outside Advantage: Can Social Rejection Fuel Creative Thought?" *Journal of Experimental Psychology: General*, 142, no. 3 (2013): 605–11. https://doi.org/10.1037/a0029728.

Knight, Elizabeth. "Uber Pays a $26 Billion Price for Its Toxic Corporate Culture." *Sydney Morning Herald*, June 30, 2017. https://www.smh.com.au /business/uber-pays-a-26-billion-price-for-its-toxic-corporate-culture -20170630-gx1x3w.html.

Knockless, Trudy, and Greg Andrews. "'The Fish Rots from the Head': Why Fixing Wells Fargo's Culture Is Taking So Long." *ThinkAdvisor*, January 31, 2023. https://www.thinkadvisor.com/2023/01/31/the-fish-rots -from-the-head-backward-why-fixing-wells-fargos-culture-is-taking -so-long-415-484357/.

Koçak, Özgecan, and Phanish Puranam. "Decoding Culture: Tools for Behavioral Strategists." *Strategy Science* 9, no. 1 (2024): 18–37. https://doi.org /10.1287/stsc.2022.0008.

Kotter, John P., and James L. Heskett. *Corporate Culture and Performance*. Free, 1992.

Kreps, David M. "Corporate Culture and Economic Theory." In *Perspectives on Positive Political Economy*, edited by James E. Alt. Cambridge University Press, 1990.

Kristof-Brown, Amy L., Ryan D. Zimmerman, and Erin C. Johnson. "Consequences of Individuals' Fit at Work: A Meta-analysis of Person–Job, Person–Organization, Person–Group, and Person–Supervisor Fit." *Personnel Psychology* 58, no. 2 (2005): 281–342. https://doi.org/10.1111/j.1744-6570.2005 .00672.x.

Kyser, Diana C. "Through the Looking Glass: Company Culture as a Reflection of Founder Personality in Entrepreneurial Organizations." Dissertation submitted to Temple University Graduate Board, May 2017.

Labov, William. "The Intersection of Sex and Social Class in the Course of Linguistic Change." *Language Variation and Change* 2, no. 2 (1990): 205–54. https://doi.org/10.1017/S0954394500000338.

Langley, Monica, and Marc Benioff. "How Salesforce Closed the Pay Gap Between Men and Women." *Wired*, October 15, 2019. https:// www.wired.com/story/how-salesforce-closed-pay-gap-between-men -women/.

Lashinsky, Adam. "How Apple Works: Inside the World's Biggest Startup," *Fortune*, May 9, 2011. https://fortune.com/article/inside-apple/.

Lazear, Edward P. "Culture and Language." *Journal of Political Economy* 107, no. S6 (1999): S95–S126. https://doi.org/10.1086/250105.

Lee, Siew Kim Jean, and Kelvin Yu. "Corporate Culture and Organizational Performance." *Journal of Managerial Psychology* 19, no. 4 (June 2004): 340–59. https://doi.org/10.1108/02683940410537927.

Leggett, Theo. "How Ford's Alan Mulally Turned Around Its Fortunes." BBC News, July 1, 2014. https://www.bbc.com/news/business-28087325.

Leon, Marielle. "How lululemon's CEO, Calvin McDonald, Has Navigated the Pandemic to Date." *Glassdoor for Employers*, October 6, 2020. https://www.glassdoor.com/employers/blog/lululemon-ceo-navigated-pandemic/.

Lesonsky, Rieva. "It's National Mom & Pop Business Owners Day, Entrepreneurs Are Optimistic, Why Culture Is a 4-Letter Word and Other Things Entrepreneurs Need to Know." *smallbizdaily*, March 29, 2017. https://www.smallbizdaily.com/national-mom-pop-business-owners-day-entrepreneurs-optimistic-culture-4-letter-word-things-entrepreneurs-need-know/.

Lizardo, Omar. "Cultural Symbols and Cultural Power." *Qualitative Sociology* 39, no. 3 (2016): 199–204. https://doi.org/10.1007/s11133-016-9329-4.

Lizardo, Omar, and Isaac Jilbert. "Organizations and the Structure of Culture." *Sociology Compass* 17, no. 4 (2023). https://doi.org/10.1111/soc4.13063.

Lu, Richard, Jennifer A. Chatman, Amir Goldberg, and Sameer Srivastava. "Two-Sided Cultural Fit: The Differing Behavioral Consequences of Cultural Congruence Based on Values Versus Perceptions." *Organization Science* 35, no. 1 (2023): 71–91. https://doi.org/10.1287/orsc.2023.1659.

Lynch, Eamon. "Lynch: Team USA Is Trying to Mimic Europe's Ryder Cup Magic, but Missing the Point." *USA Today*, September 1, 2023. https://golfweek.usatoday.com/2023/09/01/eamon-lynch-team-usa-mimic-europe-ryder-cup-magic/.

Lyons, Richard K., Jennifer A. Chatman, and Caneel K. Joyce. "Innovation in Services: Corporate Culture and Investment Banking." *California Management Review* 50, no. 1 (2007): 174–91. https://doi.org/10.2307/41166422.

Malmendier, Ulrike, and Geoffrey Tate. "Behavioral CEOs: The Role of Managerial Overconfidence." *Journal of Economic Perspectives* 29, no. 4 (2015): 37–60. https://doi.org/10.1257/jep.29.4.37.

Mannix, Elizabeth, and Margaret A. Neale. "What Differences Make a Difference? The Promise and Reality of Diverse Teams in Organizations." *Psychological Science in the Public Interest* 6, no. 2 (2005): 31–55. https://doi.org/10.1111/j.1529-1006.2005.00022.x.

Marchetti, Arianna, and Phanish Puranam. "Organizational Cultural Strength as the Negative Cross-Entropy of Mindshare: A Measure Based on Descriptive Text." *Humanities and Social Sciences Communications* 9, (2022): 135. https://doi.org/10.1057/s41599-022-01152-1.

McCarthy, Paul, Xian Gong, Fabian Braesemann, Fabian Stephany, Marian-Andrei Rizoiu, and Margaret L. Kern. "The Impact of Founder Personalities

on Startup Success." *Scientific Reports*, *13*(1), (2023) 17200. https://www
.nature.com/articles/s41598-023-41980-y.

McCord, Patty. "Stop Hiring for Culture Fit." *Harvard Business Review*,
January–February, (2018). https://hbr.org/2018/01/how-to-hire.

Mead, Margaret. *Coming of Age in Samoa: A Psychological Study of Primitive
Youth for Western Civilization*. William Morrow, 1928.

"MEASURE Magazine." Hewlett-Packard, May–June 1996. https://www
.hp.com/hpinfo/abouthp/histnfacts/publications/measure/pdf/1996
_05-06.pdf.

Meyer, Erin. *The Culture Map: Breaking Through the Invisible Boundaries of
Global Business* Public Affairs, 2014. https://erinmeyer.com/books/the
-culture-map/.

Miceli, Alex. "European Ryder Cup Team Believes Its Camaraderie Is an Edge
over U.S." *Sports Illustrated*, September 13, 2023. https://www.si.com/golf
/news/european-ryder-cup-team-feels-camaraderie-remains-an-edge.

Möller, Ulrich, and Mathew McCaffrey. "Levels Without Bosses? Entrepreneurship and Valve's Organizational Design." In *The Invisible Hand in Virtual Worlds: The Economic Order of Video Games*, ed. Matthew McCaffrey.
Cambridge University Press, 2021.

Neeley, Tsedal. "How to Successfully Work Across Countries, Languages, and
Cultures." *Harvard Business Review*, August 29, 2017, https://hbr.org/2017/08
/how-to-successfully-work-across-countries-languages-and-cultures.

Nobel, Carmen. "Introverts: The Best Leaders For Proactive Employees."
Harvard Business School Working Knowledge, October 4, 2010. https://hbswk
.hbs.edu/item/introverts-the-best-leaders-for-proactive-employees.

Ofshe, Richard. "The Social Development of the Synanon Cult: The Managerial Strategy of Organizational Transformation." *Sociology of Religion* 41,
no. 2 (1980): 109–27. https://doi.org/10.2307/3709903.

O'Reilly, Charles III. "How Microsoft Transformed Its Culture: Five Levers for
Organizational Cultural Change," *Management and Business Review*, Winter
2024. https://mbrjournal.com/2024/07/04/how-microsoft-transformed-its
-culture-five-levers-for-organizational-cultural-change/.

O'Reilly, Charles A. III, David F. Caldwell, Jennifer A. Chatman, and Bernadette Doerr. "The Promise and Problems of Organizational Culture:
CEO Personality, Culture, and Firm Performance." *Group & Organization Management* 39, no. 6 (2014): 595–625. https://doi.org/10.1177
/1059601114550713.

O'Reilly, Charles A. III, Xubo Cao, and Don Sull. "CEO Personality: The Cornerstone of Organizational Culture?" *Academy of Management Proceedings* 2022, no. 1 (2022). https://doi.org/10.5465/ambpp.2022.12573abstract.

O'Reilly, Charles A. III, and Jennifer A. Chatman. "Culture as Social Control: Corporations, Cults and Commitment." In B. Staw and L. Cummings (eds.), *Research in Organizational Behavior*, vol. 18. JAI, 1996.

O'Reilly, Charles A. III, and Jennifer A. Chatman. "Organizational Commitment and Psychological Attachment: The Effects of Compliance, Identification, and Internalization on Prosocial Behavior." *Journal of Applied Psychology* 71, no. 3 (1986): 492–99. https://doi.org/10.1037//0021-9010.71.3.492.

O'Reilly, Charles A. III, and Jennifer A. Chatman. "Transformational Leader or Narcissist? How Grandiose Narcissists Can Create and Destroy Organizations and Institutions." *California Management Review* 62, no. 3 (2020): 5–27. https://doi.org/10.1177/0008125620914989.

O'Reilly, Charles A. III, Jennifer A. Chatman, and David F. Caldwell. "People and Organizational Culture: A Profile Comparison Approach to Assessing Person-Organization Fit." *Academy of Management Journal* 34, no. 3 (1991): 487–516. https://doi.org/10.2307/256404.

O'Reilly, Charles A. III, Jennifer A. Chatman, and Bernadette Doerr. "When 'Me' Trumps 'We': Narcissistic Leaders and the Cultures They Create." *Academy of Management Discoveries* 7, no. 3 (September 2021): 419–50. https://doi.org/10.5465/amd.2019.0163.

O'Reilly, Charles A. III, and Bernadette Doerr. "Conceit and Deceit: Lying, Cheating, and Stealing Among Grandiose Narcissists." *Personality and Individual Differences* 154 (2020): 109627. https://doi.org/10.1016/j.paid.2019.109627.

O'Reilly, Charles A. III, Bernadette Doerr, David F. Caldwell, and Jennifer A. Chatman. "Narcissistic CEOs and Executive Compensation." *Leadership Quarterly* 25, no. 2 (2014): 218–31. https://doi.org/10.1016/j.leaqua.2013.08.002.

O'Reilly, Charles A. III, Bernadette Doerr, and Jennifer A. Chatman. "'See You in Court': How CEO Narcissism Increases Firms' Vulnerability to Lawsuits." *Leadership Quarterly* 29, no. 3 (2018): 365–78. https://doi.org/10.1016/j.leaqua.2017.08.001.

O'Reilly, Charles A. III, Katherine Y. Williams, and Sigal Barsade. "The Impact of Relational Demography on Teamwork: When Differences Make a Difference." *Academy of Management Proceedings* 1999, no. 1 (1999). https://doi.org/10.5465/apbpp.1999.27622078.

Perlow, Leslie A., and Liz Kind. "New HP: The Clean Room and Beyond." *Harvard Business School Case Series*, February 22, 2004.

Pettigrew, Andrew M. "On Studying Organizational Cultures." *Administrative Science Quarterly* 24, no. 4 (1979): 570–81. https://doi.org/10.2307/2392363.

Prakash, Prarthana. "Elon Musk Sends Middle-of-the-Night Demanding 'Extremely Hardcore' Work Culture at Twitter with 'Long Hours at High Intensity'." *Fortune*, November 16, 2022. https://fortune.com/2022/11/16/elon-musk-email-twitter-extremely-hardcore-long-hours-high-intensity/.

Pfeffer, Jeffrey. *Power in Organizations*. Ballinger, 1981.

Podolny, Joel M., and Morten T. Hansen. "How Apple Is Organized for Innovation." *Harvard Business Review*, November 1, 2020. https://hbr.org/2020/11/how-apple-is-organized-for-innovation.

Pontefract, Dan. "Former CEO Alan Mulally Is Who CEOs Need to Be Today." *Forbes*, July 11, 2022. https://www.forbes.com/sites/danpontefract/2022/07/11/former-ceo-alan-mulally-is-who-ceos-need-to-be-today/?sh=3916e6b66490.

PwC. "Global Culture Survey 2021." 2021. https://www.pwc.com/gx/en/issues/upskilling/global-culture-survey-2021.html.

Rafaeli, Anat, and Robert I. Sutton. "Busy Stores and Demanding Customers: How Do They Affect the Display of Positive Emotion?" *Academy of Management Journal* 33, no. 3 (1990): 623–37. https://doi.org/10.2307/256584.

Recode. "Katrina Lake: Hiring People Who Fit Your Company Culture Isn't Working For Diversity | Code 2018." YouTube. May 30, 2018, 2:50. https://www.youtube.com/watch?v=dx40NdSz5Pc.

Rivera, Lauren A. "Hiring as Cultural Matching: The Case of Elite Professional Service Firms." *American Sociological Review* 77, no. 6 (2012): 999–1022. https://doi.org/10.1177/0003122412463213.

Robin, Joanna. "Uber Chief Tells French Lobbying Inquiry Company's Culture Has Been Transformed." International Consortium of Investigative Journalists (ICIJ), May 31, 2023. https://www.icij.org/investigations/uber-files/uber-chief-tells-french-lobbying-inquiry-companys-culture-has-been-transformed/.

Rokeach, Milton. *The Nature of Human Values*. Free, 1973.

Rufo, Christopher F. "Why Boeing Killed DEI," *City Journal*, November 12, 2024. https://www.city-journal.org/article/why-boeing-killed-dei.

Scanlon, Scott A., Dale M. Zupsansky, and Stephen Sawicki. "The Importance of Culture on Today's Businesses." *Hunt Scanlon Media*, March 16, 2023. https://huntscanlon.com/the-importance-of-culture-on-todays -businesses/.

Sharf, Samantha. "Startup Lessons from WeWork Founder Adam Neumann." *Forbes*, October 2, 2017. https://www.businessinsider.in/wework-cofounders -explained-the-future-of-the-office-at-ignition-2016/articleshow /57993401.cms.

Schein, Edgar. "How Culture Forms, Develops and Changes." In *Gaining Control of the Corporate Culture*, edited by Ralph H. Kilmann, Mary J. Saxton, and Roy Serpa. Jossey Bass, 1985.

Schein, Edgar H. *Organizational Culture and Leadership*. Jossey-Bass Publishers, 1985.

Schein, Edgar H. *Organizational Culture and Leadership*. 5th ed. Wiley, 2017.

Schifrin, Debra, Glenn R. Carroll, and Jesper B. Sørensen. "Scoot: Singapore Airlines' Low-Cost Carrier Strategy." Stanford GSB Case SM-321, February 28, 2020.

Schudel, Matt. "Herb Kelleher, Visionary Co-founder and Chief Executive of Southwest Airlines, Dies at 87." *The Washington Post*, January 6, 2019. https://www.washingtonpost.com/local/obituaries/herb-kelleher -visionary-co-founder-and-chief-executive-of-southwest-airlines-dies -at-87/2019/01/04/7d3160e2-1031-11e9-84fc-d58c33d6c8c7_story.html.

Schwartz, Karen. "Tangy Touch in the Sky," *SouthCoastToday*, November 16, 1995, https://www.southcoasttoday.com/story/business/1996/11/17/tangy -touch-in-sky/50619361007/.

Sider, Alison. "Southwest Airlines Is Ditching Open Seating on Flights." *The Wall Street Journal*, July 25, 2024. https://www.wsj.com/business/airlines /southwest-airlines-is-ditching-open-seating-on-flights-25bb30fd.

Sørensen, Jesper B. "The Strength of Corporate Culture and the Reliability of Firm Performance." *Administrative Science Quarterly* 47, no. 1 (2002): 70–91. https://doi.org/10.2307/3094891.

Souhan, Jim. "Americans Have Better Ryder Cup Team, but Europe Always Has Better Teamwork." *Star Tribune*, September 24, 2021. https://www .startribune.com/ryder-cup-americans-better-team-europe-better-teamwork -jim-souhan/600100306.

Spander, Art. "Why Has Team Europe Dominated Team USA at the Ryder Cup?" *Bleacher Report*, September 24, 2014. https://bleacherreport

.com/articles/2209679-why-has-team-europe-dominated-team-usa-at
-the-ryder-cup.

Sperling, Nicole. "Responsibility over Freedom: How Netflix's Culture Has Changed," *The New York Times*, June 24, 2024. https://www.nytimes.com /2024/06/24/business/media/netflix-corporate-culture.html.

Srivastava, Sameer B., Amir Goldberg, V. Govind Manian, and Christopher Potts. "Enculturation Trajectories and Individual Attainment: An Interactional Language Use Model of Cultural Dynamics in Organizations." University of California, Berkeley: Institute for Research on Labor and Employment (2016). eScholarship. https://escholarship.org/uc/item/8bq4q6d5.

Stanford Graduate School of Business. "DaVita CEO Kent Thiry on Building a Signature Company Culture." YouTube. November 23, 2015. 56:14. https://www.youtube.com/watch?v=9CN85CFllME.

Stevenson, Alexandra, and Matthew Goldstein. "Bridgewater's Ray Dalio Spreads His Gospel of 'Radical Transparency'." *The New York Times*, September 8, 2017. https://www.nytimes.com/2017/09/08/business/dealbook /bridgewaters-ray-dalio-spreads-his-gospel-of-radical-transparency.html.

Stewart, James B. *DisneyWar: Intrigue, Treachery and Deceit in the Magic Kingdom*. Simon & Schuster, 2005.

Surowiecki, James. "What's Gone Wrong at Boeing?" *The Atlantic*, January 15, 2024. https://www.theatlantic.com/ideas/archive/2024/01/boeing-737-max -corporate-culture/677120/.

Sutton, Robert I., and Huggy Rao. *Scaling Up Excellence: Getting to More Without Settling for Less*. Random House, 2016.

Swidler, Ann. "Culture in Action: Symbols and Strategies." *American Sociological Review* 51, no. 2 (1986): 273–86. https://doi.org/10.2307/2095521.

Taylor, Richard. "The Body Shop Brand Can Be Revived, But It Can't Coast on Goodwill Forever." *The Drum*, February 13, 2024. https://www .thedrum.com/opinion/2024/02/13/the-body-shop-brand-can-be-revived -it-cant-coast-goodwill-forever.

Tushman, Michael L., and Charles A. O'Reilly III. "Ambidextrous Organizations: Managing Evolutionary and Revolutionary Change." *California Management Review* 38, no. 4 (1996): 8–29. https://doi.org/10.2307/41165852.

Tushman, Michael, Ruth Page, and Tom Ryder. "Leadership, Culture, and Transition at lululemon." *Harvard Business School Multimedia/Video Case 410–705*, December 2010. https://www.hbs.edu/faculty/Pages/item.aspx ?num=39817#:~:text=Citation,410%2D705%2C%20December%202010.

Tushman, Michael, and Wendy Smith. "Organizational Technology: Technological Change, Ambidextrous Organizations and Organizational Evolution." In *Blackwell Companion to Organizations*, edited by J. A. C. Baum. Blackwell Publishers, 2002.

Useem, Jerry. "Boeing and the Dark Age of American Manufacturing." *The Atlantic*, April 20, 2024. https://www.theatlantic.com/ideas/archive/2024/04/boeing-corporate-america-manufacturing/678137/.

Useem, Jerry. "The Long-Forgotten Flight That Sent Boeing Off Course: A Company Once Driven by Engineers Became Driven by Finance." *The Atlantic*, November 20, 2019. https://www.theatlantic.com/ideas/archive/2019/11/how-boeing-lost-its-bearings/602188/.

Valve, "Boss-Free Since 1996." https://www.valvesoftware.com/en/people#:~:text=We%20believe%20that%20the%20best,Valve%20who%20do%20just%20that.

van Eijnatten, Frans M., L. Andries van der Ark, and Sjaña S. Holloway. "Ipsative Measurement and the Analysis of Organizational Values: An Alternative Approach for Data Analysis." *Quality & Quantity: International Journal of Methodology* 49, no. 2 (2015): 559–79. https://doi.org/10.1007/s11135-014-0009-8.

Weber, Roberto A., and Colin F. Camerer. "Cultural Conflict and Merger Failure: An Experimental Approach." *Management Science* 49, no. 4 (2003): 400–415. https://doi.org/10.1287/mnsc.49.4.400.14430.

Whitson, Jennifer A., Cynthia S. Wang, Ya Hui Michelle See, Wayne E. Baker, and J. Keith Murnighan. "How, When, and Why Recipients and Observers Reward Good Deeds and Punish Bad Deeds." *Organizational Behavior and Human Decision Processes* 128 (2015): 84–95. https://doi.org/10.1016/j.obhdp.2015.03.006.

Yarow, Jay. "What It's Like When Steve Jobs Chews You Out for a Product Failure." *Business Insider*, May 7, 2011. https://www.businessinsider.com/steve-jobs-mobileme-failure-2011-5.

INDEX

GPSR Authorized Representative: Easy Access System Europe, Mustamäe tee
50, 10621 Tallinn, Estonia, gpsr.requests@easproject.com

www.ingramcontent.com/pod-product-compliance
Lightning Source LLC
Chambersburg PA
CBHW031841200326
41597CB00012B/226